"Monica Jackman's OpenMind Preschool and Kinder
tribution to helping children understand their minds a
others. She indicates many ways in which we can help
integrated into the school program and be a source for regular practice and guidance."

—**Paul Gilbert**, author of *Compassionate Mind* and *Living like Crazy*; professor of
clinical psychology at the University of Derby; visiting professor at the University
of Queensland, Australia; and president of the Compassionate Mind Foundation

"Using a developmentally appropriate and student-centered approach, this book offers practices for
very young children that build their social-emotional learning (SEL) skills using mindfulness as the
backdrop. There is also a meaty chapter detailing mindfulness practices for educators, recognizing
that teaching these skills involves embodiment of a mindful way of being. This is a must-read for
anyone working with young children!"

—**Deborah Schussler, EdD**, professor of education at Pennsylvania State University,
and faculty affiliate of Prevention Research Center and Rock Ethics Institute

"An authentic and nuanced approach to mindfulness for young children, Jackman offers an in-
depth, comprehensive program to improve children's ability to engage and learn in the classroom.
Different from other SEL programs, OMPK integrates creative, developmentally appropriate, and
meaningful activities throughout the day, contextualized so that they 'make sense' to kids. Providing
an abundant array of different activities for different situations and learners, Jackman makes implementing OMPK an easy lift for teachers. A truly terrific gift for our youngest learners and their
teachers!"

—**Karen Bluth, PhD**, assistant professor at the University of North Carolina, Chapel
Hill; author of *The Self-Compassion Workbook for Teens* and *The Self-Compassionate
Teen*; and coauthor of *Mindfulness and Self-Compassion for Teen ADHD*

"This book is a precious resource for early childhood educators who wish to teach students fundamental skills of attentional focus, self-regulation, and mindful awareness that underlie and support
learning, social relationships, and well-being. The book offers innovative and evidence-based practices for cultivating virtuous habits of attention and awareness in young children, as well as excellent
recommendations for how educators can create a compassionate classroom environment in which
children more readily learn such skills. I highly recommend it."

—**Robert W. Roeser, PhD**, Bennett Pierce Professor of Caring and Compassion
at Pennsylvania State University

"In these challenging times, *Mindfulness for Preschool and Kindergarten* provides a timely and unique
program supporting mindful engagement of all learners essential for both teachers and young children. Grounded in theory and research, this book is a comprehensive and self-contained guide for
the effective mindfulness training of teachers and children containing a detailed outline of practices
and classroom activities. Teachers will find this evidence-based book remarkably practical for developing children's mindfulness, self-regulation, executive function, and learning engagement."

—**Oleg N. Medvedev**, assistant professor of psychology at the University of Waikato
in New Zealand, and coauthor of *Mindfulness-Based Intervention Research* and
Handbook of Assessment in Mindfulness Research

"This practical, detailed, and inspirational guide is a must-read for teachers bringing mindfulness into the preschool and kindergarten classroom. Multiple examples are provided throughout of how to address specific challenging behaviors in the classroom with the most appropriate mindfulness-based, age-appropriate exercise. The OpenMind Program holds a compassionate container for both the teacher and the child, and will be of great benefit to classrooms and their broader communities."

—**Andrea Grabovac**, **MD**, clinical professor of psychiatry at the University of
British Columbia, and codirector of the North American chapter of the
Mindfulness-integrated Cognitive Behavioural Therapy Institute

"If you're an educator who wants to help your preschool students learn to cope more effectively with challenging emotions and be more focused in the classroom, this book will support you every step of the way. It provides a highly detailed and comprehensive guide to implementing the OpenMind Program, an empirically supported method to raise the social-emotional intelligence of young children."

—**Kristin Neff**, **PhD**, associate professor of educational psychology at the
University of Texas at Austin

"*Mindfulness for Preschool and Kindergarten* is a timely and authentic contribution to the burgeoning field of mindfulness-based programs for youth. Jackman has created a secular and developmentally appropriate mindfulness curricula to meet the social-emotional needs of today's children. Early childhood educators interested in learning how to embody and teach mindfulness are encouraged to read this book."

—**Joshua C. Felver**, **PhD**, **ABPP**, assistant professor of psychology and director of
clinical training at Syracuse University, and coauthor of *Mindfulness in the Classroom*

"*Mindfulness for Preschool and Kindergarten* is a gift for children, parents, and teachers! This book offers realistic exercises that intertwine conceptual and contextual learning into unique, developmentally appropriate play-based activities useful for learning in preschool and kindergarten—and for children's everyday life. The mindfulness exercises teach students to understand and communicate their emotions from a very early age."

—**B. Ann Bettencourt**, professor at the University of Missouri; associate editor
of the journal, *Mindfulness*; and author of a variety of research articles on the
topic of mindfulness

"*Mindfulness for Preschool and Kindergarten* is a timely, accessible, practical, and research-grounded resource for educators looking for comprehensive and effective guidance on supporting young children to develop key social and emotional skills of self-regulation, connection, and prosociality. Research consistently shows that fostering such skills from an early age improves children's lifelong prospects. The program presented in this book increases the likelihood of such long-term benefits by embedding age-appropriate practices into daily lives, expanding on the foundation of mindfulness through loving-kindness and gratitude practices, and a balanced approach to working with difficult emotions. The wide range of meaningfully combined practices in this book has the potential to encourage children in developing essential life skills and self-understanding from an early age."

—**Dusana Dorjee**, **PhD**, associate professor of psychology in education at the
University of York

MINDFULNESS
for Preschool
& Kindergarten

The **OpenMind** Program to
Boost Social-Emotional Learning
& Classroom Engagement

MONICA MOORE JACKMAN, OTD

New Harbinger Publications, Inc.

Publisher's Note

This publication is designed to provide accurate and authoritative information in regard to the subject matter covered. It is sold with the understanding that the publisher is not engaged in rendering psychological, financial, legal, or other professional services. If expert assistance or counseling is needed, the services of a competent professional should be sought.

NEW HARBINGER PUBLICATIONS
is a registered trademark of New Harbinger Publications, Inc.

New Harbinger Publications is an employee-owned company.

Copyright © 2022 by Monica Moore Jackman
New Harbinger Publications, Inc.
5674 Shattuck Avenue
Oakland, CA 94609
www.newharbinger.com

Cover design by Amy Daniel

Acquired by Tesilya Hanauer

Edited by Rona Bernstein

Indexed by James Minkin

Library of Congress Cataloging-in-Publication Data on file

Printed in the United States of America

24   23   22

10   9   8   7   6   5   4   3   2   1   First Printing

To all children—especially those who have struggled to learn, to belong, to understand themselves, to be themselves, and to be seen, heard, and loved no matter what—and to the amazing teachers, therapists, educators, assistants, and caregivers who support them to grow and go forth to make our world a better place.

Contents

PART 4: Bringing the OMPK Program to All Learners to Promote Quality of Life and Engagement

Foreword

When I was of preschool age, my father, who was my first spiritual teacher, said that I needed to learn to chant the 43 verses of the *Hanuman Chalisa*, a Hindu devotional hymn composed by Tulsidas in the 16th century. Although originally written in the Awadhi language, my father taught me the Sanskrit version––the language he had chanted in most of his life. When I asked him who Hanuman was, he said that he was the ocean of knowledge and that devotion to him can remove our afflictions and impurities of the mind. I learned to chant but had great difficulty translating the wisdom of the chants into my daily life. Fortunately for today's preschool and kindergarten children, such knowledge can be acquired in the classroom and practiced in daily life without having to learn foreign chants.

OpenMind-Preschool and Kindergarten (OMPK) is a mindfulness-based social-emotional learning (SEL) program for preschool and kindergarten children. Over the years, SEL practices have been integrated into and formed an essential part of preschool through high school education. While many SEL programs are available for older children, few evidence-based programs are available for younger children. OMPK is uniquely situated in this regard, being designed and tested specifically for preschool and kindergarten children. A critical feature of the program is that it is based on foundational mindfulness practices and anchored in social-emotional learning. The program provides teachers with training in mindfulness so that they can bring their embodied mindfulness into the classroom, teach the required school curriculum, and overlay mindfulness-based practices in the way they teach. This enables the children to better regulate their emotional ups and downs as they grow and develop into kind, loving, and compassionate human beings.

The OMPK program is presented in an accessible format that can be used by both novice and experienced teachers. The curriculum is designed for ease of implementation in the classroom with each of the core daily practices and supplemental learning activities having different graded variations of activities that range from easy to inspiring and thought-provoking. As a bonus, teachers can download over 150 pages of visuals, resources, and supplemental learning activities, as well as songs that accompany some of the activities. The curriculum has five overarching strengths that teachers will greatly appreciate.

The first strength is that the activities, practices, and structured support frameworks are designed to be inclusive and accessible to all learners, including those with language impairments, disabilities, trauma history, and so on. This differs from many other SEL programs that can be language-rich and require a certain baseline level of attention and expressive and receptive language that many young children may not have.

The second strength is that practices and supports are taught in a contextualized way, in the rhythm of life, rather than as scheduled or isolated lessons in a predetermined series. Many of the practices involve body-based hands-on engagement. In this way, children can learn from situations and opportunities that naturally arise, and not only understand the concepts taught, but also experience how the concepts feel. The practices are contextualized in life itself, whether it is in the classroom, at home, or in the community.

The third strength is that core practices are done daily, or as often as is appropriate because young children learn by repetition.

The fourth strength is the implementation of the 5P process that helps adults to see children who are exhibiting challenging behaviors as children who are lacking skills, a sense of safety, and/or connection. Instead of punishment or other negative consequences, teachers can support children to build missing skills and experience a better quality of life. Challenging behaviors are repurposed as learning opportunities, both for the teacher and for the child.

The fifth strength is the utilization of the CREATE framework that supports teachers to understand how to modify a learning environment or situation to help children feel engaged and successful when typical task's demands or activities may not align well with a child's abilities or interests.

It was my father's unshakeable belief that each child has innate wisdom buried deep within and that it can be awakened if given proper nourishment. Monica Moore Jackman has provided simple, tested, and effective tools for increasing the capacity of teachers to enable young children's minds to be nourished so that they are in touch with their intrinsic nature. As Martin Luther King said in another context, "we are confronted with the fierce of the urgency of now." In a world that is, in many ways, divided, we need to provide our children with the kind of wise and transformational teaching that is so well presented in this book. So, what are we waiting for? Let's embed the OMPK program as an immutable part of preschool and kindergarten education.

—Nirbhay N. Singh, PhD
  Medical College of Georgia, Augusta University

PART 1

Introduction, Overview, Foundations, and Theoretical Concepts

CHAPTER 1

Introduction to the OpenMind Preschool and Kindergarten (OMPK) Program

Young children in our world face increasing challenges and life storms, including adverse childhood experiences, trauma, social disconnection, systemic discrimination, and ongoing threats of human violence and natural disasters. As preschool and kindergarten teachers, educators, and therapists, you are on the frontlines of helping kids face these challenges, as your jobs include not only academic instruction, but also the vital task of teaching young children how to socially interact, solve problems, communicate, and work together, all while helping them feel valued, heard, protected, and supported. The weight of these responsibilities, plus the pressure of measuring and monitoring performance, can create stress and feelings of overwhelm that can at times feel impossible to manage. Over recent years, the rise in school shootings and race-based violence has added yet another challenge for teachers tasked with providing safe and nurturing learning environments. While teachers have worked tirelessly to implement new safety measures and drills, these are short-term fixes. Our current problem of human-on-human violence requires a more long-term solution—it calls for a massive change to put our efforts into building the skills that young children will need to prevent these acts of violence from continually occurring in the future.

One powerful way to change the world is to start by fostering and supporting love, kindness, compassion, acceptance, responsibility, presence, and resilience in its youngest citizens. The idea is that by teaching children to be mindful and to exhibit and practice all of these characteristics at a very young age, one in which they are experiencing an explosion of development, they will have a strong prosocial foundation on which to build the rest of their lives. In light of this, I created the OpenMind Preschool and

Kindergarten (OMPK) program to help children not only to be able to withstand inevitable life storms, but also to grow from them so that they can provide shade, shelter, and fruit for others, thereby making the world a better place. This program is for preschool and kindergarten classroom teachers, therapists, support staff, and caregivers who would like to learn to manage their own stress; to create safe, inclusive, peaceful, and mindful learning environments; to build learning readiness; to improve the development of the social-emotional, prosocial, and executive function skills of young children; and to prevent a culture of violence, oppression, and disconnection. For ease of readability, the term "teacher" in this book will refer to any adult who is helping and supporting a young child, and may include teachers, therapists, support staff, caregivers, or other educational professionals.

The OMPK program is a secular, humanist, and inclusive social-emotional learning (SEL) program, meaning that it is nonreligious, is concerned with the well-being of all people, is aimed at building common human and social values, and is accessible to children of all races, cultures, religions, and abilities. The OMPK program uses evidence-based mindfulness practices and a structured framework to provide a holistic and comprehensive program for all of us who wish to support young children's social, emotional, and academic learning, engagement, and quality of life. Used together, the practices and processes in this book can provide new tools for you to cope with stress and growing job demands; to find ways to help all learners, including the children who struggle the most; to create healthy and helpful classroom habits; and to build a culture of engagement, learning, discovery, peace, and prosocial action. Given that this is a big promise, you may already have many questions!

What Makes the Open Mind Preschool and Kindergarten Program Different from Other Programs?

There are many excellent, research-based SEL programs available that demonstrate positive outcomes in young children's social interactions, problem-solving skills, and emotional self-regulation. What makes the OMPK program stand out, however, is its unique approach to addressing accessibility and readiness in young children, the incorporation of practices into the children's daily lives, and the focus on meaningful engagement.

Accessibility and Learning Readiness

Most SEL programs involve a series of lessons that teach discrete social-emotional skills in a sequence, using structured, language-rich activities that require foundational skills and readiness. These programs are based on the presumption that children already have these abilities, which include attention, language comprehension, and even the ability to stay present in the learning area without running around, arguing, or becoming distracted by objects unrelated to the lesson. As a preschool or kindergarten teacher, you have probably experienced firsthand how difficult it can be to get a group of young children to quietly focus on a lesson, even a fun and exciting one!

The OMPK program does not just start with teaching new social and emotional material—it begins with teaching children how to be present for the learning process itself by building *self-regulation* (the ability to control impulses, emotions, and actions) and *attention.* As a parent, therapist, and instructor, I have witnessed many adults tell young children to "pay attention," and I have even said these words myself in the past. However, in all my years of experience, very few people have ever told me that they have explained and demonstrated exactly what this phrase means. We use this expression so much, and we expect children to engage in focused attention and self-control in the preschool and kindergarten setting, but the request itself gives children little idea of how to actually "pay attention." Most children eventually figure it out, but there is typically a uniform lack of explicit instruction about what it means—or more importantly, *how it feels*—to "pay attention." It can be even more confusing for children who struggle with understanding figurative language to understand this expression. I once worked with an autistic child who told me that he couldn't pay attention because he didn't have any money! His worry about his lack of money to "pay" attention actually impacted his ability to focus every time he heard these words.

Another factor associated with learning readiness is the ability to be "open" (hence, the name, OpenMind) and receptive to new ideas, information, and perspectives, especially the perspectives of others. When you want to illustrate a new lesson on a whiteboard, you do not write over the writing from a previous lesson—you first erase the board so that it is clean and clear. It is the same when working with young children who may have a mental whiteboard full of emotions, trauma history, sensory issues, and developmental impulses to move, play, or have fun. To teach a new lesson, we must be able to first help children clear their own mental whiteboards. The OMPK program uses experiential and hands-on exercises to build learning readiness and the ability to be present for and open to academic and social-emotional lessons, using structured processes and repeated practice.

Practice, Practice, Practice

If you have played sports, danced, painted, played an instrument, or learned any new language or skill, you already know that the best way to get better is to practice—a lot. Young children's brain development is use-dependent, and learning requires frequent repetition so that they can experience competence and *contextualized* understanding. Contextualized simply means that we are teaching, and children are learning, in the natural environment where a task occurs or a skill is required. For example, we can teach children about what it means to share with others during a planned Tuesday morning lesson, but when learning is contextualized, we would teach them about how to plan and problem solve how to share when materials may be limited and multiple children want the same items during center time. Teachers are very gifted at noticing when these learning opportunities arise. Yet when introducing new social-emotional skills to children, even complex skills like emotional awareness, many SEL programs attempt to teach this skill in just a few lessons, sometimes even just one. Take for example the skill of emotional awareness and labeling; most children need to practice this skill many times, in a variety of different situations throughout the day to fully be able to generalize it to other life situations.

The OMPK program uses a group of ten Daily Practices that are built into daily life so that children can practice them over and over, along with the activities they are already doing, until they begin to feel mastery of these skills. For example, in considering emotional awareness, the OMPK program provides a Daily Practice called the "Feelings Finder," which includes multiple activities to help children identify, label, and describe emotions and can be applied repeatedly, in different contexts. These learning contexts can include identifying emotions during a daily check-in, identifying the emotions of characters in a storybook as a component of literature and narrative retelling, expressing positive feelings during times of achievement and success, expressing what emotions one is feeling and where they are being felt in the body following a meltdown or conflict with a peer, and identifying the emotions in others via teacher modeling, storytelling, puppet shows, and/or facilitated perspective taking.

A second example is the practice of a foundational skill necessary for learning readiness: the seemingly simple ability to stay present in the learning area long enough to actively listen to a book being read or a lesson explained. It may seem silly, but young children often need to practice the skill of waiting. Getting preschool and kindergarten-aged children to sit still long enough to hear you read an entire book can be a very daunting task, especially considering that many children also have developmental delays, history of trauma, behavioral difficulties, or a diagnosis of attention-deficit/hyperactivity disorder (ADHD) or other neurodevelopmental disorder that may make sitting still very difficult for them. As a preschool or kindergarten teacher, you can spend much of your time just trying to get everyone to stay in the learning area, somewhat quietly, without rolling around, making noises, or recruiting friends to play instead of listen. An example of how the OMPK program may target the skill of staying present in the learning area is by using the "Bell Practices," which are play-based tasks for waiting and staying focused and quiet. For instance, you could facilitate an activity for passing a "sleeping" baby doll around a circle upon the sound of a bell; each time the bell rings, the child passes the baby to the next child quietly and slowly so as not to "wake" the baby. Once the students get better at this skill and different play-based variations of it, it can be generalized to other learning contexts. In this case, going back to story time, you could ring a bell when it is time to turn a page, and have a different child turn the page each time to increase engagement and interest. There are many variations of the OMPK "Bell Practices" that can be used throughout the day in different contexts that require waiting, such as during transitions to line up, waiting one's turn, and so on.

The most exciting part of this process is that once children start to feel competent, they often begin to intuitively and spontaneously try to teach and support others to gain these skills. I remember seeing a total transformation within a classroom in which children initially exhibited aggressive behaviors while waiting in line and putting on coats to go outside. The teacher linked the waiting activity to a loving-kindness and kindness-reporting practice, and over time, children who were able began to assist peers who were struggling to button their coats, while the peers who were being helped waited patiently and expressed gratitude for the assistance.

In addition to intentionally practicing what we want to get better at doing, it's important to be aware of what we are already practicing, perhaps unintentionally. We don't always realize that in our daily lives we are constantly practicing social-emotional behaviors—sometimes nonconstructive ones—often without even noticing. When we practice worrying, we get very good at worrying and we strengthen this ability. When we practice getting angry and taking the hurtful comments or behaviors of others personally, we get very good at reacting out of anger and striking back at others. The awareness of what we are practicing can help us know what we are (even unintentionally) strengthening, and we can begin to understand that in order to be healthy and strong we must balance our self-protective habits with our positive and prosocial habits, such as noticing moments of joy and expressing gratitude when things go our way.

Balance

Throughout this book you will see the term *equanimity*. Simply stated, equanimity is our ability to find and maintain balance, even when our world is unbalanced, and to accept our situation for what it is; think of it as staying on your feet in a rowboat in the middle of a sea of huge and unpredictable waves. The OMPK program was initially developed for children living in poverty, many of whom were living in unsafe or unpredictable environments and/or experiencing trauma, abuse, language disorders, developmental delays, and behavior challenges. While it is impossible to change our history and, often, our life circumstances, the goal is to help both children and ourselves to develop resilience and equanimity that makes us feel grounded and strong, even in the face of turbulent times.

There is a well-known Cherokee teaching in which a grandfather is teaching his grandson about how to handle the battle that occurs within the human mind. The grandfather says that there are two wolves battling: the dark wolf, which represents things such as anger, ego, greed, dishonesty, and guilt; and the light wolf, which represents things such as love, peace, generosity, and compassion. When the boy asks which wolf will win, his grandfather tells him, "The one that you feed." While it is important to practice feeding the light wolf, who brings positive aspects to our lives, we cannot completely ignore the dark wolf, as that wolf is also a part of us—a part that can protect us, strengthen us, and help us to stand up for what is right. Thus, the OMPK program helps children and teachers to acknowledge and respond to difficult feelings and circumstances while also feeding the positive skills and habits necessary to learn from and overcome these challenges.

For example, common practice is to give a child a time-out for angry behavior such as hitting a peer or to ask a child to apologize when they are still feeling hurt and emotionally overwhelmed. Instead, using OMPK interactive practices and visual tools, you can give the child a safe space and time to calm down and help the child to process the type of anger they are feeling, the other emotions (e.g., fear, overwhelm) that might have increased or triggered the anger, and the reason for the emotions. Once the child understands the reason for the anger, you can help them figure out a way to use the energy that the anger brought to solve a problem in a nonhurtful way and to engage in a prosocial action to remedy the hurtful choice. In this way, the child has acknowledged and spent time experiencing the challenging emotions, and has also had a chance to "feed" the associated positive emotions and actions, not because they are getting a sticker or a reward, but because prosocial actions themselves and the resulting benefits to others are intrinsically rewarding. As you can imagine, attaining a balance requires a lot of initial effort and considerable awareness by both the child and the teacher, but it can result in true learning and growth. This type of awareness requires mindfulness.

What Is Mindfulness?

Whenever I lead a training or course, I always begin by asking participants what they think mindfulness means, and I get many different answers. Some are spot on, because participants have prior knowledge or have looked ahead in the course book, but most are close, and relate to being focused and being present. I have met some people who were concerned that mindfulness and meditation were religious practices that could conflict with their own beliefs. While it is true that mindfulness practices and terms were initially derived from Buddhist practices, the mindfulness and meditation practices in the OMPK program are secular, or nonreligious in nature, so that they can be used by people of all cultural backgrounds, no matter their personal and spiritual beliefs.

Mindfulness is the practice of being attentive to and aware of life's present-moment events and our experiences of them as they come and go, without trying to hold on to, run away from, or control them. Mindfulness requires the ability to notice both what is happening and how we are reacting to what is happening, while simultaneously considering the effects of our actions on others. The most commonly referenced operational definition of mindfulness is "the awareness that arises through paying attention, on purpose in the present moment, and non-judgmentally" (Kabat-Zinn 1994, p. 4). Using the example in the section above, if you are trying to balance standing up in a rowboat in the middle of a stormy sea, you would need to use mindfulness to avoid toppling over. This may include awareness of your body and muscles, awareness of the size of the waves coming, awareness of your footing on the slippery floor, awareness of the force of the winds, awareness of your own fear, and even awareness of when to take cover, lie down, and hold tight if you see a large shark approaching. While this is an extreme example, mindfulness in daily life involves awareness of just as many factors; it requires us to be able to see both the individual trees and the forest simultaneously.

In the very first section, I described the OMPK program as being humanist, so to take mindfulness a step further, let's talk about the concept of "right" mindfulness—mindfulness with a moral, humanist, and ethical intention. Practicing "right" mindfulness means being able to focus on and attend to one thing while maintaining awareness of stimuli around us and within us, being ready to shift our focus as needed, and being able to do all of this while maintaining openhearted and positive intentions for others. For example, if you are walking while carrying a hot cup of coffee across your brand-new rug, you are likely to be focused on not spilling the coffee on the rug, but you must also be aware of your speed, the movement of your hand, the level of the coffee, your own worry about how clumsy you are, and any obstacles to avoid on the rug itself. However, if your new puppy suddenly darts toward your feet, your focus will probably shift from not spilling coffee on your new rug to not burning your puppy, while maintaining awareness of your own balance, your feeling of regret about buying a new rug and adopting a new puppy at the same time, and so on.

In addition to combining attention and awareness to be fully present in the moment, with positive intentions, right mindfulness also requires us to be open to and accepting of what the present moment is offering. Mindfulness helps us enter into a situation or interaction without assuming that we already know what is going to happen. It is about being present for the possibilities of each moment without always feeling the constant need to run from or prevent pain or boredom, or to seek entertainment and "good" emotions. Being mindful in no way means that we do not feel uncomfortable and volatile emotions like anger; it means that we can accept and acknowledge the anger and its function, and use that emotion as a signal of a problem that we can resolve. For instance, if you have carefully and painstakingly prepared materials for a craft-based lesson on your own personal time, and your students do not seem interested in the lesson, or accidently destroy some of the materials, it is okay to feel angry. Being mindful means that you can feel angry and express your frustration in a way that lets children know how you are feeling, without reacting in a potentially harmful way, such as yelling in a hurtful tone. You can also work to remedy the situation by modifying the activity in the moment to increase interest by following the children's lead and ideas.

Finally, while there are many parts to mindfulness, it is important to note that mindfulness is not the same as multitasking. With multitasking, the brain is trying to focus on more than one thing at the same time. On the contrary, with mindfulness, the brain is focused on one task, while maintaining awareness of, or noticing, internal and external factors. In fact, the original Pali word for mindfulness means "remembrance";

one interpretation of this is to think of mindfulness as the practice of consistently remembering to be present. Another explanation is that when we are mindful, we take note of what is happening around us, and file it efficiently in our brain for easier retrieval later. Have you ever walked into a room of your house but then completely forgot why you went in there? It is likely because you were focused on thinking about something else—mental multitasking! This is in our nature, but even though our brains are wired to reflexively shift focus to survive, and our minds are designed to wander so that we can process ideas and social situations, we can build mindfulness with practice. Mindfulness is not about having perfect focus and control, but rather it is about remembering our intentions to be present when we notice that we are mentally multitasking or spending the present moment dwelling in the past or anticipating the future.

So why teach mindfulness to children? As mentioned above, mindfulness in daily life means being able to observe the world with an open heart and sense of discovery, without an assumption of predetermined knowledge and understanding. Young children, by nature, often exhibit the type of inquiring beginner's mind that comes with exploring the world and all its sensations and wonders. Mindfulness is about observing the world with curiosity, and children often embody open inquisitiveness, because they are so often experiencing events and sensations for the first time. As children grow older, they begin to develop premature cognitive commitments to people, concepts, and occurrences and can form biases regarding the types of events and sensations that they notice, evaluate, and subsequently avoid or approach. They often become less tolerant and more set in their ways. Given that it is a natural human tendency to pursue self-preservation (to look out for ourselves) and self-gratification (to engage in actions that make us feel good) and to compete in society, children may encounter difficulty regulating and controlling their reactions in a mindful way.

Supporting Research

As a full-time clinician and mother of four, I have used these practices and processes daily in both my personal and my professional life and can attest that I have seen many children benefit. In fact, the original inspiration behind many of these practices and activities has been my beautiful, brilliant, neurodiverse son, who has taught me so much about how to address and view challenges in areas such as emotion regulation, sensory processing, flexibility, transitions, and pragmatic language skills in new and creative ways.

Thanks to a lot of incredible teachers and researchers, I can also share some research that supports the OMPK program. The OMPK program is based on research findings from a variety of disciplines—especially developmental psychology, positive psychology, and occupational therapy—and from subspecialty areas such as mindfulness and social-emotional learning. The program has benefitted from multiple revisions based on feedback from teachers who have used the program, and from researchers who have evaluated its feasibility, acceptability, and outcomes for both teachers and their students. The following paragraphs outline recent research on the OMPK program, including its replication in Korean preschools.

In a cluster randomized controlled trial, Jackman et al. (2019) assessed the feasibility, acceptability, and preliminary effectiveness of the OMPK program with 262 preschool children, 27 teachers, and 281 parents. The children were randomly assigned by classrooms to either the experimental (i.e., OMPK) group or to an active control group (i.e., comparison program). Both groups were in effect for one school year. The teachers reported that it was feasible for them to integrate the OMPK program within the school's regular curriculum. Teachers in the OMPK group of classrooms reported benefits for the children in terms of improved self-regulation, increased body and emotional awareness, improved self-calming ability, and increased empathy and awareness of the feelings of others. The teachers rated the OMPK program as very acceptable and indicated that they would recommend it to other preschool teachers. The outcome data indicated positive child outcomes for both groups, with added advantage for the children in the OMPK program.

Kim et al. (2019a) evaluated the feasibility and acceptability of the OpenMind program that was translated into Korean, culturally contextualized, and implemented as the OpenMind-Korea (OM-K) program in Korean preschools. Six preschools were cluster randomized into an active experimental (OM-K) group and a control group. The teachers in the OM-K group completed a thirty-four-item feasibility questionnaire and an eight-item acceptability questionnaire following implementation of the OM-K program over one school year. Furthermore, they were individually interviewed regarding their views of the OM-K program. The teachers fluently implemented three or four of the Daily Practices on a regular basis, and the rest of the activities as much as possible. They were able to embed the OM-K activities within the Nuri Curriculum that is mandated in all Korean preschools and adapted the activities according to the children's needs and space available in each classroom. The teachers rated the OM-K program as being feasible to implement within the Korean preschool system and as acceptable to them. All teachers uniformly reported that they would recommend the program to other preschool teachers because of its positive effects on both the teachers and the children.

In a related study, Kim et al. (2019b) assessed the parental social validity of the OM-K program. Social validity in this context refers to the parents' opinion of the social significance of the goals, social appropriateness of the program, and social importance of the outcomes for the teachers and children. Results showed that the majority of the parents' ratings were positive about the OM-K program, especially with regard to its usefulness to their children both at school and at home. They found the program to be simple and easy to use, effective, and acceptable for their children, with no adverse unintended effects. The majority of parents reported that they would recommend it to other parents. Together with the results reported by Kim et al. (2019a), these results demonstrate that the OM-K was acceptable to both teachers and parents of three- to five-year-old children.

In a randomized controlled trial, Kim et al. (2020) assessed the effects of the OM-K program on preschool children's emotion regulation, resilience, and prosocial behaviors. Two of four preschools were randomly assigned to the experimental (OM-K) group and the other two to the control group. The teachers in the experimental group implemented the OM-K program with 42 children, and the teachers in the control group provided instruction as usual to 41 children. At the start of the study, based on a pretest, teacher ratings of the children in the control group were significantly better on all outcome variables than those in the OM-K group. And although children in the OM-K group improved on all outcome variables, the children in the control condition group continued to be rated somewhat higher on all outcome variables at the first posttraining assessment. However, at the second and third posttraining assessments, the children in the OM-K group were given significantly higher ratings on lability/negativity, resilience, and prosocial behaviors than the children in the control group. This study suggested that engaging preschool children in the OM-K program enhanced their emotion regulation (lability/negativity), resilience, and prosocial behaviors (helping, sharing, cooperation, and comfort to others).

Pause for Reflection...

If you have picked up this book, you probably have already thought about the possible benefits of bringing mindfulness into the lives of the young children you support. Before I developed this program, I taught mindfulness practices to adults and older children; I wasn't sure how younger children would respond to it—especially the meditation part! I began to use the practices with young children in therapy and with my own little ones, and I was amazed at how well they soaked it all in and benefitted, especially when we went slowly and used lots of hands-on activities. If you think about the many strengths that preschool and kindergarten children have, like their sense of wonder and excitement at exploring what life has to offer and their capacity for loving everyone and making friends without bias, then it is easy to understand the following reasons for using the OMPK curriculum with young children:

1. By nature, children have a beginner's mind and sense of openhearted discovery that provide fertile and receptive soil for planting seeds of mindfulness.

2. Growing and cultivating mindfulness at a young age supports the development of SEL skills and resilience.

3. When we embody mindfulness, we can model prosocial actions for children and notice their needs and strengths more clearly.

4. If we can see with an open mind children who are struggling, we can look at challenging behaviors in a new light, as signals that alert us to what skills they need to learn.

5. When children embody "right" mindfulness, they model this way of being, effect change in the atmosphere of their culture, engage in prosocial actions, and in doing so act to make the world better for others.

With that rationale for the OMPK program in mind, we'll turn to chapter 2 to explore the foundations of the program.

CHAPTER 2

Overview and Foundations of the OMPK Program

In chapter 1, we discussed how the OMPK program is unique in that it uses an inclusive, contextualized format, rooted in repeated practice. This chapter will provide a detailed description of the five basic foundations of the OMPK program and will close with a look at the format of the program.

Our children's educational environments are rife with disparity, inequity, and inequality due to factors such as poverty, systemic racism, and ableism (i.e., prejudice or discrimination against people with disabilities). As a result, many children may miss out on the benefits of traditional SEL programs due to differences in language skills, executive function, history of or ongoing trauma, and learning styles. Instead of a "one size fits all" approach to a sequential, lesson-based social-emotional program, the OMPK program teaches ten Daily Practices, each of which offers varying options based on level of difficulty and type of learning modality. This makes it possible for you to customize lessons and practices for all types of learners and align practices with children's interests and strengths. Many activities are multisensory and body based and can be adapted according to children's needs and interests. In addition, the OMPK program incorporates structured processes that are done in real time, in context, and when the need arises, allowing you to help children who are struggling with challenging behaviors and learning readiness to grow, develop missing skills, and access new learning.

The Five Foundations of the OMPK Program

What makes the above aspects of the OMPK program possible are the five basic foundations on which it stands. These foundations are:

1. Mindfulness training for teachers, support staff, therapists, and caregivers to enable them to embody and model mindfulness and to enhance authenticity of teaching mindfulness and resilience;

2. Consistent classroom Daily Practices and practice variations for children that are integrated into the rhythm of life to build self-regulation, executive function, and engagement from the bottom up and to allow for organic contextualized learning experiences;

3. Planned practices and lessons taught in response to arising individual and classroom needs and/or anchored to academic content;

4. A five-part process for transforming children's challenging behaviors into opportunities for learning, growth, autonomy, and agency, and for creating a prosocial classroom environment; and

5. A structured format for helping children who are struggling to be more engaged and experience more inclusion and enjoyment in the classroom.

Foundation 1: *OpenMind Teacher Mindfulness Practice*

To effectively teach the OMPK practices to children, we ourselves must practice mindfulness authentically. In addition, teaching is one of the most stressful jobs out there! This is why the first part of the program has been designed for us adults who are teaching and supporting young children. It is the fundamental base for all of the other program foundations.

Young children engage in observational learning, and when we embody mindful engagement, we provide modeling and examples of the practices in action. On the contrary, when we do not act mindfully, we can send children mixed messages. For example, yelling at a group of children to talk quietly can send a confusing message, and we know that children learn more from seeing *what to do* than from being told *what not to do*. In addition, by working to maintain a mindful presence, we can create a milieu of nonjudgmental safety and connection, which further serves to foster relationship building.

The OpenMind Resilience, Equanimity, and Mindfulness (REMIND) practices were designed for teachers and other adults to build executive function skills such as attention, focus, emotional control, and mental flexibility; to increase awareness; to foster appreciation of positive emotional experiences; to help you stay present; and to establish and strengthen positive wellness habits. There are seven REMIND practices, each of which is matched to a different color of the rainbow to help you to remember the different practice options by color association. Each REMIND practice is also matched to a different wellness state that can help us stay balanced among the inevitable uncertainty, stress, and chaos that is inherent in a preschool and kindergarten classroom—and characteristic of life itself. The seven REMIND practices and corresponding wellness states are as follows:

- Loving-kindness meditation (red): Loving, kind, forgiving, inclusive

- Open monitoring meditation (orange): Present, open, nonjudgmental, flexible

- Joy meditation (yellow): Joyful, fun, lighthearted

- Embodied meditation (green): Grounded, aware, discerning

- Focused meditation (blue): Peaceful, calm, patient

- Compassion meditation (indigo): Compassionate, empathetic

- Gratitude meditation (violet): Grateful, appreciative

The OpenMind REMIND practices are unique in that they have been designed from an occupation-based perspective, which means that they can be used in the daily rhythm of life to support your engagement in daily occupations of life (work, rest, play, self-care). An occupation is any meaningful activity that occupies our time. In this way, the mindfulness practice can be an occupation in itself, such as sitting in meditation first thing in the morning to clear our minds for the day, or it can be linked to an occupation, such as engaging in compassion meditation while sitting with a friend in pain, or using informal joy practice while eating an ice-cream cone. Once the mindfulness practices are anchored to occupations or become meaningful occupations in our daily lives, they are more likely to be continued as habits and practiced regularly. Each of the seven REMIND practices includes options for formal, informal, and PAUSE practices. The formal mindfulness practices offer a way to build attention, concentration, focus, and awareness through meditation practiced intentionally, and repeatedly, from the bottom up. The informal mindfulness practices are a means to put the skills you build during formal mindfulness meditation practices into action, by applying them to daily life situations. For example, you may be able to use formal focused breathing to feel calm in the quiet of morning, before your children are awake, but it is equally important to practice mindfulness during the chaos of the busy before-school routine. Finally, the PAUSE practices offer a way to stop in daily life, notice what's happening, choose a response that is not harmful to others or ourselves, and set an intention to build a positive habit.

Foundation 2: *Practice in the Rhythm of Life*

Much like the teacher practices, the OMPK classroom practices use an occupation-based form of teaching and experience. Lessons are delivered and practiced in what we call the classroom rhythm of life (during play, academic lessons, transitions, self-care activities, recess, and collaborative group learning) instead of at a designated, separate, decontextualized, or preset learning time. The term *rhythm of life* refers to the use of activities in the naturalistic context of daily life when the need or opportunity for a learning experience occurs. For example, you may introduce an activity to encourage loving-kindness practice and nonjudgment if a child is being excluded by peers because they look different or engage in unique methods of self-regulation such as flapping their hands.

GENERALIZATION AND RETENTION OF SKILLS

The occupation-based format of OMPK aligns with the learning concept called *contextual interference,* which means that retention and generalization of skills are increased when practice schedules are random and done in context, rather than at a planned and dedicated time. Random practice schedules, wherein all aspects of a task are practiced with a higher level of contextual interference may result in poorer performance during practice trials, but result in better retention and better performance during transfer of the task to real life (Battig, 1979; Magill, 2001; Magill & Hall, 1990). This means that children can better generalize what they have learned when they learn in a natural, contextualized way than when they practice in a prescriptive and overly planned manner.

Research has shown that engagement in play, consistent practice of exercises throughout the academic day, and increasing executive challenges impact the success of executive function skills programs and gains in executive function, which are necessary for attention and self-regulation (Diamond & Lee, 2011; Diamond et al., 2007). Moreover, embedding processes into the natural rhythm of classroom life can enhance the foundational skills necessary for academic engagement and provide a context for generalization of social and emotional lessons into other areas of daily life. In line with foundation 2, the OMPK program involves ten Daily Practices and practice variations that children perform during the school day.

THE TEN DAILY PRACTICES

The Daily Practice activities help children learn to be aware of themselves and others, to give attention and awareness to what is happening in the present moment, to enhance social-emotional competence, and to act with kindness and compassion. When you work with children to practice these activities as a part of the daily routine, they can become habits that support being mindful in daily life. To ensure that Daily Practices remain child driven, and not prescriptive and teacher driven, some activities are designed to change each day or be performed as needed in the rhythm of life. Other Daily Practices include multiple variations of modality (e.g., song or visual) or rhythm-of-life context (e.g., time of day, large group, outside, following child meltdown) to ensure that they are dynamic enough to meet changing needs while remaining supportive of the foundational learning practices.

When implemented consistently, the Daily Practices become woven into the daily routine and serve to build an environment in which teachers and children notice and reinforce prosocial behaviors. In this way, the system of these practices becomes self-sustaining, as often the resulting behavioral outcomes and actions (e.g., sharing, kindness) lead to reciprocal positive acts. In other words, positive behaviors and actions can become contagious! Collectively, the Daily Practices serve to nourish the development of equanimity, loving-kindness, compassion, and empathetic joy, which help to bring people closer together in spite of the human tendency to act out of self-interest. In addition, these practices can prevent antisocial behavioral actions such as harming or taking from others and using unkind or dishonest speech.

The Daily Practices include:

1. Meditation
    a. Sitting Meditation
    b. Walking Meditation and Guided Movement
2. Are You Present for Me?
3. Bell Exercises
4. Yoga Postures and Body Awareness
5. Feelings Finder Practices
6. Super Me Practices
7. Loving-Kindness Practices
8. Gratitude and Interconnectedness Practices
9. Kindness and Compassion Reporting Practices
10. Soles of the Little Feet and Shifting Practices

These activities are designed to engage all children, regardless of ability. You, as the teacher, have the freedom to decide when and where to practice based on your students' needs for that day. Table 1 provides an overview of the types of behaviors and social-emotional skills that may increase with the implementation and integration of each Daily Practice into the classroom or family culture. These behaviors and skills serve not only to enhance learning and development, but also to improve quality of life. The table also lists challenging behaviors that may decrease with the use of each Daily Practice.

Table 1

Daily Practice	Quality of Life Indicators or Skills That May Increase in Children	Nonfunctional Behaviors or Problems That May Decrease in Children
Meditation (A): Sitting Meditation	Attention, focus, concentration, staying present, listening, self-control of body movements	Inability to sit still, difficulty waiting, impulsivity, fidgeting, becoming easily distracted, stress
Meditation (B): Walking Meditation and Guided Movement	Attention and awareness of body movements, experience of how calm movement feels, balance, control of body movements and speed of movement, inhibitory control	Impulsive movement, fidgeting, difficulty delaying gratification, poor grading and control of force and speed of body movements
Are You Present for Me?	Respect for others, ability to wait to get the full attention of others, understanding of "being present"	Impatience, interrupting, using disruptive behaviors to request attention, not being present for others and for learning
Bell Exercises	Awareness of classroom activities, attention to teacher instruction, self-awareness, intentional attention shift, being present, working memory	Decreased attention to teacher instruction, loud or disruptive classroom behavior, difficulty shifting attention, difficulty staying in the present
Yoga Postures and Body Awareness	Attention and awareness of body sensations, movements, and breath; balance; strength; control of body movements	Stress and tension, fidgeting, difficulty staying still, poor awareness and control of body sensations and movements
Feelings Finder© Practices	Recognition of emotions in self and others, emotional awareness and identification, communication of emotion with others, emotion regulation, perspective taking	Difficulty expressing and controlling reactions to emotions during times of distress, poor awareness of others' emotions, difficulty with emotional perspective taking and empathy

Daily Practice	Quality of Life Indicators or Skills That May Increase in Children	Nonfunctional Behaviors or Problems That May Decrease in Children
Super Me© Practices	Forgiveness, helping others, sharing and giving, listening, self-calming, trying, conflict resolution, using kind words and kind hands, comforting others, making compromises, supporting peers, self-kindness and self-compassion, putting forth effort on difficult tasks, making a meaningful apology, connection	Jealousy and envy, lying, using unkind words, arguing over toys, whining, yelling, physical aggression, selfish behavior, stealing, disruptive or destructive actions, negative self-talk, not trying, difficulty apologizing to others or resolving conflicts
Loving-Kindness Practices	Unconditional caring for others, feelings of acceptance for others, nonjudgment of others	Envy, difficulty forgiving others, fighting, judging others, being upset when others don't comply with one's wishes
Gratitude and Interconnectedness Practices	Grateful attitude, appreciation for others, thankfulness for things or kind acts received, noticing the positive aspects of life, awareness of social connection	Complaining, lack of appreciation for actions of others, not expressing thanks for things or actions received, feelings of entitlement, greed, selfish behavior
Kindness and Compassion Reporting Practices	Awareness of kind and compassionate acts of others, ability to notice and report positive actions and effort by others	Tattling, complaining about others for adult attention, focusing on negative aspects of others
Soles of the Little Feet and Shifting Practices	Responding instead of reacting to emotional impulses, ability to decrease suffering from difficult emotions, shifting from focus on difficult emotions to also notice positive emotions	Reacting to difficult emotions with physical and/or verbal aggression, engaging in disruptive behaviors, emotional suffering

Foundation 3: *Planned Practices That Meet an Identified Need or Teach an Explicit Lesson*

The OMPK program was designed to be both flexible and structured to enable us to be responsive to changing individual and group needs. Thus, in addition to regular mindfulness practices to build skills, the OMPK program uses planned lessons that can address present-moment concerns and be anchored to academic tasks such as language and literacy activities. For example, two of the primary OMPK Daily Practices are the Feelings Finder practices for emotional awareness and regulation, and the Super Me practices for prosocial behaviors and self-management. If children are having difficulty sharing, resulting in aggression and distress, you can use these practices as a planned lesson to retrospectively process the situation when everyone is calm and to teach and reinforce emotional and social awareness, perspective taking, problem solving, and prosocial alternatives using available classroom tools such as storybooks, puppets, and interactive visuals and objects. In addition to the Daily Practices, supplemental learning activities are available to further help you to meet identified individual and classroom needs.

The OMPK Supplemental Learning Activities complement and enhance the Daily Practices to teach children how to live more mindfully and act with equanimity, loving-kindness, compassion, and joy. These practices help children to build social-emotional skills that can support both personal well-being and academic success. Activities are organized into eight different social-emotional skill areas, or modules. These modules include:

1. Self-awareness and self-control of body and movement

2. Attention and awareness in the present moment

3. Self-calming

4. Self-regulation of emotions for making positive behavioral choices

5. Social awareness and social connection

6. Social communication

7. Positive interaction with others (conflict resolution, sharing, helping)

8. Self-kindness and self-compassion

Beyond helping children at an individual level, the focus of these practices is to help children learn how to help others and make the world a better place for others. Many of the activities include art, music, and movement modalities common in preschool class-rooms. In addition, many activities are designed to support extension lessons in academic topic areas (e.g., science, phonological awareness, preliteracy) and offer you an opportunity to use your teaching expertise and creativity. As with the OMPK Daily Practices, the OMPK Supplemental Learning Activities in each module are arranged to progress in level of difficulty so that you can match an activity to a child's developmental level and interests. Chapter 14 will give you an overview of these activities, and the full spectrum of activities, including instructions and full-color visual support tools, are available as downloadable accessories at the website for this book, http://www.newharbinger.com/49258. (See the very back of this book for more details.) Given that child learning, understanding, and retention of concepts is enhanced by teaching, each module also includes an opportunity for children to lead and teach the prosocial skills and practices (i.e., child-as-teacher practices).

Foundation 4: *Supporting Positive Behaviors*

Many people view challenging behaviors as evidence that a child is intentionally manipulating a situation, acting out for attention or to get their way, or trying to escape a situation. In these instances, adults often use rewards (such as point sheets or sticker charts) and punishment (such as withholding of recess or screen time) to lead children to stop the challenging behaviors and replace them with positive behaviors. However, keep in mind this important point: if a child does not have the present moment ability to meet the behavioral goal, they will not succeed no matter how much they want to. To use an example from my life, I have a condition called postural orthostatic tachycardia syndrome (POTS), which often makes my heart rate skyrocket when I am standing, requiring me to sit or lie down so that I do not pass out, and the heat exacerbates my symptoms. If you offered me one million dollars to run a marathon in my home state of Florida tomorrow, I would not be able to meet the goal no matter how much I may want the reward—I would likely collapse long before the three-mile mark!

A key tenet of the OMPK program is that children who exhibit challenging behaviors are demonstrating a lack of or deficit in skills necessary for self-regulation, emotion regulation, sensory regulation, problem solving, social interaction, self-regulated learning, self-efficacy, autonomy, and/or communication. Often, these challenges can arise from disparities due to factors such as implicit bias and systemic racism. For example, Black children are 70% less likely to receive an ADHD diagnosis than white children with similar behaviors and presentation (Morgan et. al., 2014). Also, compared to white children, Black children are more likely to be diagnosed with conduct disorder and less likely to be diagnosed with ADHD and to receive psychiatric treatment (Baglivio et al., 2016). As a result, minority children are more likely to be labeled as having "behavior problems" or as being "bad kids" and less likely to receive the services and interventions they need to address the true underlying skill deficits, which likely came about because of inequality. In other words, they are more likely to receive punishment than treatment. One of the main goals of the OMPK program is to create a culture of learning instead of a cycle of punishment, as punishment does not teach missing skills. Without learning, behaviors can escalate throughout the lifespan and result in increasing levels of punishment, such as institutionalization and prison.

In addition, approximately 18% of young children in the United States are living in poverty (National Center for Children in Poverty, 2018). Children living in poverty experience increased risk for developmental delays, increased stress, impaired academic achievement, and reduced measures of self-regulation (Wanless et al., 2011; Blair et al., 2011; Bradley & Corwyn, 2002; Duncan & Brooks-Gunn, 2000; Mistry et al., 2010; Raver et al., 2013). One study indicated that over 40% of children living in poverty entered school with delays in social competence and communication (Kaiser et al., 2000). These factors can lead to skill deficits that manifest as challenging behaviors, lead to more "bad kid" and "behavior problem" labels, and ultimately contribute to the continued cycle of poverty as children receive increasing levels of punishment that limit opportunity, rather than support skills.

The OMPK program views challenging behaviors not simply as triggers for working toward extinction of the problem behaviors, but as opportunities to learn foundational skills to promote success and quality of life. To help children when these challenging situations arise in the classroom, the OMPK program uses the 5P Process:

- Protect, be Present, and Prepare

- Process

- Problem Solve

- Practice Prosocial Behavior

- Praise

This process, which we will cover in Part 4 of this book, supports adults to help a child who is struggling to learn *what to do* instead of telling them *what not to do*.

Foundation 5: *Mindful Engagement*

The OMPK program was influenced by many theoretical perspectives, though the primary conceptual model underpinning the delivery of the program is that of mindful occupational engagement. The popular connotation of the term "occupation" is that of work done for pay, yet the operational definition for human occupation includes any meaningful activity or role that occupies a person's time. *Occupations* are not simple, static mechanistic tasks, but are multidimensional transactions between person, physical environment, social milieu, and cultural contexts that are constantly influenced by changing personal motivation, purpose, meaning, and values. *Engagement* speaks to the manner in which we perform an occupation; we can think of it as the degree to which we invest ourselves in a particular task. For example, have you ever been so immersed in a task, such as drawing, cooking, gardening, or reading, that you maintained focus and did it for the pure experience of it, without feeling pressure to do it? This is mindful occupational engagement! The value of engagement in occupation lies not in its purpose or outcome, but in the subjective experience that engagement brings (Hasselkus, 2006), much like mindfulness itself.

Mindful occupational engagement can be defined as "the moment-by-moment, open-hearted awareness and nonjudgmental engagement in an activity, without expectation of specific outcomes" (Jackman, 2014, p. 244). Mindful engagement is a state of being that requires active presence. In contrast, *participation* can be passive and is typically focused on a goal-directed task or avoidance of an unpleasant consequence. Children who are engaged and feel a sense of connection to learning experience more academic success than children who are disengaged (Finn & Rock, 1997; Osterman, 2000). Engagement appears to be mediated by attention and persistence. Attention can be either involuntary (e.g., captured and maintained by novelty or high-interest activities) or effortful and voluntary (Kaplan, 1995; Kaplan & Berman, 2010).

The OMPK practices and activities were designed with the goal of creating opportunities for mindfully engaged social-emotional learning to occur through activities that initially capture children's involuntary attention as a means of then practicing effortful attention. In other words, you can ease students into practicing difficult skills like waiting and focusing by starting with a simpler version of the task that is also fun. One of my favorite activities for capturing attention in young children is bringing out a new or interesting item (such as a little character made out of a puffball) or putting an everyday item (such as a slinky) in a bag for kids to pass around and feel. Then, I explain an activity or a game that they will play with the item, which requires more effortful attention that has been primed by the initial curiosity and excitement. For example, we may use the slinky or a puffball for one of the Daily Practice meditation and breathing exercises.

There is a qualitative, observable difference between a child who is participating or doing something without awareness, or with an extrinsic goal-directed focus such as earning a reward or avoiding punishment, and a child who is mindfully engaged. With the former, the expectation of a particular outcome may induce stress if the child is under a time pressure, or if the outcome is not achievable or meaningful to the child; in these cases, the child is focused more on the outcome (future reward, failure, punishment) than on the present-moment experience of engagement in the task, and this can result in withdrawal or refusal. For example, if a child who takes longer to process verbal information is pressed to quickly answer a question before being ready, they may shut down and not answer at all. Or, a child who has poor trunk control and core strength may not be able to sit unsupported on the carpet or even in a chair for long without shifting position or standing up, and therefore would be unable to "sit still" despite trying. Furthermore, if there is a mismatch between task demands and a child's skill or arousal level, they may become bored or frustrated, such as when a child finishes a center task quickly and wanders around the classroom or when a child who struggles with visual and fine motor skills throws a pair of scissors down because the task is too difficult.

In the process of mindful engagement, a child experiences enjoyment and reinforcement in the act of being present for or invested in an activity; this means that the reward is inherent in the engagement and is not dependent on the outcome of the activity or achievement of an objective.

Format of the OMPK Program

The OMPK program uses a unique and comprehensive format that differs from most sequenced, lesson-based SEL programs in that it gives you the freedom to choose the practices and practice variations that will best align with the ever-changing needs of your classrooms. To aid fidelity of implementation, Daily Practices and Supplemental Learning Activities have detailed instructions, case examples, environmental and developmental considerations, and practice options that build in a stepwise progressive manner to help you choose the practices that are the best fit each particular day and in each arising situation.

Our job of teaching and supporting children requires an incredible amount of planning, energy, and time management, so Daily Practice and Supplemental Learning Activities can be integrated into the general education lesson plans, Exceptional Student Education classroom, therapy room, and even the home routine. Given that the primary occupation of preschool and kindergarten children is to play, many of the OMPK practices use multisensory, hands-on tools, visuals, songs, stories, puppet shows, and games to teach self-regulation and promote social-emotional and academic skills that can be overlaid on common preschool and kindergarten play, social, and academic activities.

The various options for the Daily Practices and Supplemental Learning Activities are ordered according to the typical developmental sequence. However, this order is only a suggested guide, as children are different and do not necessarily follow the same developmental trajectory for all social-emotional learning domains. You have the ability to choose which options will work best with the children in your unique classroom. In Part 4 of this book, you'll learn about tools to support children with varying needs and to increase children's engagement in the classroom.

Finally, while the target audience for this book is preschool and kindergarten teachers, therapists, support staff, and other educational professionals, many of the practices—such as the OpenMind REMIND practices—can be used without modification by parents and caregivers. The classroom practices can also be modified for implementation in the home or community. On the website for this book, http://www.newharbinger.com/49258, you will find an online appendix with numerous resources, along with other downloadable tools that you can share with families to carry over helpful practices from school to home.

Pause for Reflection…

We've covered the five foundations of the OMPK program as well as the general format. What follows is a comprehensive guide to understanding and implementing the OMPK program in preschool and kindergarten classrooms. The following chapters provide instruction for teachers, therapists, and other educational professionals in how to practice mindfulness, teach mindfulness practices to young children, and apply processes that reflect the principles of mindfulness to address challenging behaviors and support engagement. In the next chapter, we will examine the conceptual foundations of mindfulness more closely.

CHAPTER 3

Theory and Concepts of Mindfulness and Social-Emotional Learning

Often, interventions and SEL programs for children come about because children are struggling, exhibit delays, have particular diagnostic labels, or are engaging in behaviors that are problematic for adults. Therapeutic interventions and educational programs for children commonly serve to increase child compliance and grow developmental and academic skills that adults have deemed important or to reduce difficult or challenging behaviors that adults have determined to be unacceptable or unpleasant. Many psychological, behavioral, and educational interventions are narrowly aimed at treating the child's difficulties, disorders, and symptoms.

Mindfulness interventions offer a broader contribution. Teaching children to cultivate a mindful way of life can help nourish individual growth, development, and personal transformation that, in turn, will contribute to positive and prosocial downstream effects on the child's community and social network. By engaging in ethically motivated actions that stem from mindfulness practice, children learn to move from potentially harmful self-focused actions to prosocial actions that are beneficial to others. When children discover how to live mindfully, they can learn not only to function better within their social environments, but to model prosocial behavior and actions for others.

I have provided numerous trainings and presentations on mindfulness and mindfulness-based interventions, and while doing so have been asked many excellent questions about mindfulness, and have also heard many misconceptions. For example, as mentioned earlier, people may be uncomfortable or uncertain about practicing mindfulness or meditation because they are worried that it may conflict with their personal religious or spiritual belief systems—or lack thereof. It is important to understand that the mindfulness and meditation practices in this book are secular, so they can be used by anyone, regardless of personal or cultural beliefs. That said, most major religions and spiritual traditions include some type of contemplative and awareness practices (e.g., centering prayer of Christianity, the Sufi practice of *muraqabah)*, so you can integrate these practices into existing religious practices if you choose. The purpose of this chapter is to give you a comprehensive working definition of mindfulness and to show you how mindfulness links to and supports social-emotional learning.

The Five Parts of Mindfulness

Research suggests that mindfulness practice involves intention, attention regulation, emotion regulation, self-awareness, reduced cognitive bias and self-referential thinking, nonattachment, and prosocial behavior (Tang et al., 2015; Vago & Silbersweig, 2012). Accordingly, the OMPK program conceptualizes mindfulness as an ethical way of being that has five parts: attention, awareness, being present, nonjudgment, and openhearted intention and attitude. The five parts work together and form a big picture that represents the practice of right mindfulness—again, that's mindfulness with a moral, humanist, and ethical intention—despite our brain's hardwired predisposition to engage in self-focused, self-preserving reactions. The pieces (figure 1) are interdependent and create a nonlinear scaffolding that enables realization of a whole that is more than the sum of its parts (figure 2). The experience of embodying mindfulness results in personal transformation that moves the heart to spontaneously act in an authentic and prosocial manner. So, let's look at these five parts one at a time, starting with attention.

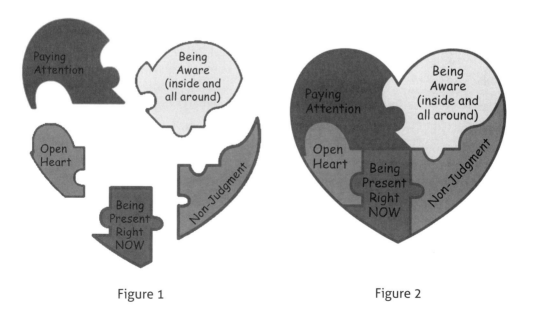

Figure 1   Figure 2

Attention

Attention refers to our ability to shift to and hold focus on one thing, such as when threading a needle. Attention helps the mind to stay focused on a task or a person, even when the mind wants to wander or daydream. Our human brains are wired to constantly scan the environment and jump from thought to thought to ensure that we are always looking out for threats to our survival. This jumping around is often called the "monkey mind." It is important to differentiate between shifting attention intentionally, with awareness (e.g., shifting focus from writing a lesson plan because someone knocks on your door) and shifting attention without awareness (e.g., getting distracted by the impulse to browse the internet in the middle of writing a lesson plan, and then, thirty minutes later, realizing you have not completed the plan). On the other hand, if we remain too focused without also having awareness, we can miss important cues from our bodies and our environment that impact the present moment.

Awareness

Awareness requires the active observation and noticing of what is happening inside of us, including thoughts, emotions, perceptions, and interoceptive (inner) sensations from the body. Awareness also involves noticing external stimuli, such as exteroceptive (external) sensations of touch, visual, auditory, olfactory (smell), and gustatory (taste) stimuli; information from the physical environment; and social signals. Something interesting to note is that our brain, often without our conscious awareness, assigns a value (good-bad, safe-dangerous, pleasant-unpleasant, and so on) to each stimulus that our sensory receptors detect. To take it a step further, *meta-awareness* is essentially our capacity to think about our thinking. It includes our ability to both notice the types of values that our brains detect (for example, coffee smells good, gasoline smells bad) and observe the way our minds think about and evaluate what we are perceiving. Awareness can be affected by factors such as pain and big emotions like fear, which tend to decrease our ability to notice other sensations and stimuli.

Being Present

When we are able to simultaneously integrate attention and awareness, we can stay present and engaged in each unfolding moment, without mindlessly drifting away to the past or future. *Being present* is the ability to stay with what is happening now, and shift the object of focus intentionally as needed while maintaining awareness. Being present in daily life can be challenging due to our minds' natural tendency to move, seek comfort, and avoid pain. Being present involves the ability to see both the trees (or "figure," in "figure-ground" terminology) and the forest (or "ground") and to intentionally shift focus as needed. For example, in the classroom, just the simple act of answering a child's question requires focus and attention on that child, but also awareness of how the child is responding, whether the child is understanding, and the ability to notice and scan for what other children may be doing. At any moment, no matter how fascinating and important the child's question is, you may need to shift your attention if Billy at the art table starts to give himself a haircut. Being present also involves staying in the current moment without engaging in mental time travel to the past and to the future.

Nonjudgment

Nonjudgment involves being able to notice, evaluate, and analyze with an open mind, without undue influence of implicit or explicit bias in attention, perception, or interpretation. Nonjudgment results in objective noticing and assessing of salient information without assumption, holding on to strong value words (e.g., "good," "bad"), or applying black-and-white, rigid belief structures. For example, a judgmental statement may sound like this: "Oh no, here comes Maxim, he is so tired; he is going to be a mess today. I bet his mom let him stay up all night. Make sure to keep him away from Hector and Samuel and don't let him have any scissors." A nonjudgmental statement would be: "Maxim's face and body look like he is feeling sleepy this morning. I'll ask him how he is feeling." Nonjudgment also involves the ability to be flexible in beliefs and thinking and to engage in compromise to serve the greater good.

Open Heart Practices

The last part of mindfulness consists of four *open heart practices,* which serves to anchor the pieces of mindfulness and form the big picture of mindfulness practice. Being present while practicing nonjudgment and acceptance can facilitate the dynamic process of equipoise, or balance, in the face of constant change. This can lead to the state of equanimity—the first open heart practice. *Equanimity* refers to the ability to observe experiences as they come and go in a state of peace and calmness and not react in a way that harms oneself, others, or one's environment. Equanimity builds the larger understanding that all things are impermanent and that everything is connected to something else. It has been defined as "even-mindedness in the face of every sort of experience, regardless of whether pleasure [or] pain are present or not," (Thanissaro Bhikkhu, 1996, p. 262). When we embody equanimity, it is much like being able to look at the dark clouds around us and know that they will pass, and while they may darken the sky and change outdoor plans, that they will bring rain to nourish the trees.

Equanimity provides a level physiological and psychological ground for us to cultivate the other three open heart practices: loving-kindness, compassion, and empathetic joy (i.e., feeling joy for others). *Loving-kindness* is unconditional caring, or the ability to give love to ourselves and to others even when getting nothing in return. *Compassion* involves the ability to notice that someone is suffering and then do something to try to relieve that suffering. *Empathetic joy* is the act of experiencing joy for someone else's success or happiness. These heart practices serve to set the intentional thermostat for moral prosocial behavior and ethical decision making.

The Five Domains of Social-Emotional Learning

Humans seek social connection; this is supported by research in evolutionary anthropology, positive psychology, social psychology, epidemiology, and studies of subjective and physical well-being. Research suggests that the human brain is wired to seek social engagement, and our neocortex size can even be predicted by the size of our social group (Lieberman, 2013). Social connection has been associated with positive mental and physical health benefits (Cacioppo et al., 2002). Conversely, social isolation and lack of social relationships has been linked to increased mortality, biological markers of disease, and reduced immune function (Ertel et al., 2009; Everson-Rose & Lewis, 2005; House et al., 1988; Kiecolt-Glaser et al., 2002; Robles & Kiecolt-Glaser, 2003; Uchino, 2006). Given that social relationships influence health and well-being, there has been an increased emphasis on educational programs that develop social skills and positive cooperative social engagement.

In addition to improving social and emotional skills, it is well established in the literature that implementing SEL programs can result in improved academic outcomes (Durlak et al., 2011), mitigate the effects of adverse childhood experiences, predict physical health, improve executive functions, and potentially affect biomarkers of stress (Diamond & Lee, 2011; Greenberg et al., 2015; Moffitt et al., 2011; Raver et al., 2011).

The Collaborative for Academic, Social, and Emotional Learning (CASEL) is a nonprofit agency dedicated to research, innovation, and multidisciplinary collaboration to ensure that all students have a right to social-emotional learning education. Over twenty years ago, CASEL initially defined social-emotional learning as having five domains of competency skills: self-awareness, self-management, social awareness, relationship management, and responsible decision making (CASEL, 2013). These domains represent global competencies meant to apply to all educational programs. Specific to early learning for preschool and kindergarten children, the Center on the Social and Emotional Foundations for Early Learning (CSEFEL) lists the following six skills as early learning competencies that promote school and community success in young children: confidence, ability to develop relationships, concentration and task persistence, effective communication of emotions, ability to pay attention and listen to instructions, and problem solving (Santos et al., 2012). All of these skills can be found within the five SEL domains, but I mention them here to highlight the importance placed on these specific skills in the early learning environment—skills heavily targeted in the OMPK program.

The five domains of social-emotional learning can be characterized by the following social-emotional behaviors and abilities, adapted from CASEL definitions:

Self-awareness: The child recognizes their own feelings, understands and talks about feelings, is aware of their own behaviors and how they affect others, has a capacity for self-reflection, understands their own needs in different situations, practices self-determination and self-advocacy, identifies their own strengths, practices self-compassion, and knows when to ask for help.

Self-management: The child understands and responds to their own feelings and feelings toward others, focuses and pays attention during lessons, has adequate attention for active learning, faces challenges with greater ease, independently self-calms, exhibits decreased challenging behaviors (e.g., aggression), exhibits decreased impulsivity, demonstrates resilience in difficult situations, follows rules in different contexts (e.g., home, school, and community), practices self-compassion, and delays gratification for an age-appropriate and reasonable amount of time.

Social awareness: The child shows empathy; recognizes feelings of others; recognizes suffering in others; recognizes joy in others; practices empathetic joy; recognizes opportunities to express gratitude; listens to and understands others; has an emerging capacity for perspective taking; accepts people from other cultures, religions, and races; accepts people who are differently abled or neurodiverse; and is aware of rules for behavior in class, at home, and in the community.

Relationship skills: The child peacefully resolves conflicts with peers and adults; works well with others; engages in collaborative learning; forms and maintains positive relationships; listens and communicates mindfully; uses respectful and kind words, tone, and voice volume; makes meaningful apologies; expresses gratitude to others; forgives others; and demonstrates respect for others' spaces, work, and bodies.

Responsible decision making: The child shares materials and task responsibility; cleans up and helps others; takes turns appropriately; makes appropriate responses to environmental demands; engages in problem solving; responds rather than reacts to situations; engages in compromise; and follows rules for behavior in class, at home, and in the community.

The Link Between Mindfulness and Social-Emotional Learning

The five parts of mindfulness practice discussed above—attention, awareness, being present, nonjudgment, and openhearted intention and attitude—clearly link to the development of the five domains of social-emotional learning, as you can see in figure 3.

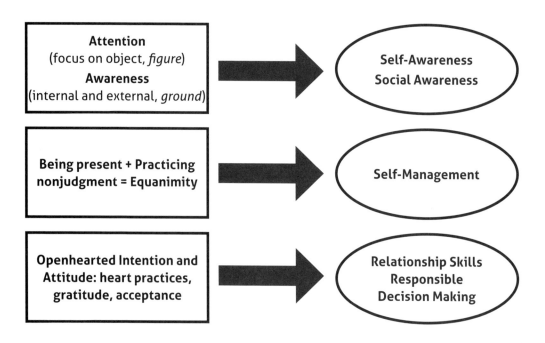

Figure 3

Mindfulness practices can work to affect the brain processes that subserve the domains of SEL in two ways: from the bottom up and from the top down. *Bottom-up practices* involve regular, repeated practice, such as when we train for a marathon by starting slow and practicing running day after day to build cardiovascular health, endurance, and strength. *Top-down practices* involve learning new techniques and strategies, such as learning what types of food to eat while training, what stretches to do before and after, the different types of running strides, how to pace our breathing, and so on. While many programs aimed at teaching social skills predominantly involve didactic, cognitive top-down methods, right mindfulness practice is rooted in the experiential practice of attention, awareness, present-moment embodiment, nonjudgment, and equanimity as a scaffolding to promote and actualize loving-kindness, compassion, empathetic joy, and ethical, prosocial actions.

Pause for Reflection…

Daily engagement in foundational mindfulness practices in the classroom by both teachers and students can create an environment conducive to teaching and learning more specific social-emotional practices, such as conflict-resolution skills and social problem solving. One of the best side effects of daily mindfulness practices is improved classroom management, as the classroom environment becomes more peaceful and children become more engaged. To make a comparison to physical health and wellness, rather than a fad diet, the OMPK program is more of a lifestyle change—it can offer a shift to a more mindful, accepting, and kind way of being and acting.

We've concluded part 1, covering the foundations and theory underlying the OMPK program and the benefits for young children. Part 2 is geared toward teachers, other professionals, and caregivers. Beginning in the next chapter, you'll learn how practicing mindfulness can not only enhance your abilities as a teacher, but also enrich your life and help you to manage the stress that comes with one of the most important and difficult jobs there is.

The OpenMind Resilience, Equanimity, and Mindfulness (REMIND) Practices for Teachers, Therapists, and Caregivers

CHAPTER 4

The Purpose of the OpenMind REMIND Practices for Teachers

The best way to teach mindfulness is to *be mindful*—we must show children what mindfulness looks and sounds like, and most importantly, let them experience how they feel when others are mindful and present for them. This is why the teacher practices are so essential to the OMPK program. The first step in teaching mindfulness to children is to develop our own mindfulness practice. This is crucial because it helps us attain three main goals: (1) to model mindfulness for the children we teach and support, (2) to help manage our own stress and notice all the beautiful moments that happen in and out of the classroom, and (3) to be present for others so that we may foster meaningful connections. And while the idea of starting a mindfulness practice may sound great in theory, you may be asking yourself how you will have time to add something new to everything you are already doing. Given how hard you work preparing and communicating with caregivers and peers, how busy and scheduled a preschool and kindergarten day is, and how challenging it can be to balance your work and personal needs, it can seem impossible to add one more thing.

As you're well aware, teachers are required not only to have knowledge about subject material, but also to have pedagogical understanding about teaching itself, to understand child development, to have emotion regulation amidst an often-chaotic environment, to make hundreds of rapid decisions in response to fluctuating student needs, to manage many relationships at once, to care for and make children feel safe, and to respond to challenging student behaviors. Working with young children is a profession that requires so much, often with very little resources. It can feel like trying to empty an ocean given only a teaspoon. And when the demands of our job are coupled with the problems that life brings, the resulting stress can seem overwhelming.

Adding to all this stress are the socially imposed and bureaucratic requirements and demands such as testing and increased data collection. While the effects of ongoing stress are often termed "burnout," some researchers and theorists prefer the term "demoralization," meaning that the job is so demanding in terms of time and labor that it prevents teachers from accessing the moral rewards of teaching, including student relationships, creativity, and fun, because they are constantly putting out fires (Santoro, 2011; Tsang & Liu, 2016). In other words, instead of placing blame or fault on the teacher for burning out, we must also consider the broken system that has helped to cause the fires! The moral aspects of teaching can be the most important rewards of our job—the ability to connect with children, to see light bulbs brighten up in young minds, to nurture and inspire. So how do we deal with the effects of stress, demoralization, and our ongoing personal and life problems? Life itself, regardless of our profession, is uncertain and ever changing. As Shunryu Suzuki Roshi is known to have said, "Life is like stepping into a boat that is about to sail out to sea and sink."

As humans, we know we are on a sinking ship—that our life has a time limit—but we set sail anyway. This takes such courage and strength, and yet we do it, day after day. We navigate our sinking ships by engaging in all the tasks needed to care for it, by enjoying the incredible scenery, relaxing over calm waters, holding the course through storms, making plans for new destinations, changing course when needed, and recruiting a strong crew to help us, especially when the ship begins to form new leaks or needs special repair. Teaching and supporting young children is a job that requires patience, persistence, creativity, compassion, connection, and resilience. The OpenMind Resilience, Equanimity, and Mindfulness (REMIND) practices, an essential component of the OMPK program, are geared toward teaching mindfulness to the adults who teach and support preschool- and kindergarten-aged children. These practices were designed to support and strengthen all aspects of teachers' ever-changing journey of life, as teaching does not happen in a vacuum, but within the larger context of our own personal adventures. This chapter will give you an overview of the REMIND practices and explain not only how mindfulness can help you as a teacher, but also how it can benefit your life.

Why Practice Mindfulness?

There are countless benefits to practicing mindfulness. Here, we will cover some of the main ones: improved ability to respond to stress, enhanced ability to teach mindfulness, improved teacher–child connection, downstream effects on others, and increased flexibility.

Improved Response to Stress

A growing body of research has shown that practicing mindfulness meditation can decrease our perceived stress, emotional reactivity, aggression, anxiety, and depression. Teachers' levels of mindfulness are inversely associated with burnout and stress; the more mindful we are, the more likely we are to report lower levels of stress (Abenavoli et al., 2013). Stress often has a negative connotation, but at its core, stress is any force that acts on us and requires a change. Stress forces can be perceived as negative, such as when we have an encounter with someone who is acting aggressively, or we are given too little time to complete a task. They can also be perceived as positive, such as when we get a promotion that requires us to learn new skills and take on added responsibilities. The stress occurs, and our bodies and minds respond to make the needed change and rebalance our systems. Stress can be a normal and healthy part of life, because the physiological changes that happen when we feel stress—such as increased heartbeat and blood pressure, muscle tension, and overall rush of energy—are designed to be short term. However, when stress becomes chronic, we can experience *strain,* which is the impact on our system from repeated or long-term stress. Strain can result in conditions like anxiety, depression, muscle pain, chronic high blood pressure, and headaches. Although practicing mindfulness will not take away the stressors in our lives, it can help us to minimize the strain on our systems by helping us to become more resilient. Mindfulness can help prevent the effects of chronic stress by teaching us how it feels to be present for stress rather than be controlled by it.

Enhanced Ability to Teach Mindfulness

The essence and foundation of practicing mindfulness is sitting and focusing on our breath. However, this is something that does not come easily to everyone, especially people who are experiencing chronic stress—it can be hard to just sit while feeling that the world is rushing on around you! Over the years I have met many people who tried but did not continue with sitting mindfulness practice because they felt like it was too difficult. This is why the REMIND practices offer many different options and give us opportunities to work the practices into our daily lives. Mindfulness practices can be formal, such as sitting and focusing on the breath, or informal, such as being present for others and actively listening. Being mindful in daily life also involves being able to notice how we are feeling in a situation and *pause* before responding, to prevent hurtful actions and regret. All of the REMIND practices have options for formal (sitting) practices, informal practices (practice in action), and PAUSE practices.

Even if you recognize all of the mindfulness concepts and can explain all of the lessons and practices for teaching the OMPK program to children, you will not have the full depth of understanding of mindfulness unless you are also practicing and experiencing it. The teacher and philosopher Krishnamurti (1972) once told a story about scholars who were discussing the concept of awareness while driving. They were so focused on their explanation of awareness, about its various aspects and definitions, and how important it was, that they ran over and killed a goat without even noticing. They were so busy analyzing the idea of awareness that they completely forgot to practice awareness! I have learned that to teach mindfulness concepts, practices, and exercises authentically, we must provide a living example of the practices in action, and we must also be able to give accurate and meaningful responses to student questions that arise during the course of mindfulness practice (McCown et al., 2010).

Think of it this way: you could read a manual on how to teach swimming, but you will not be a strong swimming teacher unless you have experienced how it feels to stay afloat, to cut through the water, to get water up your nose. Even if you are able to teach a swimming lesson based on knowledge alone, without ever having tried to swim, your students will likely know the difference. This is true for mindfulness as well; your own practice is essential if you wish to teach mindfulness principles to others. It is also a powerful tool for connection, which is so often where teaching begins.

Improved Teacher–Child Connection

The teacher–child connection is the anchor of the learning process, and research supports just how important these relationships are not only to a child's comfort and well-being, but also to academic gains. Positive teacher and child relationships and teacher responsiveness to the social and emotional needs of a child have predicted academic success in kindergarten and resulted in improved academic achievement (Birch & Ladd, 1997; Jennings & Greenberg, 2009). The classroom environment can be stressful and overwhelming at times, and when you are able to use mindfulness practices to demonstrate an engaged presence, self-regulation, positive attitude, and prosocial behaviors, children will grow just by observing these mindful responses to stress and challenges.

I experienced this when I was a new therapist working with individuals with profound intellectual disabilities; most of my clients were either deaf, blind, or both, and almost all used self-injurious or aggressive behaviors as coping skills. I learned that the only way to connect with people who had very limited communication and were living in a constant state of fear was to just be present, to sit with them and connect in stillness.

I will never forget the time we were having a treatment team meeting in a residential facility for a young man with a rare pituitary disorder. He was blind, sat in a wheelchair, and would hit himself hundreds of times a day—he was not able to regulate his temperature, energy, or appetite and was constantly in a state of movement and apparent distress. When his caregiver brought him into the meeting, she was worried he would not be able to handle being in a room full of people. However, when we started the meeting with a five-minute mindfulness meditation, he slowly calmed and became still—his caregiver and team were stunned. He felt the effects of being surrounded by peace and calm.

Furthermore, when you are practicing mindfulness, you may be less likely to use facial expressions, vocal tone, and body language that may result in unintentional harm due to *emotional contagion,* which is defined as "a process in which a person or group influences the emotions, or behavior of another person or group through the conscious or unconscious induction of emotion states and behavioral attitudes" (Schoenewolf, 1990, p. 50). In other words, our negative emotions and attitudes can be perceived and felt by others, even if we are not intending for this to happen, or we are not aware that it is happening. The good news is that when we model a kind and calm presence, these effects can also be felt by others; these are called the downstream effects of practicing mindfulness.

Downstream Effects

Beyond the direct benefits of mindfulness to us as teachers, therapists, and caregivers for increasing stress management, attention, and overall wellness, empirical evidence suggests that there are also measurable downstream benefits to others when we practice mindfulness. My mentor, Nirbhay Singh, and his research group have conducted many studies showing the measurable benefits of caregiver and teacher mindfulness practice to neurodiverse children and adolescents, and to adults with intellectual disabilities, even when the individuals themselves received no interventions. Just by training caregivers and teachers to practice mindfulness, they were able to see positive outcomes for the people they were caring for! Mindfulness-based training for caregivers has resulted in reduced use of physical restraints and emergency medications for aggressive and destructive behavior in people with intellectual disabilities (Singh et al., 2009; Singh et al., 2015, Singh et al., 2016a, 2016b) and reduced aggression, noncompliance, negative social interactions, and self-injury in children (Singh et al., 2014; Singh et al., 2013). In addition, positive behaviors, such as independent play and compliance with parent and teacher requests, have increased following parent and teacher training in mindfulness-based practice (Singh et al., 2010; Singh et al., 2014; Singh et al., 2013). This may have been because the caregivers were more mindful, stable, in tune with, and present for the people they care for, and thus could respond objectively and with kindness, rather than reacting quickly or taking an uncomfortable situation personally. It may also have been due to the caregivers' enhanced ability to be flexible and respond to emerging needs.

Flexibility

When we are more mindfully engaged with children and less attached to expectations and strict protocols, we tend to be more flexible in adapting to their unfolding needs and more likely to model functional social-emotional behaviors such as increased social awareness and decreased emotional reactivity. It is this flexibility that can enable us to see exactly what each child needs in each moment, without predetermining what may happen before it actually happens, and respond in a way that is supportive, individualized, caring, and skillful. Furthermore, when we are mindful, we may experience less *inattentional bias,* or the tendency to miss things in plain sight because we are focused on something else, and we may be less likely to be surprised by unexpected changes that can occur frequently when working with young children (Schofield et al., 2015).

Benefits of the OpenMind Resilience, Equanimity, and Mindfulness Practices

The OpenMind REMIND practices are evidence-based mindfulness practices that have been found to improve health, well-being, and quality of life, and also to decrease stress and symptoms of depression and anxiety. When used in daily life, these practices can help us to:

- cope with stress and uncertainty
- respond to difficult emotions, such as anger, anxiety, and sadness
- be resilient and bounce back when faced with pain and life challenges
- notice and grow positive emotions
- be focused and present
- form connections with others

- interact peacefully with others

- increase respect and acceptance of self and others

- solve social problems and resolve conflicts with others

As humans, our brains are wired to be restless, to rapidly shift attention, and also to have a negativity bias, which means that we tend to focus more on negative emotions and experiences. The REMIND practices have been designed to build our executive function skills such as attention, focus, emotional control, and mental flexibility. They also serve to increase awareness and appreciation of positive emotional experiences and to establish and strengthen positive habits. Collectively, these practices can help us to develop a state of *equanimity*—the ability to maintain stability and even-mindedness when faced with challenging situations, and to not get caught up in chasing pleasure and escaping from pain.

That said, I chose the acronym REMIND for this group of practices because despite how much we practice to develop equanimity and mindfulness in an effort to experience a peaceful balance, we will inevitably experience moments when we lose our balance and fall. These practices were not developed to take away all of our problems, and I cannot promise that they will help you manifest everlasting happiness, as these goals are not realistic. Instead, the purpose of these practices is to remind us that it is okay to not be okay; they can remind us to stay present for and accept all of our experiences as our experiences, even when we want to run. As Pema Chödrön wisely said,

Life is glorious, but life is also wretched. It is both. Appreciating the gloriousness inspires us, encourages us, cheers us up, gives us a bigger perspective, energizes us. We feel connected. But if that's all that's happening, we get arrogant and start to look down on others, and there is a sense of making ourselves a big deal and being really serious about it, wanting it to be like that forever. The gloriousness becomes tinged by craving and addiction. On the other hand, wretchedness—life's painful aspect—softens us up considerably. Knowing pain is a very important ingredient of being there for another person. When you are feeling a lot of grief, you can look right into somebody's eyes because you feel you haven't got anything to lose—you're just there. The wretchedness humbles us and softens us, but if we were only wretched, we would all just go down the tubes. We'd be so depressed, discouraged, and hopeless that we wouldn't have enough energy to eat an apple. Gloriousness and wretchedness need each other. One inspires us, the other softens us. They go together. (Chödrön, 2001, p. 178)

Our human brains are wired to assign particular judgment values (e.g., "good," "bad, "painful," "pleasurable") to every stimulus that enters our brain. This process occurs so frequently that we are often unaware of it—this is how our biases become strengthened. Equanimity is the ability to decouple the degree of desire or avoidance for a particular experience, and instead to objectively notice and accept it as it is, without unnecessarily adding to it. It is the ability to maintain even-mindedness in all situations, whether the situation brings pain, pleasure, boredom, or big emotions. As humans, we frequently take a burden or a hardship and we let our thoughts, worries, and stories add extra weight to it. This makes us more likely to drop the burden and flee, or let it keep us weighted down.

When I teach children about the practice of equanimity, I describe it as the ability to "be like a tree." When a storm approaches, a tree cannot escape and run from it, so the tree stays still, roots planted, and bends with the wind while observing the storm, knowing that all storms are impermanent and will eventually cease. At the center of the storm is a place of stillness and balance that is our natural state.

Equanimity is not a state of feeling neutral or indifferent, but rather the practice of returning to a place of peace and stillness to observe the storm, rather than to be controlled by it. Another aspect of equanimity is the gratitude that comes with all experiences, even difficult ones; using the former example, the tree can be grateful for new growth after the rain. This is why people undergoing tremendous hardships and injustice, for example Black, indigenous, people of color (BIPOC) women or children fighting cancer, can cultivate unbelievable strength in times of adversity and, like the tree, experience growth in the deepest soil.

Equanimity builds the larger understanding that all things are impermanent and everything is connected to something else. When you embody equanimity, you are able to practice intentional gratitude and acceptance of impermanent and ever-changing life experiences and events, rather than constantly seeking a perfect, ever-happy life. Equanimity also requires flexibility of thinking and responding, and openness in the face of strong emotions and opinions. Even the biggest trees must be able to bend in the wind, or they will snap and fall. When you embody equanimity, not only are you able to grow into a strong tree, but you can provide strength, shelter, fruit, shade, and support for the children you nurture to climb high upon you, to get a better view of the world.

The OpenMind REMIND Practices: Formal, Practice in Action, PAUSE

As I mentioned earlier, there are seven REMIND practices, and each practice is matched to a different color of the rainbow to facilitate remembrance of the different practice options by color association. The rainbow also serves as a symbol of being open to and surprised by the amazing beauty that life can offer, even in the midst of or following a storm. The seven REMIND practices can support the following wellness states:

1. Loving-kindness meditation (red): Loving, kind, forgiving, inclusive

2. Open monitoring meditation (orange): Present, open, nonjudgmental, flexible

3. Joy meditation (yellow): Joyful, fun, lighthearted

4. Embodied meditation (green): Grounded, aware, discerning

5. Focused meditation (blue): Peaceful, calm, patient

6. Compassion meditation (indigo): Compassionate, empathetic

7. Gratitude meditation (violet): Grateful, appreciative

Figure 4 gives an overview of what each practice can nurture and empower within you, so that you can then give to others.

WHEN I AM:	I CAN GIVE:
LOVING	UNCONDITIONAL LOVE, KINDNESS, FORGIVENESS, AND CONNECTION
OPEN	NONJUDGMENTAL ACCEPTANCE, COMPROMISES, AND CREATIVE LEARNING EXPERIENCES
JOYFUL	HUMOR, PLAYFULNESS, AND FUN LEARNING EXPERIENCES
GROUNDED	APPROACHABLE AND NONTHREATENING BODY LANGUAGE AND A SENSE OF STABILITY
PEACEFUL	CALM REASSURANCE AND COMFORT
COMPASSIONATE	EMPATHY, HELP, AND SUPPORT
GRATEFUL	APPRECIATION, THANKS, RESPECT, AND RECOGNITION

Figure 4

In chapter 5, you will find a description of why each practice is important and beneficial, as well as instructions for how to do the practice formally as a meditation, informally in daily life, and as a means to pause. Below, I'll give a general overview of the formal practices, practice in action (i.e., informal practice), and PAUSE practices.

Formal Practices

The formal REMIND practices offer us a way to build attention, concentration, focus, and awareness through meditation. They are done at a designated time and serve to build our capacity for focus and for experiencing each wellness state. To use a physical wellness analogy, formal mindfulness practice is much like doing a regular exercise practice to build strength and endurance. By engaging in regular formal mindfulness practices, your ability to focus on, remember, and notice these wellness states will be strengthened and come more naturally in daily life. All of the formal practices will build concentration. Some will help you to build your capacity for cultivating and sitting with the positive emotions (love, joy, peace, compassion) that are at our core but that we often do not notice, so that we can experience them more naturally and more frequently.

The guidelines below apply to any formal mindfulness practice.

POSTURE

It is important to have a stable posture when practicing formal meditation. As Kabat-Zinn says, the goal is to "fall awake"; being too relaxed can result in falling asleep. However, if an upright position is too uncomfortable, the discomfort can completely capture your attention, taking your focus away from the meditation practice, especially for beginners. Stable postures include sitting in a chair with your feet on the floor, sitting on the floor (with or without a cushion), and sitting up in bed, with pillows if needed due to physical limitations. A stable posture includes an upright spine with shoulders relaxed and back, and chin slightly tucked. If you are just beginning or have physical limitations, orthostatic limitations, or chronic pain when sitting, lying down can also provide added stability to allow you to focus on breathing without having to worry about maintaining an upright posture.

BREATHING

Each time we take a breath, we are taking in, and then letting go. We have a large muscle called the diaphragm that separates our chest cavity from our abdominal cavity;

it sits under our lungs. When we breathe in, the diaphragm contracts downward toward our belly, making room for our lungs to fill up with air and oxygen. When we breathe out, the diaphragm relaxes and can push air out of our lungs, getting rid of carbon dioxide. When breathing in, our belly should expand like a balloon filling with air; when breathing out, our belly should deflate like a balloon that has lost its air. This is called diaphragmatic breathing because we use that powerful muscle to take full and efficient inhales and exhales. However, when we are feeling a stress response, we tend to hold our breath and not use the diaphragm; instead, we use our upper chest, shoulder, and neck muscles. Not only can this tire out these muscles and lead to tension and pain, but it can make us feel shortness of breath because we are not filling and emptying our lungs completely. When this becomes chronic, it can result in something called hypercapnia, which means that we breathe quickly and not as deeply and build up carbon dioxide; this can keep the cycle of stress going. Mindful breathing with good breathing mechanics can help us to reduce the effects of stress.

Ironically, when some people begin meditation, they try to focus on so many factors that they may feel like they are breathing too fast, not deeply enough, or even too deeply, and this can result in stress! It is important to remember that our typical breathing rhythm changes from moment to moment—it isn't the same every breath, and some variation is okay. There should be a slight pause between the inhale and exhale: inhale, pause, exhale, pause, and so on. If you find that you are having difficulty with your breathing or want to make sure you are engaging your diaphragm, you can try this trick: place one hand on your chest and one hand on your belly; when you breathe in, the hand on the belly should move more than the one on your chest. You can use this as a guide for getting into a healthy breathing rhythm. It may also be easier for you to lie down so that you don't also have to think about sitting upright. Another strategy is to sit in a chair and push down with your arms on the armrest while breathing in, and release when breathing out—this will prevent you from using your upper muscles to breathe and will help you to recruit your diaphragm.

CONTEXT AND LOCATION

Ideally, a designated location for practicing formal meditation that is quiet and free from distractions is best for practicing formal meditation. However, due to the often hectic nature of life, family, and work environments, a serene and peaceful oasis for practicing meditation is not always available or practical. This is okay, as interruptions and distractions are part of daily life.

HABIT AND ROUTINE

It will be easier to maintain a formal meditation practice if it is linked to a part of your existing daily routine; this will make it a habit you are more likely to sustain. This is one of the ways that these practices are occupation based; if you can insert them in your daily routine, they become meaningful activities. Some suggestions include waking up before the rest of the household to sit in a quiet area, arriving at work a few minutes early to sit in the car and meditate, and using the moments before bed to practice.

FELT SAFETY

Many meditation teachers recommend keeping your eyes closed to block out visual distractions. However, if you have a history of trauma, or medical conditions such as vertigo, you may not feel comfortable or safe with your eyes closed. If this is the case, keeping your eyes open but cast down to reduce ambient distractions can be beneficial. At any point if you begin to experience intense emotions or memories during formal mindfulness practice, I recommend that you speak to a counselor or therapist and/or switch to an informal or PAUSE practice option.

Practice in Action

Informal mindfulness practices are a means to put formal mindfulness meditation practices into action by applying them in daily life as intentional and prosocial decisions, using them to prepare for or respond to challenges and opportunities that occur during the various occupations of daily life, or increasing our engagement in activities we find meaningful. To continue with the physical wellness analogy, informal practice is like being able to help others carry belongings or do physical tasks because you have built the strength to lift heavy objects through formal exercise. In other words, you're putting your strength into action. Of course, formal practice is not necessary to use mindfulness practice in action, but it certainly makes it much easier! Informal REMIND practices can help you to change and enrich the activities of your daily life, process the practices in context, model your practice for others, and pass along the benefits of your practice.

PAUSE Practices

PAUSE practices offer a way to stop in daily life, notice what is happening, choose a response that is not harmful to others or yourself, and set an intention to build a positive habit. Just like when you are served very hot food, the only way to eat without harming yourself is to wait for it to cool down—given time, challenging emotions and pain will also cool down. PAUSE practices can help you to notice an old, familiar, or potentially harmful habit and shift to a mindful intention. Once more thinking about our physical wellness analogy, a PAUSE practice would be like choosing to take the stairs instead of the elevator, or stopping before lifting a heavy object to make sure you are using proper body mechanics. PAUSE practices are meant to be a quick, in-the-moment shift and reset.

Pause for Reflection…

You can use the OpenMind REMIND practices individually, or in combination, depending on your needs, preferences, and goals. You can also integrate them into an existing therapy, self-improvement, or meditation program. Now that you have had an overview of the purpose, potential benefits, types, and format of the REMIND practices, we will take a look at individual practices themselves, review the instructions for doing these practices, and learn how to use them in your daily life.

CHAPTER 5

OpenMind REMIND
Practice Instructions

In the previous two chapters, we discussed why mindfulness is important, learned about the different facets of mindfulness, and took a broad look at the REMIND practices and program. In this chapter, we will focus on gaining a more in-depth understanding of each practice, including its concepts and how it relates to life, and review instructions for how to actually do each practice. One thing I love about the REMIND practices is the wide variety of options so that you can choose what practices appeal most to your needs, interests, and current life situation. Rather than being a static prescription, it is flexible and occupation-based in that it can be used to support and help you prepare for and engage in the activities you find meaningful. You can opt to highly structure your practice or to adapt your practices to your changing circumstances each day. That said, having so many choices can also feel overwhelming, so toward the end of this chapter we will talk about strategies for selecting and implementing the practices into your daily life and customizing your program for your unique needs and methods of learning. The first practice we will cover is loving-kindness, as it is the basis and foundation for every other practice, and possibly the most essential practice to use when working with young children.

Red: Loving-Kindness Practices

Love refers not only to romantic love, or fond affection for people close to us, but to having unconditional positive regard for all people, for animals, for ourselves, and for our environment. The reason this particular series of practices is first on the list is that the ability to act with genuine unconditional loving-kindness forms the foundation for the humanist aspect of the OMPK program. As humans, our brains are designed to seek social connection, as we can survive better in groups than we can alone. Love is the foundation for connection to others, and for respect, cooperation, forgiveness, and positive social interaction. Feelings of love and connection can lead to acts of kindness. Engagement in loving-kindness meditation can increase feelings of social connectedness, positive regard for others, measures of physiological and psychological health, and resilience (Cohn et al., 2009; Hofmann et al., 2011; Hutcherson et al., 2008; Kok et al., 2013; Kok & Singer, 2017). Furthermore, we live in a world of systemic injustice, inequality, and discrimination based on race, sex, culture, beliefs, sexual orientation, and religion. Loving-kindness meditation can help to decrease the implicit bias that perpetuates inequality and oppression (Kang et al., 2014). The practice of loving-kindness serves to build acceptance, caring, and positive regard for all people, which can reduce the tendency to dislike or judge people, even on an unconscious level, who are different from us.

When to Practice Loving-Kindness

This practice can be helpful when we are:

- missing someone, have had a loss

- feeling sad, lonely, or disconnected

- feeling angry at ourself

- feeling ashamed or embarrassed for making a mistake

- feeling annoyed by others

- feeling angry at others

- feeling anxious, overwhelmed, or inadequate

As I was writing the final draft of this book, I had the profound gift of helping my mother and sister to care for my father in home Hospice care. One of the things I learned was that, no matter how deep the pain cut, how seemingly unbearable and intense it felt as I watched him suffer, as I saw my mother and sister hurting, the love was always bigger. For a little over two weeks we surrounded him and each other with love; we experienced the love of family and friends; we told stories about the epic love story of my parents' marriage; we celebrated the love in the midst of the pain. These loving-kindness practices got me through those weeks and the time after, much like they have helped me through so many other difficult situations.

Loving-Kindness Mindfulness Meditation Practices

The six formal loving-kindness meditation practices described below will help you to build loving-kindness and focus through repeated practice. Much like developing "muscle memory" by practicing a physical task over and over, formal loving-kindness practice helps you to build memory of how it feels to experience unconditional caring for yourself, loved ones, strangers, people who are hurting, people who have hurt you, and the world at large. You can do these six formal practices alone, in combination, or in a sequence. If you do them in a sequence, it is beneficial to complete them in order. To begin, you can start by doing 10 breath cycles for each practice. To increase focus for a single practice, build each practice up to 5 minutes, and then to 10 minutes. End each practice by thinking or saying, *May you be healthy, may you be happy, may you be loved, may you have peace.* You can also think or say these words during your meditation practice, as you breathe in and out.

Loving-Kindness to Self

Take a moment to remember that unconditional love means loving yourself no matter what, even when you make a mistake or let yourself down. Breathe in and feel love grow inside your heart and expand to fill your whole body. Breathe out love and forgiveness, sending it to yourself, and accepting yourself as you would accept a friend who made a similar mistake.

Loving-Kindness to a Loved One or Someone You Are Missing

Breathe in and feel love grow inside your heart and expand to fill your whole body. Breathe out love, sending it to someone you care about.

Loving-Kindness to a Stranger or Person You Do Not Know Well

Breathe in and feel love grow inside your heart and expand to fill your whole body. Breathe out love, sending it to someone you don't know well who may need love, such as a nurse, a sanitation worker, a firefighter, or anyone doing important services for the community.

Loving-Kindness for Someone Who Is Hurting or Sick

Breathe in and feel love grow inside your heart and expand to fill your whole body. Breathe out love, sending it to someone you know who is sick, hurting, lonely, or has experienced a loss. Feel the connection between you and the other person.

Loving-Kindness for Someone Who Has Hurt You or Disagreed with You

Breathe in and feel love grow inside your heart and expand to fill your whole body. Breathe out love, sending it to someone you find difficult to love, to someone who shares opposite beliefs, to someone who has hurt you, or to someone who would benefit from your forgiveness.

Loving-Kindness for the Whole World

Breathe in and feel love grow inside your heart and expand to fill your whole body. Breathe out love, sending it to the whole world (animals, people, nature).

Loving-Kindness in Action

Loving-kindness in action practices help you to apply what you have cultivated in formal mindfulness practice to situations and occupations of your daily life. Acting in kindness can help others to feel safe and connected. The practices below may take extra effort, especially during challenging times, but they can be very rewarding to both others and yourself.

Make Space for Loving-Kindness

When you notice you are overthinking a difficult emotion, or are stuck in a cycle of a difficult emotion, and it is affecting something in your daily life (e.g., your ability to meet with an upset parent), label the emotion (e.g., sadness, shame, fear). Determine what type of love you may need in the moment (e.g., love for yourself if you are feeling shame, love for the parent who has hurt you with unkind words). Breathe in and feel love grow inside your heart, expand to fill your whole body, and mix in with the difficult feeling. Breathe out the difficult emotion, noticing it and letting it go. Repeat for 10 breath cycles, and return to the task knowing you have made space for loving-kindness and can offer it moving forward. In the most difficult times in my life, I have realized that intense pain, anxiety, anger, and sadness and intense love can happen at the same time; they can co-exist in a way that expands us and makes us more open and whole.

Kind Acts

There are three main categories of kind acts: giving, helping, and caring. Examples for giving include providing financial assistance, food, or usable items that someone else may need or giving compliments, smiles, or praise. Examples of helping include assisting others to solve a problem, meet a goal, or complete a task they cannot do alone. Examples of caring include forgiving someone or yourself, asking someone how they are doing, and wishing someone well. A growing body of research shows that kind acts result in health benefits not only for the receiver, but also for the giver.

Loving-Kindness PAUSE Practices

The following PAUSE practices may seem simple, but they are not always easy! However, they can serve to help you shift in the moment from potentially harmful reactions to beneficial responses.

- When you notice that you are feeling down or disconnected or are dwelling on negative thoughts or feelings, pause and remember that *no feeling lasts forever.* Stop and take three loving-kindness breaths (to self, to other, or to make space) and remember that loving-kindness is always accessible and available.

- When you notice that another person is annoying you or you are angry at yourself, pause and remember that *the person is doing the best they can with what they have going on.* Take three loving-kindness breaths, and with each breath, send to yourself or the other person the words *May you be healthy, may you be happy, may you be loved, may you have peace,* and set an intention to act with love, kindness, and acceptance to yourself or the other person.

Orange: Present and Open Practices

Earlier I mentioned that we tend to live with a "monkey mind"; our minds jump around to different thoughts, feelings, and happenings without much of our awareness. Staying closed in our own minds can lead to reactions that can cause regret, make it difficult to notice and consider the perspective of others, and affect our ability to listen to and be present for others. In addition, as humans we tend to rapidly habituate, or get used to, our physical environments, which can decrease our external awareness. For example, if you buy a brand new comfortable couch after years of sitting on an uncomfortable, broken couch, you will likely notice and admire it frequently—at first. However, eventually, the couch fades out of the foreground of awareness, and you grow to not notice it as much. When we stop noticing what is right in front of us, dwell on the past, and worry about the future, or when we stay attached to our own thoughts and goals without consideration of others, we can feel overwhelmed, restless, and stressed. The present and open practices help us to notice what is happening inside of us and all around us, without judging and holding on to thoughts too tightly. Present and open practices encourage us to be aware in the present moment, to be available to others, to be flexible, and to be nonjudgmental in our actions.

Aspects of Present and Open Practice

Given that this is the largest group of practices—and that they are often the more challenging and novel types of mindfulness practices—we'll begin with a deeper explanation of the characteristics of present and open practices.

INTEGRATING ATTENTION AND AWARENESS

If attention is viewed as a focus on the "trees," awareness can be regarded as the ability to notice the "forest." Mindfulness cultivates our ability to see both the forest and the trees. Mindful awareness includes internal (i.e., interoceptive awareness of internal body sensations like pain, heartbeat, and hunger; awareness of thoughts, urges, and judgments) and external (i.e., exteroceptive sensory input, sensory stimuli, awareness of the physical and social environment, and pragmatic awareness) factors, as well as those factors that include a combination of both (e.g., empathetic awareness). To capture a beautiful photo, we must be able to focus and hold the camera steady on the target image, but also be aware of all the options, and be open enough to see beauty from any potential source. We must also be able to shift the camera when the lighting changes or the object of focus moves. Being present and embodying mindfulness in daily life requires us to balance attention and awareness simultaneously. Extreme concentration without awareness can lead to the inability to respond adaptively to salient internal and external cues and stimuli. In other words:

> We can concentrate on what we are doing, but if we are not mindful at the same time, with the ability to reflect on the moment, then if somebody interferes with our concentration, we may blow up, get carried away by anger at being frustrated. If we are mindful, we are aware of the tendency to first concentrate and

then to feel anger when something interferes with that concentration. With mindfulness, we can concentrate when it is appropriate to do so and not concentrate when it is appropriate not to do so. If we are concentrating on what we are doing and then something else happens, we can reflect on how to solve that other problem, or do that other thing, without getting into a terrible state about it and without upsetting others. (Sumedho, 1990, p. 48)

Research has shown that engaging in a brief mindfulness awareness practice can reduce inattention blindness (concentrating so hard on one thing that we miss other important information) and increase our ability to notice an unexpected distractor during a goal-directed task (Schofield et al., 2015). This is especially important when working with young children, as distractions are constant, and you can often feel like you are putting out fire after fire! In daily life, the challenge of integrating attention and awareness can be even more difficult when we spend so much time engaged in near-point focus activities that are urge driven, such as when using smartphones and tablets. When we become focused on an electronic activity that is guided and maintained by impulse and pleasure-seeking behavior, such as scrolling through social media, clicking on hyperlinks and videos, we often block out ambient input. Have you ever been so engaged on a computer or a smartphone that when you stopped using the device, you felt completely bombarded by stimuli? Often this contrast between our inner and outer worlds can feel overwhelming, which is why many of us retreat to the comforts and entertainment of screen time in the first place. With mindfulness practice, we can build the capacity to more steadily balance focus and awareness.

LISTENING MINDFULLY

In the age of social media connection, text messaging, and virtual communication, people in cultures with easy access to technology may spend less time engaged in face-to-face communication. Listening mindfully requires us to be present while another person is talking, without presuming what that person will say, and to wait until the person has finished speaking to prepare our response. Have you ever been listening to someone speak to you about a controversial topic, or offer possible solutions to a common problem, and you find yourself tuning out because you are already thinking about what you want to say next? Often when someone brings up a topic, it can spark an idea in our own minds, and we may want to share it right away so we don't forget it; this can be especially true if we have attention or working memory problems. (Working memory is the ability to hold onto information necessary for a task at hand long enough to use it.) When this happens, we have to make a choice to continue listening or to hold on to our counter point. This can be difficult in real time but is not as much of an issue in a social media format, as people are able to talk over each other digitally.

During real-time communication, when we have difficulty with focusing attention, holding onto ideas in working memory, and inhibiting distractions from our inner thoughts and worries, we can engage in mindless modes of communication—our minds wander, we "tune out," and we wait for our turn to talk instead of mindfully listening. This can make the other person feel not respected or heard, and can make us miss important elements of what they have said. The OpenMind REMIND practices can help you to build mindful listening by increasing awareness of your inner thoughts and of what is happening around you so that you can stay present for the other person. When we listen mindfully, there is a quality of our presence that makes others feel valued and appreciated, and it helps us to stay open to new ideas. A related aspect of mindful listening is the ability to practice nonjudgment, so that we do not presume what the other person will say before they say it or assume the other person's intentions.

NONJUDGMENT

To define nonjudgment, I'll first describe its opposite. The human brain is wired to establish and use bias at the most fundamental level to inform our survival by acting to approach or avoid a given stimulus or situation. For each incoming stimulus, our brains assign a valence, or rating, and engage in valuation, which can be defined as "a simple form of meaning analysis in which something is judged as helpful or harmful in a given instance, producing some change in core affective state" (Barrett, 2006, p. 39). In other words, our brains are constantly labeling each stimulus that we encounter as either "good—this can help me," or "bad—this can hurt me." Due to this process and our own unique personal and cultural experiences, over time, we form biases.

Biases impact social cognition (i.e., how we think about and perceive social situations or information) and can often cause an automatic, unconscious influence on our judgment and behavior. For example, people have been shown to make a judgment about a person's level of trustworthiness and other personal characteristics within 100 milliseconds of seeing the person's face (Willis & Todorov, 2006). Just seeing an unknown person's face, a superficial representation, causes our brains to make a judgment about that person's character within a fraction of a second—and we are not even always consciously aware of it. Implicit bias is a type of unconscious bias based on stereotypical beliefs about a group of people (e.g., BIPOC, the LGBTQ community). This type of bias can influence behavior, decision making, and ultimately our ability to engage in prosocial behavior. Implicit bias is automatic and often does not correlate with the beliefs that we express.

While a full discussion of cognitive biases and attribution errors is beyond the scope of this chapter, it is interesting to get an idea of just how many types of biases we face. Some examples include:

- *attention bias due to salience* (increased attention toward very noticeable or important information, such as stimuli perceived as threatening),

- *correspondence bias* (attribution of a person's behaviors to stable personal characteristics instead of external forces that may have caused the behaviors),

- *confirmation bias* (believing that something that aligns with our beliefs is proof that our beliefs are true), and

- *self-serving attributional bias* (attributing success to our own efforts and denying responsibility for our failures) (Fiske & Taylor, 2017).

Another form of bias is *negativity bias,* which is the tendency for us humans to pay greater attention to negative events, notice negative events more easily, focus more attention on negative events, and give more weight to negative stimuli and information that can represent immediate or potential threat (Baumeister et al., 2001; Gilovich, 1983; Öhman et al., 2001; Peeters & Czapinski, 1990; Pratto & John, 1991; Rozin & Royzman, 2001). Engagement in a brief mindfulness practice has resulted in a decrease in negativity bias and an increase in categorization of "positive" outcomes (Kiken & Shook, 2011). Given that formulation of judgment and bias helps to inform our immediate survival, it is unrealistic to think that practicing mindfulness will eliminate all judgment; however, mindfulness does involve increasing the awareness and recognition of our own judgments and biases with the goal of preventing automatic reactions that can be harmful to others. It can help us to recognize our biases, judgments, and perceptions, and instead make an objective assessment and evaluation.

DECENTERING

The OpenMind REMIND practices that involve *decentering* can help you to step back from your emotions so that you can objectively notice and evaluate them, rather than be controlled by them; see your present situation more clearly; and be more open to all experiences. Because we are often driven by our emotions, it can be easy to become caught up in them, and our perceptions of them. For example, we can become sad that we are feeling sad, or angry at ourselves for getting angry. The basic process known as affect labeling—simply stated, putting our feelings into words—has been found to decrease responses in the amygdala (the part of the brain responsible for regulating emotions) to negative affective images (Lieberman et al., 2007). Further, individuals who have an increased ability to label and communicate emotions rather than simply react to them have demonstrated improved emotional coping skills (Barrett et al., 2001; Gentzler et al., 2005). Decentering—and the resulting emotional processing and coping we experience—enables us to stay present for what is happening, and prevents us from being carried away to the future or past.

When to Practice Being Present and Open

These practices can be helpful when we are:

- feeling bored, restless, or distracted

- overwhelmed and wanting to settle our mind

- thinking the same thoughts over and over

- stuck on a problem or in a conflict with someone else

- stuck in our head

Present and Open Mindfulness Meditation Practices

These formal Present and Open practices include two aspects: the first part is a formal focused awareness practice, and the second part allows for your reflection about the practice. Because it is a formal practice, I recommend using a timer so that there is a beginning and end to the practice. The times recommended below for each formal practice are merely suggestions, and you may increase the number of minutes as your focus and awareness improve.

Listening to What Is Happening Around You

Sit quietly and set a goal for listening and noticing all of the sounds around you for 2–5 minutes. As you notice a sound (e.g., clock ticking, bird chirping), label it and continue listening. Notice how you may form a thought about the sounds you hear. After the timer is up, practice recalling all of the sounds you heard, and notice how you may not have been able to hear them if you were not listening. For each sound that you heard, try to notice if you had a thought about the sound after you heard it. For example, if you heard a siren go by outside, you may have noticed yourself having a thought about wondering what happened to cause an emergency. As you get better at the listening practice, try to notice both the sounds and the thoughts in the moment as you are practicing.

Watching the Sky

On a cloudy day, sit quietly and set a goal for watching and noticing the open sky for 2–5 minutes. Notice the color of the sky; the movement of birds; and the way that clouds change shape, dissipate, expand, or darken. After the timer is up, notice how the picture of the sky in any moment was impermanent and ever-changing.

Open Monitoring Meditation

Start by telling yourself that your goal is to notice everything that is happening inside you and around you, and to let your mind watch and explore whatever happens, like a moviegoer, scientist, or detective. Begin to breathe and notice the sensation of your breath in and out. If you have a thought or emotion, notice and label the thought or emotion, and let it be what it is. Notice any stories that your mind tells about a thought, feeling, or sensation. Begin with 10 breath cycles of noticing and labeling thoughts, feelings, and sensations inside and around you, and then build to 5 minutes and then 10 minutes. After the meditation, you can reflect on what you noticed in your mind, much like you may reflect on a movie you have watched.

Orange Elephant Meditation (Noticing Thoughts)

This exercise can show us exactly how much our minds wander. The visual is an "orange" elephant to correspond to the associated color of the meditation practice. Sit quietly and begin by imagining or visualizing an orange elephant. Set a timer and sit quietly for 2–5 minutes doing open monitoring meditation, starting by labeling the thought, "orange elephant." Notice how your thoughts stay on the initial thought, wander, and/or return to it; notice whether you were thinking in words, pictures, or both. After the timer is up, notice what you are thinking about or imagining—rarely will your mind still be on an orange elephant unless it has jumped back in remembrance! Try to remember the train of thought that followed your initial thought and notice how your mind wandered from thought to thought. After you have tried this practice, you can start with another phrase or question you may have; you do not have to stick with "orange elephant"! Picture the concept or situation in your mind that you wish to examine more closely and then set an intention to see the situation clearly and notice what arises in your mind.

Present and Open in Action

While the Present and Open formal mindfulness practices are intended to be done in a planned and timed format to build foundational awareness skills, the Present and Open in Action practices are designed to be used during real-life, everyday activities as the need arises. These practices can help bring you back to the present when you find you may have drifted, and help you to break the habit of mental time traveling to escape from the present moment when it is unpleasant or uncomfortable.

Sitting with Boredom or Restlessness

Whenever you are bored or restless, instead of looking for entertainment or distractions (such as scrolling on a smartphone), try to notice how it feels to be bored, and what kind of thoughts you may have if you give your brain a chance to be bored for 10 breath cycles. Practice sitting with the feeling of boredom when you notice yourself looking for distractions or entertainment.

Opening Up a Window

Many, many years ago, I wrote the following poem:

> *Mind grips vise-like,*
>
> *The tightening fear ancient.*
>
> *Impatient I pace within*
>
> *brain cells, encaged in*
>
> *such frustrating casings*
>
> *of thoughts, bone and skin,*
>
> *I need to open, and let more space in.*

We live in such a big world, and yet we can spend so much time inside the confines of certain places within our heads—places like worry, perseveration on a particular goal or cultural standard, or pain. It can feel crowded and stifling. When you notice that you are cycling through the same thoughts over and over, or that you are stuck inside your own head instead of taking part in the present moment around you, take a moment and envision yourself opening a window in your mind. Look and listen to the sensations around you and notice ten different things you may hear, see, taste, smell, or feel. This can allow you to let more space into the window of your mind and give you the freedom to notice what is happening in other places within you and around you.

Closing the Tabs

This practice is similar to the practice above but uses a slightly different visual. When you notice that your thoughts are racing, visualize all of your thoughts, worries, and things on your to-do list as open windows on the computer screen of your mind. One by one, visually "close out" each window until there is a blank screen, and then open up a new window for noticing the present moment.

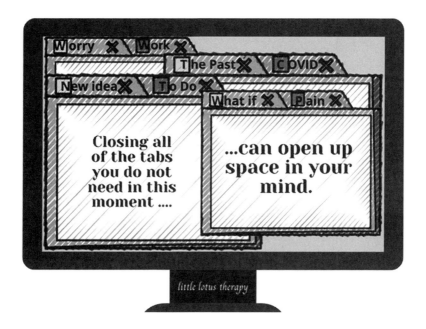

Being Present

When others are talking to you, instead of waiting your turn to talk, practice being present and still, and looking at and listening to the other person, as if you are watching a fascinating movie, an overtime period of a football game, your child taking their first steps. When you are doing an activity (e.g., washing dishes), be present and aware of that activity instead of lost in your thoughts and emotions. Notice the temperature of the water, the smell of the dish soap, the smoothness of the dish.

Listening for Your Own Bell

At the beginning of the day, choose a stimulus that occurs throughout the day to serve as your own reminder to be present, much like a meditation bell gives us a signal to be aware and to begin meditation. The stimulus "bell" can be something like an alert notification on your smartphone, a feeling of pain or physical discomfort, or even an action you may do like looking at a clock to check the time. Every time you notice this stimulus, pause and be present to take 5 mindful breaths.

Noticing Your Own Judgment, Perception, and Bias

When you are in a situation in which you are feeling defensive, argumentative, or emotionally charged, take a moment to notice your thoughts about the situation, your perceptions of the situation (e.g., the stories you may have created about the situation, the things you have added), and consider the other person's perspective. When I am in a situation like this, I try to remember that no one is ever 100% right and that there can be different levels of truth to even completely opposite sides of a story. Instead of making up your mind right away, label your emotions, thoughts, biases, and perceptions, and choose a response that facilitates resolution, compromise, or silence.

Decentering and Rating Big Emotions

When you are feeling overcome by a difficult emotion, think of it as a passing cloud rather than a permanent part of your landscape. Notice the size of the cloud, using a five-point scale; for example, a small bit of anxiety would be a 1, a full-blown sense of panic would be a 5. Take a few moments and "watch" the cloud. Notice how it changes shapes. Then reassess the emotion and its intensity. I like to use this visual when teaching others about how impermanent our emotions can be:

Present and Open PAUSE Practices

The Present and Open PAUSE practices can help you to stop when you notice that you are about to react in a potentially hurtful way because you are feeling stuck on your own thoughts, feelings, or ideas; are not aware of the bigger picture; are not being present; or are making a judgment about a person or situation. They offer a means to quickly shift to a more mindful way of responding in the moment.

- When you are feeling overwhelmed or worried about something another person has done, pause and remember that you are only responsible for how you react, and not for the actions of others. Take three breaths and notice if you are dwelling on the past, worrying about the future, or wishing you could change another person. Shift and set an intention to listen to, observe, and act in the present moment.

- When your mind is racing and you are feeling stress, guilt, or shame, remember that you are not your thoughts or your emotions, and often your thoughts are not true. Tsoknyi Rinpoche, a Tibetan teacher, is known for the phrase "real but not true" to describe the way we can view the upsetting thoughts we have. When you are having thoughts about situations, especially when they are about fear or shame, pause and think that they are real but not true. Shift and set an intention to stop adding to your own thoughts or believing thoughts that are not true, and return to the present moment.

- When you are stuck in a way of thinking about only one way to solve a problem, or on wanting something you cannot have, pause and remember that you are seeing the situation from only your perspective. Take three breaths, shift, and set an intention to notice your own biases and perceptions of the situation and to be flexible in your thoughts.

Yellow: Joy Practices

As mentioned in the previous section, our natural negativity bias can make us notice negative things more often, and talk about and think about negative situations longer than we do positive situations. This is because negative events can be harmful, and our brains want to protect us from these things. This can lead to our not noticing or thinking about positive events or situations that bring us joy. In addition, some people who have experienced loss or who have anxiety become worried when they experience joy because they do not want to lose the feeling of joy again. But much like the sun that is the symbol for this practice, joy is always possible. Even when the sky is cloudy, the sun is still behind the clouds, and they can part at any second to reveal its brightness.

Many people also do not celebrate the joy of others. From an evolutionary perspective, we are designed to compete with others for survival. This can lead to feeling resentment and jealousy when others experience joy. The joy and empathetic joy practices help you to feel and notice joy in life and also to celebrate the joy of others. Joy is different from pleasure in that you typically feel pleasure when you meet a goal or get something you want, but you can feel joy anytime, even when you are hurting. When you practice feeling joy, often it can lead to a state of happiness. As the Dalai Lama said, "We create most of our suffering, so it should be logical that we also have the ability to create more joy" (Lama et. al, 2016).

Finally, a big part of joy is laughter, and laughter is one of my favorite things about being human! Not only does laughter make us feel happy, but it is also a way to relieve tension and pain—it can actually help us to increase our pain threshold and have an opiate-like effect. We start to laugh at around three months of age, and laughter is a huge source of social bonding.

When to Practice Being Joyful

These practices can be helpful when we are:

- feeling sadness, grief, disappointment, or loss
- feeling hopeless, like everything is going wrong
- feeling jealous of others
- feeling like we want to experience more joy in daily life

Joy and Empathetic Joy Mindfulness Meditation Practices

The formal Joy practices help you to develop an awareness of how joy feels. They are focused practices designed to cultivate the feelings of warmth and lightness that joy brings. At times, life can move so fast and our stress can feel so heavy that we zoom through the natural and organic opportunities to experience joy around us, or fail to notice potentially joyful experiences because we have made up our mind about a situation, or are busy thinking of the past or worrying about the future. I remember being eight months pregnant with my third child and delayed in the Newark airport for twelve hours with my then teenaged daughter and toddler. If you would have told me that I would find joy in that situation, I would have thought it impossible, but we ended up having dance parties, laughing at the hopelessness of leaving that terminal any time soon…we still laugh about it! Regular formal joy practice can help you to notice and recognize opportunities to celebrate joy in daily life. Although it may feel odd at first, the following practices are best done while smiling because our perception of our own emotions is influenced by our bodies, including our own facial expressions.

Noticing Joy in Self

Take a minute to think about a person (e.g., a laughing child) or experience (e.g., a butterfly landing on a flower, a funny situation) that brings you joy. Smile. Breathe in and feel joy begin inside your heart and expand to fill your whole body, and smile. Joy can feel warm, bright, uplifting, and light. Breathe out joy, sending it to yourself. Repeat for 10 breath cycles. Increase to 5 minutes to build focus, concentration, and cultivation of the feeling of joy.

Feeling Joy for Others

Breathe in and feel joy begin inside your heart and expand to fill your whole body, and smile. Breathe out the wish of joy and happiness for someone you care about. Repeat for 10 breath cycles. Increase to 5 minutes to build focus, concentration, and cultivation of the feeling of joy.

Breathe in and feel joy begin inside your heart and expand to fill your whole body. Smile. Breathe out the wish of joy and happiness for someone toward whom you feel jealousy. Repeat for 10 breath cycles. Increase to 5 minutes to build focus, concentration, and cultivation of the feeling of joy.

Joy in Action

Joy in Action practices are a way for you to recognize opportunities to put joy before complaining and jealousy in real-life occupations and situations. They are designed to help you to laugh and smile through even dark times. These practices can help you to share, celebrate, and model the appreciation of joy in daily life.

Starting with Joy and Sharing Joy

Because of our human tendency toward negativity bias, when someone asks us how we are doing, we often begin with what is wrong. When discussing your day with significant others, friends, or family, begin by sharing a moment of joy that happened to you, and ask others about moments of joy that they experienced throughout the day.

Showing Empathetic Joy

If another person succeeds, wins a game, or comes out on top in an argument or discussion, instead of feeling jealous or resentful, try to feel and express joy for the other person. We can experience joy even when we are unhappy, simply by seeing other people being happy.

Share Jokes and Funny Stories, Be Silly

Take opportunities to laugh at yourself, to lighten a heavy mood with humor, to be ridiculous instead of self-conscious. Some of the best moments of social bonding happen over laughter. Make time to see the humor even in seemingly hopeless or impossible situations. Even in times of pain and suffering, there can be a release in laughter.

Joy PAUSE Practices

The Joy PAUSE practices remind you to notice the fleeting moments of happiness that you may miss if you are engaging in habits of overthinking, complaining, and over-focusing on a particular goal or problem. They can help you notice old patterns of the negativity bias and quickly shift to a more joyful state.

- When you notice that you are experiencing a moment of joy (e.g., hearing a funny joke, eating an ice-cream cone, seeing a rainbow or a puppy), pause and remember to slow down and enjoy the feeling for as long as it lasts, rather than rush through it. Set an intention to notice positive moments.

- When you notice that you are frowning, having negative thoughts, or feeling jealous of someone else, pause and remember that you can choose to shift your thoughts to embrace a positive moment in the present, or celebrate the joy of others instead of feeling envy. Take three breaths, shift, and set an intention to smile or celebrate another person's success.

Green: Grounded and Embodied Practices

As thinking beings, we tend to get caught up in our thoughts and spend much of our time living in our heads and time-traveling (living in the past or in the future). This can decrease our awareness of what our bodies are doing and feeling, and it may lead to physical problems such as muscle tension, indigestion, and headaches, as well as send out unintended signals of distress or threat. For example, when we are worried about a problem, we may frown or tense up our bodies in a defensive stance that can send out a message to other people that we are unapproachable or upset.

Research has suggested that our emotional expressions and movements can be "contagious" to others, partly because of our *mirror neuron system,* a group of specialized neurons that can cause us to often engage in mimicry of other people's facial expressions without even realizing it. Grounded practices can help you notice what is happening in your body and get back into your body when you get too caught up in thoughts and act without awareness of your body sensations, movements, body language, and facial expressions.

Awareness of Our Bodies

Awareness of our bodies requires moment-to-moment integration of sensory information, including *interoceptive* (heart rate, temperature, pain, gut sensations), *somatosensory* (tactile input), *proprioceptive* and *kinesthetic* (joint and muscle input, body movement), *vestibular* (position of head in relation to gravity), and *special sense* (vision, hearing, taste, olfaction) information. Body sensations and emotions have commonly been regarded and studied as separate phenomena, though there has also been a long history of interest in the theory of embodied emotion (how we experience emotions as physiological sensations in our bodies). Research shows a connection between the physiological sensations that inform perception and the identification of emotion (Craig, 2009; Critchley & Garfinkel, 2017; Damasio, 1999; James, 1890; Seth, 2013; Zaki et al., 2012). For example, many people may feel anger as muscle tension or feel fear as gastrointestinal pain or nausea.

Interoceptive awareness is our ability to perceive the internal sensations of our bodies, such as hunger, heartbeat, or the urge to empty our bladder; these sensations can contribute to our homeostasis, motivations, and emotions (Suzuki et al., 2013). Our body sensations can affect our decisions and actions, even when we are not aware of them. Fluctuations in interoceptive signals can affect our body states, express themselves as emotions and feelings, influence how we interpret stimuli, and play a role in our decision making (Bechara et al., 1994; Damasio, 1994; Damasio 1999; Damasio et al., 1996). Again, this often happens without much of our awareness because when we live in our minds, we can develop a disconnect from our bodies.

Evidence suggests that engaging in what we call embodied mindfulness practices, such as the body scan, increases interoceptive awareness of somatic sensations and can lead to increased emotion regulation (Farb et al., 2013; Holzel et al., 2011; Kerr et al., 2013) and better decision making. It is important to view sensations from the body and perceptions of emotions as a linked continuum. When identifying emotions, it can be helpful for us to notice not only what emotions we are feeling, but also *where* we feel them in the body, and *how the sensations that accompany them change* in location and intensity in accordance with their impermanent nature. Often, we try to avoid the unpleasant sensations that come along with emotions, such as the heaviness in the chest that comes with sadness, the tension and burst of intense energy that comes with anger, the racing heart and dizziness that comes with anxiety. When we do not give ourselves a chance to experience these feelings, we may not be able to process the emotions themselves. Grounded practices can help you to listen to and work through challenging emotions by leaning into and exploring their physical cues.

Pain vs. Suffering

Our emotions and thoughts are also closely linked to our experience of physical pain. Our pain can be acute (e.g., a recently fractured ankle); chronic (e.g., recurring headaches or myalgia); or structural (e.g., nerve pain due to herniated discs or stenosis). Pain is a primitive signal designed to alert us to the fact that something is wrong—we have injury, illness, inflammation—and therefore the signal is loud and uncomfortable. Pain is an inevitable part of life. However, when our minds amplify the pain signals, tell stories about the pain, and worry it will never end, or when we overmedicate, we can experience suffering along with the pain.

There is a Buddhist teaching about two arrows: if an arrow is shot and it hits us, we have pain; if we get caught up in worrying about the pain, we will not have the awareness to dodge the second arrow that is coming right behind it—the arrow that causes suffering. By guarding the pain and surrounding it with muscle tension and worry, we can trap it there and make it last longer than it may otherwise. The grounded practices may not prevent you from feeling pain, but they can help you to avoid being hit by the second arrow.

When to Practice Being Grounded

These practices can be helpful when we are:

- having stressful or racing thoughts

- feeling like we are moving too fast, or are completely exhausted

- feeling big emotions like worry and anger that are giving us physical pain and discomfort

- feeling pain, tension, dizziness, or other unpleasant physical sensations

Grounded Mindfulness Meditation Practices

Given that we spend so much time with our thoughts, it can take a lot of time and repetition to get back into our bodies and to build somatic (i.e., body) awareness. This can be especially important if you have a condition such as chronic pain or illness that impacts your control over your body. These formal practices will build your ability to notice the sensations that your body is experiencing internally (i.e., interoceptive stimuli), as well as from the environment (e.g., touch input), and to process them objectively and with a clearer awareness.

Body Scan Meditation

This practice was adapted from the Mindfulness-Based Stress Reduction Program developed by Jon Kabat-Zinn (1990). Sit up tall in a chair with your feet on the floor or stand up in a mountain pose. Take a deep breath and then drop your awareness to your feet. Notice your feet on the ground, how the ground feels under your feet, and how your feet feel (e.g., hot, cold, bouncy, heavy). Take another breath, move your awareness to your legs, and notice how they feel (e.g., strong, weak, wobbly, balanced). Take another breath and move your awareness to your back. Notice how it supports you and how it is positioned (e.g., straight up, slouching forward, leaning). Notice how the muscles and spine feel. Take another breath and move your awareness to your belly. Notice how it feels when you breathe in and out and notice any sensations in your belly (e.g., butterflies, hunger, pain, emptiness, nausea). Take another breath and move your awareness to your hands. Notice where your hands are resting and how they feel (e.g., sweaty, relaxed, fidgety, cold). Take another breath, move your awareness to your arms, and notice how your arms feel and how they are positioned (e.g., bent, straight, tense, tired). Take another breath and move your awareness to your chest. Notice how it feels when you breathe in and out and whether you can feel your heartbeat. Take another breath, move your awareness to your neck and throat, and notice how they feel (e.g., strong, tight, like your throat has a lump in it, relaxed, dry). Take another breath, move your awareness to your face, and notice how the breath feels going into your nose and out of your mouth. Notice how your face feels (e.g., itchy, cold, relaxed, smiling, frowning). Take another breath and drop your attention back down to your feet. Notice how they are connected to the ground and how you are strong and balanced.

Pain Meditation

There is a theory in chronic pain research called central sensitization, which means that people who experience conditions like fibromyalgia and chronic migraine can become hypersensitive to pain signals. Typically, pain signals a problem in the body, but with sensitization, these signals can become intensified. The increased pain intensity can then cause further mental amplification of the pain signals because of worry about the cause, nature, and progression of the pain. In addition, we can "guard" the pain by contracting the muscles around the areas that hurt, which can lead to more pain from chronic muscle tension, and trap the pain in our mind by creating a wall of worry around it. You can use this practice for chronic or acute pain to help you to objectively notice the pain signals, without further mentally strengthening them, and to also notice how your body may be guarding against the pain.

When you are feeling pain or discomfort, do a brief body scan to notice where the pain is. Breathe into the pain and notice the qualities of how it feels (e.g., burning, dull, aching, sharp), and notice its size, depth, and shape. Breathe out and relax the muscles around the pain, and relax your mental hold, knowing it is impermanent. Repeat for 10 breath cycles and build up to 5–10 minutes. Notice how the pain changes as you breathe.

Embodied Emotional Awareness, AKA Feel the Feelings

When you are feeling overwhelmed by unpleasant physical sensations that accompany emotion (e.g., numbness, heaviness, racing heart, nausea, lump in the throat), sit or lie down and notice these sensations as they arise and change in intensity or location. Sit or lie for 10 breath cycles and build up to 5–10 minutes. Allow yourself to lean into the sensations, support yourself, and experience them without trying to change them (e.g., cry if your body is telling you to cry, lean against the chair back if you are feeling weak, place your hands over your heart if it is aching). Notice how the sensations change as you breathe.

Hmmmmmmmeditation

Many cultural practices use chanting or movement that require concentration and awareness of the body—think about the Maori haka, the Gregorian chants of the Catholic church, and yogis who chant, "Om mani padme hum." Our voices can bring awareness and presence in our bodies. My son Miles developed this particular practice to help him to feel more present in his body.

Begin by sitting with your feet planted on the ground. Inhale and feel your feet rooted to the ground; exhale while making a "hmmmmmmm" sound that vibrates in your throat. Start with 2–5 minutes and increase the time if you find this practice beneficial.

YOGA, QI-GONG, AND MINDFUL MOVEMENT

Practices like yoga and qi-gong provide a means to become aware of body position, movement, and breathing, and to sync them together. They offer a way to focus on the breath while the body is in motion or in different positions. While formal instruction is beyond the scope of this chapter, these practices offer a means to become more grounded and balanced in your body. There are many in-person and virtual classes, as well as countless videos and courses to learn body-based meditation practice such as yoga and qi-gong. If you do not have yoga experience, you may want to start by reviewing and trying the yoga postures for children included in online appendix E of this manual, available at http://www.newharbinger.com/49258.

Grounded in Action

Because we often neglect the sensations from our bodies when we are mentally focused, we may tend to ignore our somatic signals until they intensify and tell us that there is a problem. For example, have you ever been in a stressful social situation, or worked too long at a computer all day, only to find later in the evening that your muscles are sore from tension, or you have developed a headache? This is because when we are stressed, our muscles may contract to give us a sense of groundedness and stability, especially the muscles of our jaw, neck, and shoulders. You know the expression "carrying the weight of the world on your shoulders"? This is what it often feels like! When we use the wrong muscles, or a harmful posture such as forward head posture, or "tech neck," it can result in physical pain. In addition, when we are unaware of how we are moving, we can send unintentional messages to others. Have you ever felt overwhelmed because you felt pressed for time, and realized that you were moving or speaking very quickly, or felt frustrated and realized you were using an annoyed or loud tone, or that your facial expression looked angry? The Grounded in Action practices can help you build aware-ness of your body in everyday life to prevent these types of outcomes from occurring. They can also help you to notice body signals without overreacting to them in a way that can cause additional pain or suffering.

Body Language and Facial Expression

When you are interacting with others, it is important to be aware of your body language and facial expressions. Sometimes when we are engaged with others, we do not realize that our facial expressions and body language are reflecting tension, emotions, and pain. This can communicate a negative message to others that we do not intend to communicate. There have been times when I have been in a lot of pain, and my son Maxim has asked, "Mom—are you upset?"; this is always a wake-up call to relax my face and the muscles I am using to guard the pain.

When you notice that you are feeling overwhelmed or stressed, be aware of tension and emotion in your face and body. Take 5–10 breaths in which you inhale and feel the tension, and exhale while you relax to give the pain some space. Adjust your expression and posture to reflect strength, openness, and calmness.

Informal Walking Meditation

When you notice that you are rushing and moving quickly, make an effort to slow your movements down and be aware of how you are moving and what it feels like. Try to time your breathing with your steps and walk mindfully instead of moving fast and without awareness.

Check the Alarm and Turn It Off

When you are experiencing pain or symptoms that send alarm signals, such as an increased heart rate or shortness of breath, these can feel very real and indicate an actual emergency or a false alarm. For example, if I am nervous before giving a presentation, my heart rate may go up a little and I can label this as anxiety, or a false alarm signal that feels real but is not true. However, due to an autonomic condition I described earlier called POTS, sometimes when I stand up my heart can spike up to as high as 200 beats per minute! This is because of a real event, either blood pooling in my legs or low blood volume, which causes my heart to beat rapidly to get blood back to my brain and heart. When this happens, I need to respond by lying back down or getting to the ground, elevating my feet, drinking more water and consuming salt, or scheduling IV fluids.

When you notice that you are experiencing symptoms such as pain, dizziness, stomach pain, nausea, or increased heart rate, you can assess them and make a decision about whether they seem to indicate an actual alarm—in which case you can respond and/or seek medical intervention. However, if you notice that the symptoms are familiar and seem to be more of a false alarm, visualize yourself entering a code to deactivate the alarm. Breathe and remember that the signals may feel real but are not true.

Listen to the Pain

This practice is related to the practice above but a little different. When you notice that you are feeling pain, stop and listen to what it is telling you with its alarm signal, choose the best response to it, and then thank the pain for doing its job. For example, if it is a new pain, you can make an appointment with a doctor. If it is a familiar pain for which treatment in the past has helped, make an appointment with a practitioner such as a physical therapist or chiropractor. If it is related to posture (like sitting at a desk too long), then stop, stretch, or change position. And finally, if it is chronic pain, listen to how it feels and then try to breathe into it, understanding that it is familiar and that it makes you stronger. Once you have listened to the pain, you can stop any stories or worry about it because you have taken an action in response to the signal.

Body and Feelings Check-In

When you are feeling uncomfortable, stressed, or overwhelmed, stop and complete the Thoughts, Emotions, and Sensations Self-Monitoring Tool found in appendix A, available at http://www .newharbinger.com/49258. Review all of the feelings and body sensations you are experiencing in the moment. If you are feeling one, rate how intense it is on a scale from 1 (a little) to 5 (a lot). Repeat this check-in later in the day and compare what has changed.

Grounded PAUSE Practices

The Grounded PAUSE practices offer a means to shift from being too much in the mind to being anchored in the body. These practices can facilitate a quick shift from thoughts and worries to awareness of what is happening in the body in real time.

- If you are feeling antsy or fidgety, are having trouble focusing, or are thinking too much and feeling overwhelmed, pause and remember to pay attention to what your body is doing. Drop your awareness to your feet and take three slow breaths while you notice how your feet feel, and how they are connected to the ground. Shift and set an intention to move mindfully throughout the day.

- If you are feeling like your mind is racing, stop and find your heartbeat. Count to twenty beats. Shift and set an intention to move more slowly throughout the day.

- If you are feeling pain, pause and notice if you are holding your breath. If you are, take three deep breaths into the pain and set an intention to pause often and make sure you are breathing deeply.

- If you are feeling pain or tension, pause and remember that no pain lasts forever, and pain is constantly changing. Breathe in and notice the pain, and breathe out while relaxing the muscles around the pain. Make adjustments to your position and posture as needed and set an intention to have a strong and upright posture and breathe deeply throughout the day.

Blue: Peaceful Practices

We live in a world that tends to be fast-paced and busy. Typically, our human brains focus in a way that is reflexive, in which endogenous (internal) and exogenous (external) stimuli "capture" our attention (Barrett et al., 2004; Egeth & Yantis, 1997). This form of automatic processing as our attention gets captured tends to be passive and short-lived, and typically exerts a subconscious influence on our thoughts, emotions, perceptions, and actions—as if our minds are pulled in different directions in automatic pilot instead of voluntarily driving and shifting to different focus points. In addition, we are pressured not only by our own expectations, fears, desires, goals, and motivations, but also by society's expectations and beliefs about what we should believe, how we should live our lives, and what we should achieve. This can cause us to feel anxious and overwhelmed and cause our minds to race.

The Peaceful practices use focused meditation, or *samatha* (tranquility), meditation. They help us to calm the body and settle a racing or troubled mind by focusing our attention on one thing, our breath. Deep breathing can help us to feel peaceful because it can tap into our parasympathetic nervous system, which is responsible for calming the body and acting like a brake pedal for the flight, fight, fright, or freeze reactions of our sympathetic nervous system. When you can focus on the breath, it becomes an anchor and allows you to be still and stay present while your thoughts and emotions settle. Practicing staying focused on the breath can also strengthen your attention span and your ability to focus in daily life.

The Peaceful practices involve building concentration and attention. The act of practicing concentrating on an object of attention is called focused attention meditation practice. Mindfulness interventions, both brief and intensive, that use focused attention meditation show significant improvement in measures of mindfulness, as well as in measures of cognitive factors such as working memory, attention, and visuo-spatial processing when compared to control groups (Chambers et al., 2008; Zeidan et al., 2010). A systematic review by Chiesa et al. (2011) showed that mindfulness-based interventions produced significant improvements in measures of attention, meta-awareness, and working memory. Increased practice of focused attention meditation results in a state in which "attention rests more readily and stably on the chosen focus…the ability to sustain focus thus becomes progressively 'effortless'" (Lutz et al., 2008, p. 167). This skill can also generalize to the ability to remember to return our focus to living ethically and to maintain focus on remembering the ethical consequences of our behavior (Anālayo, 2016). Finally, engagement in focused attention meditation can result in decreased activation in the amygdala following a potentially emotionally distressing situation (Desbordes et al., 2012), which means an improved ability to stay calm in a crisis or difficult situation.

Intentional focused attention is essentially what it sounds like: the practice of actively controlling our attention to focus on a particular object or situation. This is essential to our ability to inhibit impulses and distractions, listen intently to someone else, and concentrate on daily tasks that require sustained focus. When you are able to develop endurance for holding attention on a targeted object, you are better able to control your mind from wandering, control your body movements, cultivate patience, and enhance your self-efficacy (i.e., belief in your own abilities) and interest during tasks that are challenging or seem boring. In sum, the Peaceful practices improve your ability to be okay to sit and stay, instead of constantly running away.

When to Practice Being Peaceful and Focused

These practices can be helpful when we are:

- feeling like the world and our minds are moving too fast

- feeling distracted and having difficulty staying focused

- feeling too much energy (e.g., racing heart) and can't stay still

- having difficulty letting go of a troubling thought

- having feelings of anger, fear, or regret that make us feel overwhelmed and prevent us from focusing

Peaceful Mindfulness Meditation Practices

The Peaceful formal meditation practices build what many people find to be the most difficult aspect of mindfulness: focused attention. The primary practice of focusing on our breath may seem simple, but it is not easy. When you start, you may find that you become distracted multiple times, and this is absolutely normal. Even the most experienced meditators I know, who can meditate for hours at a time, have difficulty maintaining focus sometimes. The most important aspect of these practices is to start with short amounts of time, and increase as your focus endurance improves.

Focus on the Breath

Sit up tall on the floor, on a cushion, or in a chair; or kneel on a cushion; or lie down if needed. It is important that your posture is upright, aligned, and stable enough to support healthy and calming breaths. It is also important that you are stable yet relaxed so that you are not holding tension for too long. You can use pillows or a backrest if you need help staying upright. Breathe in and feel your breath move into your body at the tip of the nose, down into the lungs to expand the lungs and push the belly out, pause, and then breathe out and feel your breath move up your body and back out through your nose or mouth, and pause again. When you breathe in, your belly should expand like a balloon, and when you breathe out, it should deflate. You will notice that there are different parts—the inhale, a pause, the exhale, a pause. If your attention shifts to a thought or distraction, that is okay, it is normal—just remember to move your attention back to your breath. Repeat for 10 breath cycles to begin, and then progress to 5 minutes and then to 10 minutes. When you are first starting, it may help you to count your breaths, or to label each part of the breath, such as "inhale, pause, exhale, pause"; this is okay. The goal is to eventually just focus on the sensations of breathing in and out.

For a calming effect: Breathe in for a count of 4 and breathe out for a count of 6 or 7. If you are feeling a lot of pain, anxiety, or panic, breathe out and softly say, "shhhhh" during the exhale. The sound and feel of the breath can help to calm the body and act as a signal to be quiet and still and can make it easier to focus on the breath.

Heartbeat Meditation

Sit or lie down and find your heartbeat. Place your hand over your heart or pulse point and breathe in and out, placing your attention on your heartbeat. Repeat for 10 breath cycles and build up to 5–10 minutes, maintaining your focus on the rhythm of your heart.

Peaceful in Action

The Peaceful in Action practices can help you to transfer a sense of stillness, patience, and presence to the activities of daily life. These two simple practices can help you return to a calm focus when you may be feeling scattered or in distress, and complete daily activities with a slower and more mindful pace.

Letting It All Settle

If you are in a situation where you are waiting (e.g., in line, at a stoplight in traffic), feeling anxiety, feeling angry, or feeling overwhelmed, instead of engaging in racing thoughts, having an outburst, or seeking entertainment from a smartphone or other source, take the opportunity to stop, to build focus and calm. Visualize your mind like a snow globe that has been shaken up, or a clear river whose bottom has been stirred up and is swirling with mud. Focus your attention and awareness on taking 5–10 breaths while your mind settles like the snow or water and becomes clear and focused.

Serial Multitasking

When you are trying to do too many things at once that split your focus and make you feel scattered (i.e., simultaneous multitasking), identify the first and most important task for you to do and shift your focus to that task only. Set a time limit or goal and maintain focus on that task until the time or goal is completed, even when you are distracted by an impulse to research a new idea, or engage in a different task. Then shift your focus to the next task, and repeat. When you come to a stopping point, take three calming breaths, and focus on breathing in and out.

Peaceful PAUSE Practices

The Peaceful PAUSE practices offer a means to quickly shift from an old pattern, behavior, or impulsive reaction to an intention of stillness and focus.

- If you notice that your mind and body are racing, or if there is an emotion or thought that keeps playing over and over in your mind, pause and remember that the world is not moving fast; your mind is moving fast. Visualize your mind as an agitated animal (e.g., a bird) darting about and upset. Take a deep breath in and then breathe out and softly and gently say, "shhhhh" to the "animal" as you breathe out. Take three breaths and set an intention to focus on one thing at a time.

- If you notice that you feel upset by something someone else has done and have the urge to react with anger, pause and remember that the urge will pass if you let it settle. If you eat hot food too soon it will burn you, but if you wait it will cool down on its own. Shift your attention to your breath and take three breaths before responding. Set an intention to pause before responding when you feel upset.

Indigo: Compassion Practice

When we know that others are suffering, it can make us feel uncomfortable or powerless, especially when we do not know how to help them. The ability to notice other people's pain, emotions, and state of mind is called empathy. Empathy is important because it connects us to others. However, too much empathy can cause distress, sadness, and empathy fatigue. Compassion is a fourfold process that first requires awareness of another person's suffering, followed by empathy, then the desire to help relieve the person's suffering, and, finally, the motivation to engage in an act to help relieve the person's suffering (Jinpa, 2010). It has been posited that "compassion is not only the answer to other people's suffering, it is also the answer to our own" (Kyabgon, 2007, p. 12). Training in compassion meditation and practice has been associated with increased happiness, mindfulness, and positive affect following an empathetic response to another's suffering, and reduced emotional reactivity, worry, and emotional suppression (Desbordes et al., 2012; Jazaieri et al., 2014; Klimecki et al., 2012).

Compassionate action—even just offering quiet reassurance, sitting in silent support giving your presence, or sending love—can help to balance out the weight of empathy. Practicing compassion can help you to connect to your own suffering and the suffering of others; to feel the suffering; and to send out lightness, space, peace, kindness, and love. Compassion meditation can help you to be present for the suffering of others, to connect to them and give support through their suffering, and to send them peace. If you have ever sat with someone at the end of their life, or someone in unbearable pain, you may know that it can feel helpless, hopeless, like there is nothing to do. Compassion practice offers us a way to be present with the suffering of others, and to send them love and support.

When to Practice Being Compassionate

This practice can be helpful when we are:

- experiencing pain and suffering

- wanting to help others to relieve their suffering

- feeling empathy fatigue, or overwhelmed with empathy

- feeling helpless because someone we love is suffering

- feeling responsible for the happiness of others

Compassion Mindfulness Meditation Practices

Much like the other formal practices, compassion meditation practices enable you to build a strong foundation for acting with compassion. Empathy is one of the factors that socially binds us; however, when we experience empathy too deeply because we are emotionally sensitive, or chronically due to life roles such as caregiving and helping others, the empathy alone can drain us and leave us feeling emotionally overwhelmed. Too much empathy can be harmful, but compassion can be restorative. In addition, when we experience empathy, we often feel an obligation to "fix" the other person who is suffering or the situation that is causing suffering. Most often, this is not possible. Instead, compassion is about being able to stay present with a person who is suffering without feeling the need to dramatically change their situation. Diane Musho Hamilton described this brilliantly: "With time, we come to understand that simply being present to each other is our most basic moral obligation. There may be occasions when we can lend a helping hand. There may be instances when we are obligated to interfere, but more often than not, simple presence provides a context for others to listen to themselves, and that is the real service" (Hamilton, 2013, pp. 88–89). For additional reading on a difficult topic, Joan Halifax, a Zen Buddhist nun, has written a deeply moving book called *Being with Dying,* which addresses how to offer compassion to ourselves and others, especially when they may be facing an end-of-life situation (Halifax, 2008).

Many people have told me that compassion practices are the most difficult of all the mindfulness practices. As we have discussed several times throughout this book, our tendency as humans is to run from pain, not to willingly seek it out! If these practices are too painful for you, you can shift back to the loving-kindness practice for sending love to someone who is hurting. The formal Compassion practices will help you develop the capacity for being able to offer quiet support to others in the midst of empathy and suffering.

Compassion for Self

Breathe in and think about a painful emotion you are having (e.g., shame, regret, anger) or situation you have experienced. Feel the pain as you breathe in; the air may feel heavy, sad, burning, or tight. Breathe out and send yourself relief, lightness, peace, forgiveness, acceptance, and open space. Breathe for 10 breath cycles to begin and build up to 5 and then 10 minutes.

Compassion for Others

Breathe in and think about a friend or loved one who is suffering and experiencing pain, helplessness, fear, or other difficult emotions. Feel the other person's pain as you breathe in; the air may feel heavy, sad, burning, or tight; as you take in the pain, imagine that you are receiving it so that the other person can have relief. Breathe out relief, lightness, peace, healing, and open space, sending the other person love. Breathe for 10 breath cycles to begin and build up to 5 and then 10 minutes.

Compassion in Action

Compassion in Action practices help you to integrate compassion into your everyday life activities. These simple practices offer you a way to spread compassion to others as the opportunities arise. Used regularly, they can connect formal practice to compassionate action. Many years ago, I was fortunate to meet a magnificent woman named Sara Schairer, who created wristbands to help remind people to put compassion in action, or to "compassion it." These wrist bands can be a great tool for noticing and celebrating opportunities to be compassionate in life (see https://www.compassionit.com for more information).

When You Notice Suffering

If you learn of another person suffering during the course of the day (e.g., see an ambulance going by, hear about a tragedy or natural disaster), recognize how the other person or people may be feeling and then send loving-kindness for 5 breath cycles. If you have downtime or are waiting, think of a friend or loved one who is suffering and send a message of love and comfort.

How Can I Help?

If you notice that another person is upset, struggling, or hurting, ask if there is anything you can do to help. If the other person says no, ask if they would like you to stay with them or listen. Remember that you do not have to solve or take away that person's problem, and often just asking what you can do can serve as a compassionate act in itself.

When Someone's Suffering Makes You Feel Uncomfortable, Anxious, or Angry

Sometimes the suffering of others can make you feel uncomfortable or trigger you in some way. For example, if a child is having a tantrum or meltdown, instead of becoming upset, tell them that you feel compassion for them, and offer help when they are ready (e.g., "You are throwing your cars; it looks like you are hurting. I feel so much compassion for you. I am here when you are ready for a hug or help").

Compassion PAUSE Practices

Compassion PAUSE practices are a means to recognize patterns of reaction that can lead to empathy fatigue or increased suffering and shift to an intention to practice compassion instead. Used in the moment, the following PAUSE practices can help you to respond to a situation and to yourself with compassion instead of running from the situation, using negative self-talk, taking on too much of another person's pain, or trying to force assistance or resolution before its time.

- When you notice yourself feeling overwhelmed by the pain of another, pause and remember that you are not responsible for taking away the other person's pain, but that you can be present with the person and offer yourself as comfort. Set an intention to be present for others who are hurting and know that it is not your responsibility to take all of the pain away.

- When you notice that you are angry at yourself for a mistake you have made, pause and remember that you are not alone and that other people have made the same mistake. Set an intention to forgive yourself and remember that mistakes are how we grow.

Violet: Gratitude Practices

Because of our tendency to have a negativity bias, it is easy for us to fall into a cycle of complaining. When people ask us how we are doing, we often begin with the parts that we find painful or negative. We often dwell on negative things that happen, annoyances, losses, and disappointments instead of celebrating positive things that happen, ordinary gifts we receive, and kind actions others do to help us. In addition, we live in a society that values getting more and achieving more, and this creates a belief that happiness is linked to success, money, and status. Contrary to these values and tendencies is the practice of gratitude, which has been associated with increased job satisfaction, positive affect, and well-being (Emmons & Mishra, 2011; Lai & O'Carroll, 2017; Waters, 2012).

Gratitude practice helps us to remember to feel grateful and to focus on what we have, rather than what we don't have. It helps us to notice, celebrate, and be thankful for both the beautiful experiences in our lives and the challenging experiences that help us to grow. A lesson that illustrates this is the lotus flower. The lotus is a beautiful flower that grows out of the mud. The difficult circumstances in life can be like the mud that causes the beautiful lotus to blossom. There are two kinds of things we can have gratitude for, each with its own way of feeding our growth. First, there are the positive things we are grateful for that are obvious, like loved ones, food, water, shelter, beauty around us, pleasant surprises, and meeting goals. These are like the sun—they make us grow tall and reach for the light. Then there are the challenging times, the failures, the mistakes, and the pain that we feel grateful for because we learned valuable lessons from them. These are like the rich soil and rainstorms that make us grow stronger by pushing our roots deep into the darkness.

When to Practice Gratitude

Gratitude practice can be helpful when we are:

- longing for something we don't have

- feeling negative, empty, sad, disappointed, or jealous

- going through a rough time in life

- wanting to express thankfulness for a kind act or gift

Gratitude Mindfulness Meditation Practices

The formal Gratitude meditation practices build comfort and ease with expressing gratitude. Regular practice in sitting with gratitude can help you to counteract the natural human tendency to complain and to want more. These practices can also develop the ability to see the lotus through the mud that life can offer, and thus increase feelings of gratefulness for life's challenges.

Gratitude for the Positive

Sit, kneel, or lie down comfortably and take a few breaths while noticing how you are feeling. Then think about something (e.g., a glass of clean water) or someone (e.g., a kind coworker) you are grateful for, or an action someone has done that makes you feel thankful (e.g., your partner or child cleans up the kitchen). Breathe in and feel grateful for the person, event, or action, and breathe out while expressing thanks, gently saying or thinking, "Thank you." Begin with 10 breath cycles and build up to 5 and then 10 minutes.

Gratitude for Difficult Situations

Think about a difficult situation that has happened and reflect on how it challenged you and helped you to grow or learn. Breathe in and feel grateful for the opportunity to learn and grow, and breathe out while expressing thanks, gently saying or thinking, "Thank you." Begin with 10 breath cycles and build up to 5 and then 10 minutes.

Grateful in Action

Grateful in Action practices help you to embed gratitude into your daily life. These short practices provide a means for noticing opportunities to express thanks and to model the practice of gratitude in context for others.

Thanking Others

When someone does a kind act for you, or has a different opinion than you, take the time to thank the person for helping you, or for helping you to grow, and include the specific reason why it has been so helpful.

Sharing Gratitude with Others

When others ask us how we are doing, we often begin by talking about our problems, pain, or challenges. When someone asks how you are doing, try to start by sharing a recent moment or situation that you are grateful for. If you share a painful or challenging experience, try to end with something that the experience has taught you that makes you feel grateful.

Grateful PAUSE Practice

This simple PAUSE practice enables you to stop the reactive habit of complaining and shift to a positive intension of feeling grateful:

- When you notice that you are complaining in your own mind or to others, pause and remember that the situation can be a wonderful teacher, and can make you stronger. Take three breaths and feel gratitude for something positive in your life. Set an intention to notice opportunities to feel and express gratitude.

Rainbow Mindfulness Meditation Practice

The rainbow meditation practice combines all of the meditation practices and is ideal for beginners and children. There are three options for this practice, ranging from simple to more challenging. The practices can be combined with hands-on objects such as meditation beads to help with pace and focus in the beginning stages.

Option 1: Basic Rainbow Meditation

This is a short practice with seven focused breaths. To begin, breathe in and feel love expand, and then breathe out. Continue with each associated color word (loving, present, joyful, grounded, peaceful, compassionate, and grateful).

Option 2: Brief Rainbow Meditation with Lotus Breathing

This practice option uses your hand as a visual to pace and guide your breathing. It starts with the hand closed and fingers together, palm up. When you breathe in, your fingers expand like a lotus flower opening, and when you breathe out, your fingers close again. This can be used to count and pace breaths:

- Breathe in and open your hand and breathe out and touch your thumb and index finger; breathe in and open your hand and breathe out and touch your thumb and middle finger; repeat twice more, touching your ring finger and then your small finger—this makes a 4-count breath cycle.

- For an 8-count breath cycle, do this exercise with both hands.

- Repeat the lotus breathing (4 or 8 count) for each practice (loving, present, joyful, grounded, peaceful, compassionate, and grateful).

Option 3: Rainbow Meditation

This practice involves doing 10 or more breath cycles of each of the seven REMIND practices. You can use the formal meditation practice instructions for each of the seven practices, or a more basic form of the practice, such as breathe in and feel _____ grow, breathe out.

Option 4: Black (Strong): Putting the Rainbow Together

This practice was designed to remind you that when you use and practice all of the colors—red (loving), orange (open), yellow (joyful), green (grounded), blue (peaceful), indigo (compassion), and violet (grateful)—together, you can cultivate an inner strength. Black is the color that represents all colors. This is the final intention practice that reminds us that when we cultivate all of these practices, we can become strong in our values, presence, and actions, no matter our circumstances. To practice this, breathe in and feel your body become strengthened by your breath, breathe out and think or say, "I am strong." Repeat for 10 breath cycles and believe in your own inner strength.

The OpenMind SOS Strategy: A Top-Down Practice

If you think back to the opening section of the previous chapter, you may remember the metaphor that compares life to stepping out onto a sinking ship. We accept the challenge, and yet at times, we recognize how perilous our situations can be, and we feel distress. In the early 1900s, SOS became the international signal for distress, a call for help. While some people think that SOS is short for phrases such as "save our ship" or "save our souls," the letters were actually chosen because they make a simple pattern in Morse code: three dots, three dashes, three dots (. . . - - - . . .). The minds who gathered together to develop this international code recognized that people in distress needed a simple, easily transmittable, effective, and recognizable signal to send a message for help.

In addition to its value in Morse code, the letters SOS also are both a palindrome (read the same way backward and forward) and an ambigram (read the same way right side up or upside down). This has utility and value in situations where people may be stranded and need to write a signal on the ground that can be read by potential rescuers coming from any direction.

SOS has been used for over 100 years to signal distress and bring help and rescue in the midst of crisis. But what about everyday emotional distress that requires rescue, often from our own patterns, overthinking, and habits? Emotions and emotional distress are two separate and distinct entities. Emotions are healthy messengers that help us to survive, gain clarity, adapt, fight injustice, connect with others, and heal. Emotional distress, however, is the suffering that comes with habits such as overthinking, self-criticism, dwelling in the past, worrying about the future, and mistaking our thoughts for facts.

Much like a physical crisis, when we are experiencing emotional distress and feeling overwhelmed, we need a pattern that is simple and easily recognizable to send a signal to ourselves that we are in need of help to overcome the distress. The OpenMind SOS strategy is a simple process for working through emotional distress. Used regularly, this process may even help us to prevent distress by creating and establishing a healthy habit for responding to challenging emotions as they arise. This method uses the following three steps and incorporates a variety of the OpenMind REMIND practices:

S: Stop, Settle, Seek Safety: The first step when responding to emotional distress is to pause, allow physiological aspects of emotion (e.g., racing heart, surge of anger-related muscle tension, intense welling of tears) to settle, and seek an area that feels safe if needed.

O: Observe, be Open (and Objective!): Objectively observe and label your thoughts, bodily sensations, emotions, and perceptions of the situation, and also consider the perspective of others.

S: Shift, Surrender, Solve: Shift your mindset from one of active distress to one of acceptance or resolution. This can include surrendering to the emotion and allowing it to run its course, letting go of thoughts and beliefs that are not true, or problem solving an action to answer the call of the distress signal.

Practicing the OpenMind REMIND practices regularly will help you to build the skills to master the SOS strategy and to use it and model in everyday life to help both yourself and others around you.

Pause for Reflection...

This chapter offers many options for beginning a mindfulness practice or for enhancing a practice you may already have. While the intention is to offer many different options, as everyone is unique and may respond better to some options than others, it can seem overwhelming to determine where to start. My suggestion is to choose a "color," or wellness state, that you would like to develop, and initiate one of the formal practices. Try the practice every day for at least a week, and then begin to integrate the "in action" and PAUSE practices that go along with it into your daily life. Once you become familiar with the different practices by trying them out and experiencing them, you can ask yourself each day what you need to practice to strengthen yourself and to benefit those around you, and then choose the corresponding practices. My own children use this method for their daily formal mindfulness practice—they typically choose three to four colors and do a brief meditation for each.

If you can, determine a specific and planned time to practice formal mindfulness each day to build a strong and healthy habit. For me, this is first thing in the morning and just before bed. This regularity can transform the practice from an activity you are doing to a meaningful occupation in your life. Once you have begun working to cultivate each wellness state through formal practice, you will typically find it is easier to embed each of them into real-life situations. It can be helpful to take few minutes at the end of the day to reflect and notice opportunities that arose for practice in action and PAUSE practices; be aware of whether you were able to use the practices and, if so, how they may have been beneficial. It is also important to remember that these practices were meant to REMIND you to cultivate mindfulness, and the reason for this is that it is very easy to slip up, or to be caught up in the storms and challenges our sinking ships throw our way, and forget to be present. Using these practices will not guarantee an easy sail, but they will help you to make the most of your whole beautiful voyage.

In part 3, you will learn about the OMPK ten Daily Practices. The OpenMind REMIND practices you've just learned will give you an experiential context for understanding the purpose and function of these practices for children, and also give you a strong foundation for maintaining and modeling equanimity and patience as you teach these practices.

PART 3

The OMPK Daily Practices for Teaching Mindfulness and Creating a Prosocial Classroom

CHAPTER 6

Daily Practice Overview

This chapter provides an overview of the ten Daily Practices, which form the foundation of the OMPK program. The Daily Practices are fundamental activities practiced consistently and frequently so that they create a shift in classroom culture and foster the development of mindful habits to nurture social-emotional learning and growth. Young children's brain development is dependent on use, and learning requires a lot of repetition so that children can experience competence and understanding. You likely already have a robust classroom schedule that requires an incredible amount of planning, energy, and time management; therefore, the Daily Practice activities are offered in a format that allows for integration into your existing lesson plans and classroom schedule. In chapters 7 through 10, you will find references to materials such as visuals and songs that you can download from the online appendix of this book at http://www.newhar binger.com/49258.

When used on a regular basis, the OMPK Daily Practices can help to:

- build children's foundational skills for focus, attention, and self-regulation

- improve children's emotional, body, and social awareness

- strengthen social connection and bonding

- reinforce and encourage prosocial behaviors and choices

- support academic and social engagement

- enhance classroom management

- create a peaceful and engaged classroom environment

Daily Practice Format

The purpose of these activities is to enhance your existing academic curriculum, thereby growing children's emotional resilience and fostering mindful engagement in academic and social environments. Each activity description provides you with an overview of the activity's purpose and alignment with specific social-emotional learning domains. It also illustrates how you can use the activity in the classroom setting. The OMPK program is centered on the belief that learning should be child driven and, for this reason, gives you flexibility by offering choices for learning modalities and contexts for learning (large group, small group, outside, meals and snacks, transitions, work time). Because the needs and interests of individual children and the classroom itself are constantly changing, and children may be at different developmental levels, each Daily Practice includes multiple options to allow you to choose the practice variation that works best in the moment.

The primary learning modalities within the OMPK program include the following:

- play-based and experiential activities
- music and songs
- puppets and role-play
- visual aids and physical aids or supports
- classroom books and stories

The Four Daily Practice Groups

It can feel overwhelming to try and learn about all ten Daily Practices at once, especially since there are multiple options for most of the practices! For this reason, the practices are divided into four groups, each containing similar and related practices. You can think of these as "food groups" for the mind and body; a balance of practices from each of the groups can offer a comprehensive mindfulness-based social-emotional learning "diet." The ten Daily Practices are divided into the following groups:

Daily Practices 1 and 2: Practices for building focus, attention, and classroom presence

Daily Practices 3 and 4: Practices for developing awareness and self-management

Daily Practices 5 and 6: Practices for teaching and supporting emotional awareness, emotion regulation, and prosocial behaviors

Daily Practices 7–10: Practices for growing a peaceful and connected classroom environment

We will cover the instructions for each practice group in separate chapters, beginning with Daily Practices 1 and 2 (chapter 7) and progressing on to Daily Practices 3 and 4 (chapter 8), Daily Practices 5 and 6 (chapter 9), and Daily Practices 7–10 (chapter 10). This will allow you to reflect on the practices in one group before moving on to the next. It will also help you to reference each practice group more easily as you begin to integrate the practices into your classroom. Following the practice instructions for each group, we will cover helpful hints for how to implement them into your daily schedule, routine, and classroom habits and use them as the need arises.

Organization of Instructions

For each of the ten OMPK Daily Practices, you will find separate instructions for each practice option. Within each Daily Practice, practice options are ordered to follow a general growth trajectory that accounts for both chronological and developmental age as well as development of learning readiness, social-emotional skills, and ability. In many of the practice groups, the options progress from less challenging to more challenging. However, this order is only a suggested guide for implementation, as children do not necessarily follow the same developmental sequence for all social-emotional learning domains. Given that you, as the teacher, are the expert in terms of the social, developmental, and academic needs of the children in your classroom, you have the freedom to choose specific options each day. In addition, while instructions are provided to guide you through how to teach and implement each practice, you may feel comfortable modifying them somewhat to meet specific needs and strengths as you become more familiar with the practices themselves.

The Daily Practice descriptions include the following components:

Title. This section includes the name of the Daily Practice.

Description. Each practice or practice option description provides information on *why* the practice is included; *when and where* the activity can be used with existing lesson plans and rhythm-of-life learning; *how* to set up, teach, and lead the practice in the classroom; what materials are needed, and the social-emotional competencies the practice helps develop. The sections include:

- **Why:** A brief narrative explanation of activity purpose and application. It is important to explain the purpose of the activity to children before having them engage in the practice, and share with them the skills or benefits they will gain from the practice. This can serve to increase their understanding and motivation to engage in the practice.

- **When and where:** Lists an example or examples of the context (e.g., large group, 1:1 following child meltdown), developmental need or readiness (e.g., when children are feeling fidgety, when children have mastered a simpler version of the practice), and/or related motivational factors (e.g., when children want to sing a song) in which the activity may be beneficial.

- **How:** Lists the steps for facilitating the practice activity and supporting a child or children to engage in the activity. *Remember that these instructions are a guide and that you can modify the language as needed to meet the needs of your students.*

- **Materials:** Lists the suggested supplies and materials needed for each activity.

- **Social-Emotional Competence:** Lists the social-emotional skills that make up the five areas of social-emotional learning.

Bonus Boxes: In addition to the above sections, many of the Daily Practice options have accompanying boxes describing additional opportunities for that practice that also help you to see how the practices can be used in context, with actual examples from real classroom situations:

- **Opportunity for Growth and Engagement.** Young children are learning how to manage themselves, get along with others, listen to others, and follow directions. This can result in problems or difficult situations, and we view these as *opportunities to grow.* Each Opportunity for Growth and Engagement section includes examples of common classroom situations and challenges.

- **Natural Learning Opportunity.** These sections link the difficult situation or challenge directly to a specific skill that you can address and teach using the Daily Practice.

- **Practice Modification.** These sections describe how to modify a Daily Practice to create a learning opportunity and teach a new lesson through play and engagement that is directed at the specific challenge.

- **Academic and Developmental Skills.** These sections list the specific skills that can be strengthened during the challenging situation and resulting learning opportunity.

This consistent format for the Daily Practice instructions will help you to learn and implement these practices more efficiently. Let's get started.

CHAPTER 7

Daily Practices 1 and 2
Building Focus, Attention, and Classroom Presence

The first group of the Daily Practices includes Practice 1: Meditation, and Practice 2: Are You Present for Me? These two practices are at the foundation of the entire OMPK program in that they help children to build fundamental skills of attention and focus. Not only do these practices work to build attention and presence for taking in new information and for learning, but they are critical for engagement, self-management, and social connection. To be present for others, whether to receive instruction, to work and play collaboratively, to engage in conversation, or to ask for and receive assistance, we must be able to focus long enough to take in and process important and meaningful stimuli and information. Joan Halifax (2008) wrote about a sign in her meditation center that says, "Show Up." Showing up is the first basic step to being more mindful, and these first two practices were designed to build young children's capacity for showing up for you and for each other. And while these are the first practices we are covering, and a great place to start, it is important to note that these particular practices may take the longest to develop and require the most practice.

Daily Practice 1: Meditation

The meditation, or concentration, practices serve as the core of the OMPK program. You can view these options as modifications of the OpenMind REMIND practices for teachers that have been adapted especially for preschool learners. There are two types of meditation: (A) sitting meditation and focus, and (B) walking meditation and guided movement.

Part A: Sitting Meditation and Focus

This meditation is known as a *samatha* meditation, which involves focus and concentration on one thing. Often in meditation, this one thing is the breath. Initially, most young children (and most people in general new to meditation!) have difficulty focusing on their breath alone, so the meditation practice options enable you to meet the child at their level and progress from there. These practices are adaptations of the Peaceful (blue) REMIND practices. Most of the practice options use a meditation bell or chime to stop and start the practice. The type of bell pictured in option 1 below is called a Tibetan singing bowl; it has a long sustaining ring that has a pleasant sound.

Practice options 1 to 7 use developmentally appropriate activities to practice single-pointed focus (focus on one thing) related to the breath with sensory prompts, movement, and pretend play. They are listed in order of difficulty and developmental level, and build up to traditional sitting focus on the breath (option 8). You have the option of choosing the activity that best suits the children in your class at any given time to meet them where they are in terms of readiness, ability, and environmental context. Using the easier practice options can help children to build up their capacity for sitting meditation. However, even after children have shown competency with option 8, you may want to use other practice options based on children's interests and needs. In other words, even if children have shown competency with a less challenging practice, you can always go back to these practices if the situation calls for it, or if the children request it. Activity descriptions include pictures so that children can also choose meditation practices from a picture board (see appendix B at http://www.newharbinger.com/49258).

Option 1: Attention to the Sound of the Bell

Why: This practice option provides a way for young children and children new to meditation to have the experience of single-pointed focus. The activity involves focusing and listening to the starting and stopping of a ringing bell. It is also a way to help children understand the concept of "attention."

When and where: Large group, small group, outside; when children have not had experience with meditation and/or have difficulty with focusing and paying attention for more than a few seconds.

How:

1. Demonstrate the sound of the bell and how it starts ringing and then fades to silence.

2. Talk about the concepts of focus and attention: when we keep noticing the sound of the bell, we are focusing on it; we are giving it our attention. The activity of listening to the sound of the bell will put these concepts into context.

3. Ask children to focus and keep their attention on the sound of the bell by listening, and to put a hand up when the sound starts, and then lower the hand when the bell is quiet or stops making a sound. Ring the bell and model this practice.

4. Repeat step 3 based on children's interest, and increase the number of repetitions as attention skills increase.

5. *Variations:* Ask children to raise their hand when the bell starts and put their finger on their nose when the bell stops. For added difficulty, ask children to wait when the bell rings, and then to raise their hand or put their finger on their nose when the bell *stops* ringing.

Materials: Bell

Social-Emotional Competence: Listening, awareness, following directions, focus, concentration, inhibitory control

Option 2: Breathing with a Visual Prompt (Hoberman Sphere)

Why: This practice option uses a novel and visually interesting dynamic object (i.e., Hoberman sphere, or breathing ball) to capture children's attention for a guided breathing meditation. It helps children to build focus on another object and person and control their body and breathing. (If you do not have a Hoberman sphere, you can substitute a slinky or any other object that expands and contracts.)

When and where: Large group, small group, outside; when children have not had experience with meditation and/or have difficulty with focusing, paying attention, controlling their bodies, and following directions but enjoy watching new and interesting objects.

How:

1. Demonstrate how the "breathing ball" (i.e., Hoberman sphere) opens and closes.

2. Explain that the breathing ball is going to show children how and when to breathe. When the ball opens, children breathe in and their bellies get big. When the ball becomes small and closes, children breathe out and their bellies get small.

3. Repeat this based on children's interest, and increase the number of repetitions as their attention skills increase.

4. Variations:
   - In large or small groups, you can pass the ball around and have each child take a turn leading the breathing with the breathing ball, or you can select a child (who is putting forth effort) to lead.
   - If you do not have any equipment, you can use your body as a visual. Start by squatting down and contracting into a ball. Then stand up, open your arms, form a large circle above your head, and inhale; exhale as you contract back down. If children need an opportunity for movement, they can follow you and try to match their movements and inhalations and exhalations to yours.

Materials: Hoberman sphere (i.e., breathing ball) or other object that expands and contracts, such as a slinky

Social-Emotional Competence: Listening, awareness, following directions, focus, concentration, inhibitory control

Opportunity for Growth and Engagement: Moving or breathing too fast during meditation, decreased control or grading of movements (i.e., using an inappropriate degree of force for the practice)

During listening time or meditation time, many children have difficulty sitting still, following the teacher's directions, and breathing at the same time that the ball opens and closes. They often breathe too quickly and move their arms around instead of keeping them still. They do not seem to understand the reason or purpose for the practice.

Natural Learning Opportunity: Support children to experience the practice of controlling their breath and timing and to have a movement experience that helps them to better understand how to follow someone else's lead.

Practice Modification: Meditation (Breathing with a Visual Prompt)

Slinky or Snake Breathing

Explain to children that breathing along with the breathing ball can be tricky because we may want to go at our own speed and may have a hard time following the breathing ball by watching it only. The purpose of the breathing ball is to help us grow our skills for slowing down and following directions, and not to quickly get finished with doing all of the breaths. The cool thing about the breathing ball is that the whole class can breathe together at the same time and take giant classroom breaths together! Even though there are not enough breathing balls for everyone to have one, we can all have a cool object that does the same thing as the breathing ball! In this practice, all children receive an object, such as a small slinky or a paper accordion snake, to open and close like a breathing ball. The child uses the object to move and breathe in time with the adult to have a physical and visual experience of when to inhale and exhale. For additional fun and pretend play, the child can breathe in and then breathe out while making a snake sound, "sssssssssss." To help children increase control of their hands, tell them that they have to hold the "snakes" very gently so that the snakes don't get hurt. Supporting the children to make a paper accordion snake offers additional opportunities for engagement in art, creativity, focus, sequencing, and fine motor opportunities for learning.

Academic and Developmental Skills: Fine motor control, bilateral coordination, cutting, folding, gluing, creative expression

Option 3: Lotus Breathing

Why: This practice option uses a dynamic visual (i.e., the child's hand) to support guided focus on the breath. In this exercise, the child's hand acts much like the Hoberman sphere in that it opens and closes—so it is an ideal practice when an object like a slinky or Hoberman sphere isn't available. The lotus breathing practice uses a simple hand movement to serve as a physical and visual cue for attention to the breath. The hand movement is child directed and not dependent on the teacher for prompting, though it can also be done in time with the movements of a teacher or peer.

When and where: Large group, small group, outside; when children may be ready to transition to self-directed guided breathing but continue to need visual and movement supports.

How:

1. Demonstrate how to breathe like a lotus flower by holding your hand palm up with fingertips together and inhaling as your fingers open to make the lotus "bloom," and then exhaling while closing your fingers back up.

2. Repeat as needed based on children's interest and activity level, and then instruct the children to sit and breathe with their hand in a "lotus flower" to reinforce the lesson on breathing. Use the bell to start and stop.

3. Grade the practice as children become more skilled at focusing on "lotus breathing." For example, start with 5 breaths and progress to 10, 15, 20, or use an amount of time such as 30 seconds, 1 minute, 2 minutes.

Materials: Bell (optional)

Social-Emotional Competence: Listening, awareness, following directions, focus, concentration, inhibitory control

Option 4: Breathing with a Visual Prompt: Rainbow Breathing

Why: This practice option uses a visually interesting dynamic object (e.g., rainbow picture, rainbow-colored beads, rainbow-colored glitter bottle) and consistent sequence to capture children's attention to a guided breathing meditation. It helps children to follow a sequence (rainbow color order) for tracking their breathing and to also learn positive character traits associated with each color.

When and where: Large group, small group, outside; when children have not had experience with meditation and/or have difficulty with focusing, paying attention, controlling their bodies, and following directions but enjoy watching and engaging with colorful and interesting objects.

How:

1. Review the rainbow color order (red, orange, yellow, green, blue, indigo, violet).

2. Explain that children will take a breath for each color, and then introduce a visual (e.g., rainbow picture, rainbow-colored beads, rainbow-colored glitter bottle) as needed and/or pair the breath with an object such as the breathing ball or the child's hand (lotus breathing), as in options 2 and 3.

3. Repeat this based on children's interest, and increase the number of repetitions as their attention skills increase.

4. As children show signs of readiness, introduce the associated character traits for each rainbow color (red = loving, orange = open, yellow = joyful, green = grounded, blue = calm, indigo = compassionate, and violet = grateful).

5. Variation: in large or small groups, pass the interactive rainbow visual around and have each child take a turn saying the color and character trait and leading a focused breath.

Materials: Rainbow visuals (e.g., picture, beads, glitter bottle); Hoberman breathing ball or slinky

Social-Emotional Competence: Listening, awareness, following directions, focus, concentration, inhibitory control

Option 5: Breathing with a Bell Prompt

Why: This practice option serves as a guided meditation on the breath using an auditory signal (the sound of the bell) to prompt inhalation and exhalation. It is a way to develop focused listening skills without visual distractions.

When and where: Large group, small group, outside; when children may be ready to listen to a sound prompt and try breathing with their eyes closed, or when children get very distracted by visual objects or movements around them.

How:

1. Explain that the "breathing bell" is going to let children know how and when to breathe. When the bell rings once, the children breathe in, and their bellies get big. When the bell rings again, the children breathe out, and their bellies get small.

2. Demonstrate the breathing bell, putting your hand on your belly and having the children do the same to feel the inhalation and exhalation. It may be easier for children to start with their eyes open and then progress to having their eyes closed if they feel comfortable.

3. Repeat this based on children's interest, and increase the number of repetitions as their attention skills increase.

4. Variation: in large or small groups, you can pass the bell around and have each child take a turn leading the breathing with the breathing bell.

Materials: Bell

Social-Emotional Competence: Listening, awareness, following directions, focus, concentration, inhibitory control

Opportunity for Growth and Engagement: Aggressive play and seeking social interaction and attention from others

During large group, one older child is pushing others, taking toys away from other children, and attempting to distract the group. Children are becoming upset and the teacher is feeling overwhelmed.

Natural Learning Opportunity: Support the child to develop a sense of agency and receive positive social attention and praise by teaching peers, cooperating with the teacher, and having a leadership role.

Practice Modification: Meditation Teacher with Breathing Bell

Ask the child who is acting disruptive if they may help to lead the class in the meditation. They may sit at the front with the teacher and show the children how to breathe in and make their bellies big using the breathing ball. Then, give the child the bell while you take the breathing ball. Use the breathing ball to cue the child when to ring the bell for the inhale and exhale. This allows the child an opportunity to gain the attention that they are seeking, while also contributing to the class and cooperating with the teacher as a coleader. Once the child feels comfortable with leading the practice, they can also do this with an individual child or small groups as needed in the rhythm of life.

Academic and Developmental Skills: Expressive language, cooperative learning, following directions, leadership skills

Option 6: Birdie Breathing

Why: The "Birdie Breathing Song" serves as a story to describe a nature-based depiction of posture (like a tree) and give a concrete instruction for maintaining focused attention to the breath. Using a "shhh" at exhalation provides extra sensory input for children who may have difficulty with focusing on breath alone. This also helps to put focus on the exhalation, which tends to have a calming function. *Finally, the practice teaches children that practicing breathing can be a way to help others by being more calm and present.*

When and where: In large or small groups, when children may be interested in singing and story time and have been able to engage in some of the other practice options.

How:

1. *First time:* Tell a story about birdies flying around and how they can get tired and need to rest. The "Birdie Breathing Song" is how we help them to calm down and rest.

2. Make a "birdie" with your hands by linking your thumbs together to serve as the body of the bird and moving your other fingers to act as the wings of the bird.

3. Ask children to sit and help to sing the "Birdie Breathing Song."

4. Model the correct meditation posture to "sit or stand up tall like a tree" and give prompts and praise to children on their posture as needed.

5. Demonstrate the hand movements as you move through the song and ask the children to do this with you. You can download and play the audio track for the "Birdie Breathing Song" at http://www.newharbinger.com/49258, where you'll also find the song lyrics in appendix C.

6. Ring the bell after singing. Tell the children that at the sound of the bell, they will breathe with a quiet "shhhh" on the exhale. (As children improve, help shift the focus from the "shhh" to the breath.)

7. Breathing can be done in increments of 30 seconds, 1, 2, or 5 minutes, and there are versions for different breathing increments; select the song version based on the children's readiness and needs.

8. After the song, discuss how sitting and breathing helps us to calm down.

Materials: Meditation bell, "Birdie Breathing Song" audio download, OMPK Song Lyrics (appendix C)

Social-Emotional Competence: Listening, awareness, following directions, focus, concentration, control, compassion

Option 7: Birdie Breathing with an Object

Why: This practice serves as a transition from the "Birdie Breathing Song" to traditional sitting meditation on the breath by using an object (e.g., small fluffy ball) to represent the bird used in the song. The focus is on using the breath and movement of the belly to put the bird to sleep. It can also serve as a practice exercise for keeping the hands still for children who pull or crush objects or put them in their mouth.

When and where: At the beginning of the day, outside, in small groups, prior to work time; when children fidget and have difficulty keeping their hands still during sitting breathing practice.

How:

1. *First time:* Tell a story about birdies flying around and how they can get tired and need to rest.

2. Model the correct meditation posture to "sit or stand up tall like a tree" and give prompts and praise to children on their posture as needed.

3. Pass around small objects such as puff balls, paper balls, or rocks, and allow each child to take one. This object will be the "birdie" and will sit in the child's hands ("nest"), which will rest on the belly.

4. Tell the children that when you ring the bell, they will focus on breathing, and that the movements of the belly breathing will rock the birdie to sleep. Emphasize that children should keep focusing on the breath so that the birdie doesn't wake up.

5. Use the bell to stop and start meditation. Breathing can be done in increments of 30 seconds, 1, 2, or 5 minutes. The "Birdie Breathing Song" is optional.

Materials: Meditation bell; small puff balls, rocks, paper balls, or other small objects; "Birdie Breathing Song" audio download, OMPK Song Lyrics (appendix C; optional)

Social-Emotional Competence: Listening, awareness, following directions, focus, concentration, control, compassion

Option 8: Sitting Meditation

Why: In this practice, children are engaged in sitting meditation on breath, much like the Peaceful (blue) REMIND practice. This practice helps children build the ability to focus, concentrate, wait, and inhibit behavioral impulses and reactions to distracting stimuli.

When and where: At the beginning of the day, in small groups, prior to work time; when children are ready to sit calmly and breatho without the need for visual, sound, or movement prompts or supports.

How:

1. Model the correct meditation posture to "sit or stand up tall like a tree" and give prompts and praise to children on posture as needed.

2. Explain that when you ring the bell, children will focus on breathing in and out. They can count breaths if they are able to count.

3. Tell the children that when the bell sounds, they should close their eyes and focus on breathing. When the bell sounds again, children will open their eyes.

4. Use the bell to stop and start meditation. Breathing can be done in increments of 30 seconds, 1, 2, or 5 minutes, or more.

Materials: Bell

Social-Emotional Competence: Listening, awareness, following directions, focus, concentration, waiting, inhibitory control, compassion

Part B: Walking Meditation (Kinhin) and Guided Movement

Why: This practice involves focusing on walking and movement as the object of meditation. This can help children develop precision and control of their body movements and the ability to be aware of themselves in relation to their physical and social environment.

When and where: At the beginning of the day, in large group, during transitions, outside time; when children may have a need to stand up and move rather than sit in meditation; when children are having difficulty controlling and being aware of their movements and bodies, which may result in an unsafe classroom environment.

How:

1. Explain to children the importance of focusing carefully on walking and moving, and give examples of why it is important to pay attention to their bodies and environment while walking (e.g., so they don't step on toys or bump into others).

2. *Walking meditation:* Tell children that when the bell sounds, they will take a small step forward and then stop until the bell rings again. With each step forward, they will also take a breath. Ask the children to line up in single file (straight or circular) with about an arm's length between them. Use the bell to prompt the children to take a step. Vary the spaces between the rings to ensure that they maintain attention. As the children build skills at walking meditation, you can vary the practice, for example, asking the children to take a step when the bell stops ringing.

3. *Guided movement:* Use a visual or physical prompt to help children time and control their movements. For example, have children do squat down and stretch up movements in time to the Hoberman sphere.

Materials: Bell

Social-Emotional Competence: Listening, body awareness, following directions, focus, concentration, waiting, inhibitory control, social awareness

Opportunity for Growth and Engagement: Dangerous play and unsafe use of materials

During work time, three children are playing in the block area. They become very excited and begin to throw blocks, slam blocks into the furniture, and run around and crash into blocks to make the blocks fall down. They are having fun, but they are making the area dangerous for other children by blocking the walkways and throwing blocks into other work and play areas. They do not seem to be aware of their bodies or to notice the effects of their actions on their friends, teachers, or environment.

Natural Learning Opportunity: Support children to be more aware of their movements, to grade and control their movements, and to understand the impact of their movement and actions on others.

Practice Modification: Walking Meditation and Guided Movement—Ninja Tower

Explain to the children that even though being silly, moving fast, and playing rough can be fun and helps our bodies get strong, we need to be careful how we play when others are around. Tell children that they are going to play a game called Ninja Blocks to practice a new way to build tall towers with friends. Ninjas move carefully and notice everything that is happening to do really cool things. Have children (in a pair, small group, or large group) get into a circle and put blocks in the middle. Explain that when you ring the bell, everyone will breathe in together, and you will point to someone who is standing quietly like a ninja to have a turn to build a special ninja tower. It may be helpful to demonstrate this first. Ring the bell and point to the first child standing quiet and still; the child will step forward and pick up a block from the middle while everyone breathes in. When the bell rings again, everyone breathes out and the child places the block down to build a tower, and then steps back into the circle. This continues until everyone has a chance to place a block on the tower (if you do this with a pair of children, or in a small group, it may be easier to have children take turns). After everyone has had a turn, you can reverse the activity as follows: on the inhale ring, have a child pick up a block from the tower, and then, on the exhale ring, have them place it in a bin or shelf.

Academic and Developmental Skills: Problem solving, turn taking, cooperative learning, visual spatial skills, fine motor skills, following directions, management and cleanup of materials

Daily Practice 2: Are You Present for Me?

Why: Daily Practice 2 involves teaching children what it means to be present for others. It helps children learn to request another person's attention by asking if the other person can be present. It also teaches the child to be able to wait for the other person to be present if that person is engaged in another activity or is with another person. Finally, given that young children frequently have a difficult time staying present, adults often given reminders for them to look, listen, and stop moving. Typically, as adults, we use multiple words for this, like "eyes on me, quiet voices, listening ears, and still body." But when we are too wordy, kids can miss the whole message. When we teach children that to "be present" means to listen to others with our whole self—we look toward the person (some children may feel discomfort or be too distracted by direct eye contact), listen, face the person with our bodies, and stop doing other things so that they feel respected and so that our hearts and minds are open—they begin to understand the qualitative aspects of what it means to "be present." In this way, when we do prompt them, we can communicate a whole message with just a few simple words. They also begin to realize that being present is a gift that we give to others.

When and where: As needed in the rhythm of life when the opportunity arises, when a child or teacher would like to request present-moment attention from another person or persons.

How:

- *When first introducing the practice:*

   a. Explain to the children what being present means by first doing a demonstration. When I introduce this practice, I use my smartphone for the example, as this is what so many people are present for these days! I pretend to be looking at a phone screen and ask a child to ask me a question while I act very distracted; I may ignore the question and say, "What?!" or answer the question in a silly way—if they ask me what my favorite color is, I may say, "an elephant or puppy." Then I ask children if they think I was being present for them. It is amazing how often they get the idea even when they haven't heard the word "present" in this way before.

   b. Next, discuss what being present means (i.e., looking, listening, paying attention, and not doing something else). Often children will say a present is a gift that they open, which introduces the opportunity to share how when we are present for someone, it is like we are giving them a gift of our attention.

   c. Repeat the initial demonstration (in my case, I repeat the exercise where I am looking at my phone and ask a child to ask me a question), but this time, demonstrate being present (e.g., I put down my phone, turn toward the child, and answer the question). Ask the children if you were present that time.

d. Talk about how it feels when people are present for us, and when they are not present for us.

- Explain that people can't always be present for everyone, all of the time, but that there is a way to ask if someone can be present by saying, "Are you present for me?" Next, tell the children that if the teacher or peer they are asking says yes, they can ask for help or assistance or start talking. If the other person says no, they will tell the child when they *can* be present (e.g., "I can be present right after I finish cleaning up this spilled water). You can also discuss signs and signals of whether someone is present for you; for example, if the other person is talking to someone else, they may not be present in that moment.

- Support children to ask, "Are you present for me?" as the opportunity arises, and answer appropriately. If a child asks another child, "Are you present for me?" support the other child to respond appropriately as needed.

- Variation: Do a "present check" before large-group instruction (e.g., "If you are present for me, touch your ears," "If you are present for me, wiggle your fingers").

- Praise and give reinforcement when children are being present for you, such as, "Wow, thank you for being present, group number 2!"

Materials: None

Social-Emotional Competence: Self-awareness, social awareness, inhibitory control, waiting, respect for others, empathy, perspective taking, shifting attention

Opportunity for Growth and Engagement: Being inflexible and unable to shift attention from a preferred or desired activity

Several children are focused on engaging in a preferred or desired activity (e.g., playing with cars, being silly) and are not able to be present for the teacher to explain the small-group art activity.

Natural Learning Opportunity: Support the children to recognize their desire to engage in the preferred activity and how important it is to them. Help the children to understand that sometimes we must wait to do something we really want to do, and everyone has different things they may want to be present for, but we must work together to be present for each other to make sure everyone gets a chance.

Practice Modification: Are You Present for Me? Shifting and Waiting

In a large group, review the practice of being present. Explain that sometimes our brains or hearts may want to be present for something (e.g., a child wants to go outside), but we might have to be present for something else because it is important to another person (e.g., the teacher wants children to eat lunch first so that they have enough energy to play outside). Have the children take turns identifying something that they want to be present for in that moment. Then explain how we can notice what we want to do, and then decide to wait and be present for something that may be more important to someone else first. When this happens, the child can express the desire and then shift to being present (e.g., *I want to go outside but I can wait and first be present for lunch time*). Explain to children that being able to wait to do something we really want to do until others are ready is making a kind and helpful choice, and that it feels good to be present for others.

Academic and Developmental Skills: Expressive and receptive language, cause and effect, problem solving

Helpful Hints for Implementing Daily Practices 1 and 2

It is important to remember that these first two practices are designed to be used not with the goal of adding on one more thing to check off your seemingly never-ending to-do list, but as tools to help build children's capacity for attention, focus, and presence. Here are some suggestions and reminders for adding Daily Practices 1 and 2 into the rhythm of the day:

1. Start slow and introduce one meditation practice at a time, beginning with the suggested sequence of options. You may want to do one practice for a week or more until you see signs that children are ready for a new or more challenging practice.

2. If most of the class is ready for a more challenging meditation practice, you can always start with an easier one, like listening to the sound of the bell, so that the children who may not be quite ready can stay engaged, and then follow it with the next practice for the rest of the class.

3. At first you may notice that it is easier to plan the meditation practices in advance, but with experience you will learn to use the practices in the rhythm of life as opportunities for learning arise. For example, you may initially use the meditation practice during the morning meeting to start the day with focus and calm. However, if you notice that after recess, the class seems antsy and is having trouble being present for instruction, you can add the meditation practice to help them to calm themselves and focus; this may be the time for walking meditation or one of the meditation practice variations that use movement.

4. Before starting the meditation practice, remind children the reason and purpose of the practice, even if it is a brief and simple explanation (e.g., "We are going to do Birdie Breathing to help us get better at waiting and being calm"). When children know the reason for a practice, they may be more motivated to engage in it.

5. Remember that some children may not be able to sit "still"; in this case, provide postural assistance as needed (e.g., cushions or wall support for the child to lean against), and support children to use self-regulating movement (e.g., ricking, flapping) as needed during meditation practices.

6. While the instructions for Daily Practice 2, "Are You Present for Me?" may seem lengthy, remember that once children know what it means to be present, all you need to do is use the phrase in context. You can ask the child if they are present, support the child to ask others if they are present, and reinforce children who are present by thanking them. You can use the Super Me practices in chapter 9 to provide specific reinforcement for being present.

7. These meditation activities and exercises are called "practices" for a reason! The first time you try them, they could look like a disaster! This is completely normal, and every "disaster" provides an opportunity for learning, teaching, and growth.

8. As children learn these practices, be sure to praise effort and engagement over performance.

CHAPTER 8

Daily Practices 3 and 4
Developing Awareness and Self-Management

Daily Practice 3, Bell Practices, and Daily Practice 4, Yoga and Body Awareness, teach children to be aware of what their bodies and minds are doing by using multisensory and movement activities. These practices offer a way to further put Daily Practice 2, Are You Present for Me? into the context of daily life. Daily Practices 3 and 4 both incorporate attention and awareness and are designed to be simple, quick ways for children to practice shifting into a mode of being present. In addition to helping children build skills, these practices can also aid in transitions and serve as classroom-management strategies.

Daily Practice 3: Bell Exercises

Bell exercises have numerous applications. In this section, I'll provide general instructions for Daily Practice 3, including examples of specific prompts. Following these general instructions, you will find more detailed instructions for specific bell exercises that can target inhibitory control skills, such as waiting, stop and go, slow movements, focused attention in context, and voice volume.

General Instructions

Why: The bell is like a signal to be present, and you can use this tool to help children practice intentionally being present multiple times throughout the day. Bell exercises involve a daily instruction for external awareness, movement, or social connection that will happen when the bell rings throughout the day. The instruction for what happens when the bell rings should change daily, or weekly, but the practice of listening to the bell, remembering what to do, and responding will be the same. This enables the children to develop mindful awareness of what is happening in their bodies and environment in the present moment and to practice stopping, shifting, and being present throughout the day. You can also use this opportunity to have children practice a discrete skill throughout the day, such as air writing the letters of their name. The bell is an excellent way for helping a noisy classroom shift into a mode of being present, without having to use words and language or raise your voice. In OMPK training, we jokingly say, "Instead of a yell, use the bell!" Finally, certain types of bell exercises, presented in the next section, can help children practice building self-control.

When and where: At the start of the day; as a transition activity; outside; when the need for awareness, movement, or social connection arises; as a tool for classroom management and bringing children back to the present moment.

How:

1. Give a reminder that the purpose of the bell is to practice being present and to grow our brains for controlling our bodies, voices, and attention. At the beginning of the day, tell the children what the bell exercise is for that day, which might incorporate movement (e.g., jump up high, spin around three times, and squat down); awareness (e.g., name three things you hear); social connection (e.g., high five a friend, give a friend a compliment); or academics (e.g., point to something that is green, or something that starts with the letter of the day). Then demonstrate the bell exercise and remind them of the rules for bell instruction.

2. Throughout the day, ring the bell and either support the class to recall and respond to the daily prompt as a group (e.g., "Put your hands on your shoulders and march in place while counting to 10") or support individual children, as appropriate, with random requests (e.g., "Malcolm, can you tell me three things you can hear?"; "Rachelle, can you say something

kind to a friend?"). After they do the exercise, thank the children for being present and remind them what they should do next (e.g., "Thank you for being present! Now let's go back to our centers").

3. As children become more familiar with the bell exercises, support them to engage in selecting the daily bell responses. In my experience, children love selecting the bell exercise of the day, and you can help by giving them a list to choose from.

Materials: Bell, Inhibitory Control Bell Exercise Reference Cards (see online appendix D at http://www.newharbinger.com/49258)

Social-Emotional Competence: Listening, awareness, following directions, being present, working memory, shifting attention

Opportunity for Growth and Engagement: Chaotic loud classroom environment and difficulty gaining attention of the class

During small-group time, the class is somewhat chaotic, and children are running around, screaming, climbing, and engaging in activities that are not considered safe. The class comprises mostly three- and four-year-old children who have difficulty being present when the teacher speaks. The teacher speaks loudly to attempt to gain attention, yelling in order to be heard over the children. The children still do not respond when the teacher requests that they all come to the large carpet for large group (story time).

Natural Learning Opportunity: Use the bell as a way to gain attention before transitioning to another activity, to a quiet voice level, and to practice being present.

Practice Modification: Bell Exercise—The Quiet Bell

If the environment is loud, ring the bell and have the children do the daily bell exercise (e.g., give themselves a big hug). Once the children are present, tell them that they are going to practice walking to the carpet with the quiet bell. The practice is to take a "tiptoe" step toward the large group carpet each time the bell rings softly. Explain that they must be very quiet to be able to hear the bell, since it will be so soft. Give specific praise to children who are moving quietly (e.g., "Kalani, thank you for keeping your mouth quiet and hands still while you tiptoe; you can really hear the quiet bell!"). This practice combines walking meditation with a bell exercise.

Academic and Developmental Skills: Transitions, listening, following directions, grading of gross motor body movement, balance

Bell Exercises to Build Inhibitory Control and Improve Classroom Management

The following are specific bell exercises that can be used to help children build inhibitory control, better known as self-control. Inhibitory control has been described in the literature as having five general subskills: waiting, making slow movements, stopping and going when prompted, maintaining focused attention, and controlling voice volume (see chapter 11 for references to supporting research). Inhibitory control largely underlies the ability to be present for others and for academic and social learning and to follow classroom behavioral expectations. Like with any other developmental skill, children make the most gains in inhibitory control when they have repeated practice throughout the day, and often children with the biggest deficits make the greatest gains with practice. As with bell exercises in general, these tend to work best when you explain and review how to do them at the beginning of the day, and then practice them a few to several times throughout the day. For each exercise, after the last ring of the bell (give a verbal prompt that it is the last ring before ringing), have the children go back to their previous activity and working position (e.g., at the table, in centers).

In addition to the instructions for the exercises below, you can find printable Inhibitory Control Bell Exercise Reference Cards in online appendix D, at http://www .newharbinger.com/49258.

Bell Exercises for Building the Skill of Waiting

Waiting is a very tough skill—not only for young children but also for adults! With technology, there is so much instant gratification that some children do not get a lot of opportunity to practice this important skill. These exercises target the skill of waiting for a prompt, which is the bell or a verbal prompt. You can vary the amount of time that you have children wait for the prompt, but typically it is good to start with a few seconds and progress from there.

Option 1. Raise Hand Your When the Bell Stops. When the bell rings, children stop, freeze, listen, and wait; when the bell stops, they raise a hand. Repeat as needed.

Option 2. Waiting Hands. When the bell rings, children freeze and put their hands in a designated position (e.g., on their hips, on their head). When you say, "Move," they tap, clap, or move their hands back and forth fast until you say, "Wait." Repeat as needed. (A variation of this is Waiting Feet. The exercise is the same, but instead of moving their hands, children run in place when you say, "Move.")

Option 3. Waiting Frogs. When the bell rings one time, the children squat down. When the bell rings two times, they jump up. Repeat as needed.

Option 4. Freeze-Unfreeze. When the bell rings, children freeze (they can hold the position they are in or hold a designated yoga posture). When the bell rings again, they unfreeze. Repeat as needed.

Option 5. Head, Shoulders, Knees, Toes. When the bell rings, children put their hands on their heads. Then, they must wait for the bell to ring again to move their hands to their shoulders, then their knees, toes, eyes, ears, mouth, nose. Repeat as needed.

Bell Exercises for Practicing Slow Movements

So often, young children move quickly! They may rush through an exercise or activity to get it done fast. The pace of our culture moves pretty rapidly as well. These exercises help children become more comfortable with controlling and grading their movements by going slowly.

Option 1. Slowga. When the bell rings, children move into a yoga posture (e.g., tree) and then watch for you to model the slow transition into a second posture (e.g., child's pose). You can choose the two postures and tell them ahead of time. For ideas, refer to the OMPK Yoga Posture Cards in online appendix E (http://www.newharbinger.com/49258).

Option 2. Slow Arm Movements. When the bell rings, children put their arms down by their sides and look toward you. Then they follow as you move your arms up slowly and then clap overhead, and they clap when you clap. Next, the process reverses, and they follow as you move your arms slowly back down to clap again. Repeat as needed.

Option 3. Slow Mirror Movements. When the bell rings, children put their arms down by their sides and look toward you. Then they follow your slow movements (you can move your arms, legs, body, or face; the idea is that you are moving slowly and they are copying you).

Option 4. Slow Deep Breaths to Hoberman Sphere or Slinky. When the bell rings, children look toward you and sit up tall like a tree in their chairs or on the floor. When you open the Hoberman sphere or slinky, children breathe in. When you close it, children breathe out. Repeat as needed.

Bell Exercises for Stop and Go

The exercises below involve alternating between initiating and stopping a task in response to cues. This can help children to practice listening for and following an instruction and intentionally controlling their impulses to stop or start. These practices link closely with waiting, and they incorporate waiting for cues to stop and start.

Option 1. Walking Meditation. The first time you ring the bell, the children stand up, put their arms down by their sides, and look toward you. Then, each time you ring the bell (or each time the bell stops ringing), they will take one step and stop. Repeat as needed.

Option 2. Red Light, Yellow Light, Green Light with Walking Feet. When the bell rings, children put their arms down by their sides and look toward you. Then give a verbal or visual instruction. If you say, "Green light" or hold up a green sign, children take three regular steps; if you say, "Yellow light" or hold up a yellow sign, children take three slow steps; if you say, "Red light" or hold up a red sign, children freeze. Repeat as needed.

Option 3. Red light, Yellow Light, Green Light with Walking Fingers. When the bell rings, children put two fingers in the air and look toward you. You then lead the exercise for Red light, Yellow Light, Green Light, but instead of taking steps with their feet, children take steps with their index and middle fingers on the floor or on the forearm of their opposite arm.

Option 4. Moving Up and Down to Slinky or Hoberman Sphere. When the bell rings, children squat down on the floor and look toward you. When you expand the slinky or Hoberman sphere, children slowly rise to standing; when the ball or slinky contracts, children follow the pace of the object to squat back down. Repeat as needed.

Bell Exercises for Focused Attention

Focused attention is the ability to filter out ambient information and concentrate on one identified thing. Daily Practice 1, Meditation, also works on building focused attention, though the context is a bit different because the focus is mostly on the sound of the bell or a moving item and in most cases is linked to the breath. These bell exercises expand this skill in that focused attention is applied to movement and body-based tasks.

Option 1. Find three things that are ____ (e.g., red, small): When the bell rings, children look to you for instruction. Ask children to scan the classroom to find three things that belong in a particular category (e.g., are big, are blue, are animals, are made out of wood). Use call and response to ask children to respond with answers.

Option 2. Sound and Movement Matching (OpenMind drum shaker sounds paired to different movements)**:** This activity has been a huge hit in every classroom I have tried it in! You can make a simple OpenMind drum shaker for this exercise by taking a sturdy clear plastic cup (or doubling two cups to make it more stable) and filling it partially with beans, rice, or small beads. Cut off the narrow part of a standard balloon and stretch the remaining part over the top of the cup to make a drum "skin." You can tape around the edge of the balloon to keep it stuck to the cup. If you aren't able to make a drum shaker, any type of drum or shaker will do.

Step 1. Pairing sounds and movements. Identify three to four different sounds and pair each sound to a specific movement. For example, if you are using an OpenMind drum shaker, a shaking sound will prompt children to shake their bodies, tapping the drum three times will prompt children to stomp three times, and pulling up on the balloon drum skin to make a thump sound will prompt children to jump three times.

Step 2: Practicing throughout the day. When the bell rings, children stand up and look at you. Provide a sound prompt; children respond with the paired movement. Repeat as needed.

Option 3. Do the Opposite (e.g., I clap one time, you clap two times; I say sit up, you sit down)**:** When the bell rings, children stand up, put their hands together, and look toward you. When you clap once, children clap twice; when you clap twice, children clap once. Repeat as needed.

Option 4. Balance the _____: When the bell rings, children stand up and look toward you. Then give a verbal instruction for a balance activity (e.g., stand on one foot, balance a block on your head, balance a crayon on your finger). When you ring the bell, children hold this balance position until the bell rings again.

Bell Exercises for Controlling Voice Volume

Option 1. Whisper ABCs or other song: When the bell rings, children freeze and wait for your prompt. When you say, "One, two, ready, whisper!" children whisper the ABCs or another classroom song.

Option 2. Hum Along to the Bell (changing volume): When the bell rings, children freeze and look to you for instruction. Then you ring the bell at a specific volume, and children respond by humming at a matching volume (e.g., if you ring the bell softly, children hum softly). Repeat as needed with varying ring volumes.

Option 3. Tiptoe to a Friend and Whisper Something Kind: When the bell rings, children tiptoe to a designated friend and whisper a kind greeting, compliment, or phrase of encouragement.

Option 4. Slow Movement and Quiet Sounds—Hands Up, Clap, "Ooohhhhhh": When the bell rings, children put their arms down by their sides and look toward you. Next, they follow you as you move your arms up slowly, and then they clap overhead when you clap. After the clap, verbally make a slow quiet sound (e.g., "ooohhhhhh," "shhhhhh") as you slowly move your arms back down and clap again. After the second clap, children go back to their previous activity and working position (at table, in centers).

Daily Practice 4: Yoga Postures and Body Awareness

These practice options are modifications of the Grounded (green) REMIND practices and help children to improve awareness of the body Often when young children are learning new skills that require new cognitive processes and concentration, they may show decreased awareness of their bodies. For example, a young child who is sitting on the floor and concentrating on a new STEM building task that requires fine motor control and pattern copying may have decreased awareness of their body. This could result in the child leaning against a peer, or even having an accident (despite being toilet trained) because they did not notice the signal from their bodies due to increased concentration on the building task.

Option 1: Yoga Postures

Why: Yoga serves as a daily practice to strengthen and support children's self-calming skills, awareness of the body, attention to the breath, and balance. It is a way to transition from a focus on the breath in sitting or still meditation to a focus on the breath while moving the body. The postures can be used for transitions, as a waiting strategy, or in the rhythm of life to support academics or play time.

When and where: Daily—large group, small group, transitions, outside, as needed.

How:

1. Select a yoga posture (see sample poses in online appendix E) based on the identified position (i.e., lying down, sitting, standing) or associated skill-building factor (resting and calming, balance, weight-bearing). The cards are in appendix E for your reference and can be printed in a double-sided format.

2. Depending on the setting, modify the pose as needed to support the desired outcome (e.g., calming, focus, balance, increased weight bearing and grounding, relaxation, fun and silliness).

3. If desired, modify this practice to incorporate play and sensory awareness (e.g., when in down dog, have children inhale and then exhale while making doggie sounds, like panting; when in child's pose right before nap time, have children listen to and feel their heart beat).

4. Encourage children to select yoga poses as they become more familiar with the different postures.

Materials: OMPK Yoga Posture Cards, online appendix E (http://www.newharbinger.com/49258)

Social-Emotional Competence: Body awareness, environmental awareness, self-regulation, inhibitory control, listening, following directions, sequencing, and organizing

Option 2: Seeing with My Hands

Why: This is an activity to bring children into their bodies, to teach them to be aware with their bodies, and to have a beginner's mind (an attitude of curiosity and openness). It also encourages tactile discrimination and matching of objects. It works on the distinct sense called *stereognosis,* which is the ability to know what objects are based on how they feel—such as when putting your hand in your pocket and being able to identify different coins without looking.

When and where: Large group, small group, as an activity for individual work and exploration time.

How:

1. Identify five pairs of matching objects (e.g., two flat blocks, two cube blocks, two small balls, two puff balls, two markers). Place one set (five objects) in an opaque bag and the other set (five matching objects) on the floor or table.

2. Ask a child to reach into the bag and "see with their hands," and without looking, try to point to its match on the floor or table.

3. Children can take turns, and you may add objects or repeat the activity depending on interest.

Materials: Pairs of classroom objects of various materials, shapes, sizes, and textures

Social-Emotional Competence: Body awareness, attention, environmental awareness, nonjudgmental awareness

Option 3: Mindful Eating

Why: This activity is an adaptation of the raisin exercise in the Mindfulness-Based Stress Reduction program by Jon Kabat-Zinn (1990). The purpose of the exercise is to increase awareness of how food looks, smells, feels, and tastes. This can also be done with a bite-sized food to incorporate an academic lesson (e.g., categorization of crunchy versus chewy foods, foods that start with the letter "c").

When and where: Large group as a learning activity, small group at mealtime or snack time; when children eat rapidly and do not take the time to enjoy their food.

How:

1. Introduce a bite-sized food item and ask children to pretend that the food is from a magical forest and they have never seen it before.

2. In sequence, first ask the children to first *look at* the food item to notice how it looks, and then discuss its visual properties (e.g., color, size). Then, have the children *touch* the food

item and notice how it feels with their fingers, and discuss the tactile properties (e.g., rough, cold, smooth). Next, ask the children to *smell* the food and notice how it smells, and discuss its smell properties (e.g., sweet). After this, ask the children to *taste* the food by first touching it to their tongues, and then taking a bite and holding it in their mouth for a few seconds, and discuss how is tastes (e.g., sweet, salty, sour). Finally, ask the children to chew slowly and be aware of the *texture,* and after they have swallowed the bite, discuss these properties (e.g., crunchy, chewy).

Materials: Bite-sized food items

Social-Emotional Competence: Body awareness, attention, nonjudgmental awareness

Option 4: "Body Move Song"

Why: This is an upbeat song that uses large body movements paired with body vocabulary as an introduction to body awareness. It helps children be aware of what is happening to their bodies when they may be fidgeting, wiggly, or seeking movement input.

When and where: Transition activity, large group, outside; when children are ready to learn about body part vocabulary and body movement vocabulary; when children are demonstrating that they need to get up and move.

How:

1. Introduce the song with a recognition of its purpose (e.g., when children are demonstrating a need to get up and move, say, "I see your bodies are moving—do we want to do the 'Body Move Song'?"). You can shape this so that eventually, children can request the song or similar movement-based activities as a means of self-regulation.

2. Demonstrate the movements and song lyrics as needed.

3. When doing this song as an outside activity, encourage the children to be as expansive and silly as they would like, while still being aware of their bodies and environment.

Materials: "Body Move Song" audio download and OMPK Song Lyrics (online appendix C), both available at http://www.newharbinger.com/49258

Social-Emotional Competence: Body awareness, environmental awareness, impulse control, control and awareness of body movements in relation to others, self-regulation, listening and following directions

Option 5: "Pass the Water Song"

Why: This song introduces the concepts of attention and self-awareness, including the vocabulary words for "attention" and "aware," while offering a fun hands-on experience of how these concepts work together.

When and where: Transition activity, large group, small group, outside; when children may be having difficulty grading and controlling their body movements and have decreased body awareness. This can also be used as a transition strategy without the music and song.

How:

1. Begin with presenting the concepts of attention and awareness, and discuss why it is important to have attention and awareness (e.g., so we can focus on what we are doing, so that we don't bump into our friends or step on their work).

2. Fill a cup with water and explain that when we are carrying or moving a cup with water in it, we must move slowly and carefully so it does not spill. Demonstrate the task of lifting the cup up and down and then passing it once around the circle.

3. Support children to engage in singing the "Pass the Water Song" and imitating the movements in the song.

4. Have the children sing the song in small-group circles of four or five children each. This can be done in a small-group format, or in a large group with children divided into small circles.

Materials: Cup, water, "Pass the Water Song" audio download and OMPK Song Lyrics (online appendix C), both available at http://www.newharbinger.com/49258

Social-Emotional Competence: Body awareness, environmental awareness, impulse control, control and awareness of body movements in relation to others, listening and following directions

Option 6: Body Scan Meditation

Why: Body sensations tell us about emotions, danger, pleasant experiences, and what is happening around us, and they give signals about what our body needs to feel safe and balanced. The body scan is an exercise to practice noticing what is happening in our body and to improve body and emotional awareness.

When and where: Daily—large group, small group, transitions, outside; when a child may be having uncomfortable body sensations or has limited body awareness of body sensations. This practice may be better to introduce after children have practiced some of the easier practice options above.

Note: When leading the body scan activity, try to link it to an activity that may augment body cues to make it easier for them to notice. For example, have the children scan their bodies before or after eating when they may more easily notice hunger or fullness; guide them to scan their bodies after recess or dancing to notice their muscles firing and hearts beating more quickly.

How:

1. Ask children to sit in meditation posture (sit up tall like a tree).

2. Explain to children that they are going to practice noticing how their bodies feel, and they are going to be like reporters or scientists. It may be helpful to talk about what it means to notice, and why this is important (to see, hear, and feel what is happening).

3. Ask children to close their eyes, and then ask them to notice a part of the body (e.g., tummy). Use the bell to start and stop; let children observe the body area for about thirty seconds.

4. After the bell rings, ask children how the body part felt, and give prompts as needed (e.g., "Did your tummy feel hungry? warm? full?"). Continue with different body areas based on children's interest and ability.

Materials: Bell

Social-Emotional Competence: Body awareness, environmental awareness, self-awareness, self-regulation, inhibitory control, listening

Option 7: Large Group Mindful Movement Exercises

Why: These exercises help children to apply what they have learned about the bell exercises and body awareness in the context of a large-group activity or during a functional transition.

When and where: Daily—large group, transitions, outside time; when the class may have difficulty being aware of their bodies or focusing as a group.

How:

Note: Instead of numbered steps, the instructions below are provided for different versions and applications of large-group mindful movement exercises:

•   **Walking Meditation for Transitions:** For this exercise, follow the instructions for walking meditation (see Chapter 7, Daily Practice 1, Part B) practice during transitions to line up or move between centers or to different learning areas (e.g., from classroom to outdoor play).

•   **Pass the ____ (Balloon, Ball, Bell):** For this exercise, have the children sit or stand in a large group circle. Then present an object (e.g., ball, baby doll, new classroom object) to one child. When you ring the bell, the child passes the object to the next child, and the child receiving the object waits for the next bell prompt, and then passes the object along. The process repeats until the object is passed around the entire circle. This exercise can also be done using the bell as an object to pass. For this variation, give one child the bell and mallet and prompt the child (by pointing or clapping) to ring the bell. The child then passes the bell to the next child, who waits for the prompt to ring the bell and then passes the bell along.

- **Freeze Dance:** Children stand in a large group and wait for the music to begin. When you start the music, children begin to dance. When you stop the music, children freeze. Repeat the exercise based on children's interest and engagement.

- **Red Light Green Light:** This version of the classic game is ideal for outdoor play. Children run when they hear "green light," walk slowly when they hear "yellow light," and stop when they hear "red light."

- **Simon Says:** This version of the classic game is ideal for priming and preparing children to receive classroom instructions. Say, "Simon says," and then give an instruction (e.g., "Simon says touch your head"). Children follow the instruction. When you do not say, "Simon says," children ignore the instruction and freeze. Repeat the exercise based on children's interest and engagement.

Materials: Bell

Social-Emotional Competence: Body awareness, environmental awareness, self-regulation, inhibitory control, listening, following directions, sequencing, and organizing

Opportunity for Growth and Engagement: Self-hitting and head banging during feelings of anger and fear

A child often becomes frustrated during challenging tasks and begins to hit themselves in the head or bang their head on the floor or nearby objects. They frequently come to school with bruises on their head and body. They are able to indicate that they feel angry and scared during these times.

Natural Learning Opportunity: Help the child to notice the body sensations associated with the difficult feelings so that they can develop safer coping strategies and alternatives to self-harm.

Practice Modification: Body Scan—Looking Inside to Turn on New Lights

When the child is in a calm and alert state, remind them of a recent episode of self-harm using a nonjudgmental tone (e.g., they hit themself in the head when they could not cut out a circle). Explain that it is okay and when something like that happens, it gives us a new chance to grow and learn about ourselves. Tell the child that they are safe now, and ask them to express which feelings they were feeling when the episode occurred, using visuals as needed. Then, explain that if we really look inside, we can notice different things about these feelings in our bodies. This is like turning on a light when we feel scared in the dark. Give an example (e.g., "When I feel angry, my jaw and teeth squeeze tight, and I want to scream the hot angry out".) Ask the child to sit up tall like a tree, and practice noticing how their head feels when they are feeling calm for about thirty seconds. Use the bell to start and stop the body scan practice. After the bell rings, prompt the child to describe and/or draw how their head felt when they were calm. Then ask how it feels different when they are angry or upset, and use prompts as needed (e.g., "Does your head feel hot or cold, tight or heavy? Does the angry feel like it is trying to push out?"). Explain that these feelings can feel yucky or scary but we don't have to hurt ourselves or others. Give the child an example of a positive coping strategy (e.g., "When my jaw is tight and angry and I want to scream mean words at someone, I stop and open my mouth to stretch and then breathe until it feels relaxed and the angry goes away. Then I can turn on a light because I noticed how it feels"). Support the child to engage in problem solving, when they notice the angry and scared feelings in their head, to find new ways to act that do not involve self-harm, but instead involve seeking safety and practicing co-regulation or self-calming strategies.

Academic and Developmental Skills: Noticing, describing, cause and effect, problem solving, art, and self-expression

Helpful Hints for Implementing Daily Practices 3 and 4

Much like the first two practices, the goal of Daily Practice 3, Bell Practices, and Daily Practice 4, Yoga Postures and Body Awareness, is not to add on to your daily schedule, but to enhance it. Teachers typically report that these two practices work very well as classroom management strategies in the moment, but they also help to build skills over time. Below are recommendations for implementing these practices:

1. With the bell practices and yoga postures, it is best to select what you will do in advance—typically during morning meeting or your first large group session. At first, while everything is new, it may be easier for you to select the bell practices and yoga postures based on children's need and interest.

2. Children learn best by repetition, and it may be helpful to use the same bell practice or one to two yoga postures for more than one day until children feel comfortable with them. You can also make a yoga posture a bell exercise.

3. Once children begin to feel comfortable with the choices for bell practices, yoga postures, and body awareness exercises, they enjoy being able to select them. You can create different classroom jobs for leading yoga, ringing the bell, and choosing the daily bell practice or yoga posture.

4. Remember that these practices can be a way to integrate fun with building skills for being present and practicing awareness and self-control.

CHAPTER 9

Daily Practices 5 and 6
Teaching and Supporting Emotional Awareness, Emotion Regulation, and Prosocial Behaviors

The purpose of Daily Practice 5, The Feelings Finder Practices, and Daily Practice 6, The Super Me Practices, is to help children to build emotional awareness and emotion regulation and to engage in and be reinforced for prosocial actions, all within the context of everyday activities and learning. Children have big feelings, and difficulty identifying, understanding, and managing these feelings can lead to challenging, hurtful, or disruptive behaviors. In addition, positive emotions can lead to natural engagement in prosocial behaviors. Because our emotions so often drive our behaviors, these two practices are closely linked and presented together.

Daily Practice 5: The Feelings Finder Practices

These Daily Practice options help children to learn different emotions; associated facial expressions, posture, and voice tone; awareness of where emotions are felt in the body; awareness of the intensity of emotions; and awareness of the emotions of others. They can also help children to communicate how they are feeling when they are in distress or cannot verbalize emotions, to more objectively notice their emotions, and to understand that feelings come and go—because no feeling lasts forever. They help you to teach children the purpose of our emotions and the idea that we can often have many emotions, even positive and painful emotions, at the same time. Finally, these practices offer a way for children to experience perspective taking by seeing how others are feeling.

The way that you teach these is unique in that you can link the lessons and descriptions to an appropriate and meaningful context that provides children many cues for learning. For example, you can connect the practices to a book in which a character feels angry by discussing how the character's face looks, going around the class and having the children practice making an angry face, talking about the purpose of anger (to get a burst of energy) and where we feel angry in our bodies, exploring why the book character got angry, discussing times children have felt anger and how it went away, and problem solving ways to cope with angry feelings. Many of these practices can be embedded in the activities you are already doing and the emotional situations that naturally arise when working with young children.

Option 1: Feelings Finder Visual Tools (Incident Specific)

Why: This is a multisensory activity to help teach children about different emotions and the associated facial expressions and body postures that go along with them. It also helps children to be aware of and express which emotions they are feeling, how big the emotions are, and where in the body they are feeling them. In addition, the format of the visual tools teach children about the impermanence of emotions. The practice instructions refer to the use of a Feelings Finder board, which is a magnetic whiteboard that uses moveable emoji magnets to allow children to identify which emotions they are feeling and where they are feeling them in the body, or a paper-based version of the tool (see below for instructions).

When and where: As needed when a child is having a difficult time emotionally but is calm enough to participate, or when the child is experiencing positive emotions; the Feelings Finder board or cards should be in a place that is visible or accessible but can be moved to and used in any location.

How:

To make a Feelings Finder board: Although you may purchase the Feelings Finder magnets and outline for classroom use on a portable whiteboard or classroom whiteboard from https://www.littlelotustherapy.com, you can also make your own version using the Feelings Finder materials included in the online appendix of this book at http://www.newharbinger.com/49258. The basic concept of this practice is that it uses the outline of a body and emoji visuals to enable children to identify which emotions they are feeling and place them on the outline according to where they are feeling them on their body. This hands-on practice of moving and placing emotions on a representation of one's body can act as a means of decentering, or objectively noticing emotions as impermanent and not constant aspects of the self. In appendix F, you will find a key of emojis, called the Feelings Finder Faces Key, and in appendix G, an outline of a body that is intended to be neutral in terms of race and gender. You can print and laminate the emojis from appendix F and cut them out, and print the body outline for children to have individual copies to color and decorate to reflect them as individuals (e.g., skin color, hair texture and color). Another option is to use an electronic version of the tool that you can download here http://www.newharbinger.com/49258; to use this version, you can click on the desired emoji and drag it to where it is being felt on the body; you can also make it bigger or smaller to represent emotion intensity.

To use the Feelings Finder board:

a. Present or review each emotion face to the child and ask the child to name it. You can use the emoji key in online appendix F with just the emoji faces, or the Feelings Finder Characters Key in online appendix H and the Feelings Finder Character Cards in online appendix I to also show body posture for different emotions and to provide guidance and description if the child needs help to define a feeling. You can have multiple copies of the small emojis from appendix F so that children can express the intensity of the emotions they are feeling. Explain that the number of faces indicates intensity (one face = some, two faces = a lot).

b. Discuss how we can feel emotions in our bodies and give examples as needed (e.g., "Sometimes I feel happy in my face and heart").

c. Model use of the board by describing how you feel *right now,* and place the emotion faces accordingly.

d. Then, ask the child to think about how they feel *right now,* and ask if they want to show their feelings on the Feelings Finder board or visual.

e. Thank the child for showing their feelings, and then support the child to explain as needed.

f. If the child is too upset or not ready to use the Feelings Finder tools, they can use the Feelings Finder Size Strips in appendix J to indicate which feelings they are feeling and how big the feelings are, or the Feelings Finder Character Cards (appendix I) to identify their emotions.

g. *Practice variation for the whole class:* Use the Feelings Finder Character Cards (appendix I) as a feelings check-in. Place the cards on a whiteboard or bulletin and encourage children to "check in" first thing in the morning and throughout the day by pointing to the emotions they are experiencing or by placing a magnet or clip with their name on it by the emotion cards they are feeling.

Materials: Feelings Finder board (magnetic, paper, or electronic), Feelings Finder Faces Key (appendix F), Feelings Finder Outline (appendix G), Feelings Finder Characters Key (appendix H), Feelings Finder Character Cards (appendix I), and Feelings Finder Size Strips (appendix J)

Social-Emotional Competence: Emotion identification, emotion expression and communication, emotional awareness, emotional reactivity

Opportunity for Growth and Engagement: Overwhelming emotions; becoming upset about having difficult feelings

A child has difficulty regulating strong emotions. For example, when they become angry, make a hurtful choice, and are reprimanded, they become angry that they feel angry and got into trouble. The child's behavior tends to escalate until they do something explosive (e.g., hitting, destroying property). During these times, they may be too upset to use the Feelings Finder board or materials appropriately (e.g., may throw the board or pieces).

Natural Learning Opportunity: Support the child to be able to identify their emotions and express how intense they are by using a visual to represent intensity of emotions (appendix J). Then, help the child to see that the emotions decrease in intensity over time and to understand that they are impermanent.

Practice Modification: Feelings Finder Size Strips

When the child is in a calm and alert state, show them the Feelings Finder Size Strips and explain that sometimes we feel big feelings, and sometimes we feel small feelings, but no feeling lasts forever. Our feelings are always changing, getting bigger or smaller, and are coming or going away. Ask them to identify which feelings they are feeling and how big the feelings are on the size strip. Tell them that when they feel really angry, it may feel very big, but it will go away if they don't feed it and wait and use a calming strategy (e.g., breathing, jumping, hugging themselves). In the rhythm of life, if the child appears to be getting upset, support them to express and measure their feelings using the Feelings Finder Size Strips.

Academic and Developmental Skills: Expressive and receptive language, problem solving, categorization, size discrimination, decision making

Option 2: Feelings Finder—Teacher Lesson

Why: This practice uses the Feelings Finder visual materials (online appendices F–J) to explain different emotions and the associated facial expressions and body language. It also involves providing examples and prompting a discussion of how and where emotions may be felt in the body. It can be used in reference to real people or to book characters, toys, or puppets. Books are wonderful ways to pair lessons for individual feelings, as they provide a context, visual representation, and dialogue to go along with emotions. In addition, identifying characters' emotions can aid children in the important academic skill of narrative recall.

When and where: Large group, story time, small group, work time, outside, transitions; when children are experiencing new or difficult emotions.

How:

1. Introduce emotions and discuss associated facial expressions, body language, and meaning. Initially, it may be best to introduce one emotion at a time. You can use puppets, songs, books, and the Feelings Finder Faces Key or the Feelings Finder Characters Key to help teach children about different emotions. Given that anger is a difficult and common emotion, the Types of Anger visual (appendix K) can be helpful in supporting the child to determine the reason and possible source of anger. This visual includes pictures for nine different types of anger, such as "mangry" (feeling mad at myself) and "langry" (feeling angry because of losing or not meeting a goal).

2. Provide examples of situations and resulting feelings and emotions (e.g., "Yesterday there was a storm with very loud thunder and big lightening. I felt scared at first and my face looked like this").

3. Call on children as needed throughout activity (e.g., "James, have you ever felt scared before? How did your face look?").

4. Discuss how we can feel emotions in our bodies and give examples as needed (e.g., "Sometimes I feel scared in my tummy. When I heard the thunder, I felt scared right here in my tummy").

5. Encourage discussion and sharing about how children feel different emotions (e.g., "Has anyone ever felt scared? Where do you feel scared in your body?"). Be sure to include positive emotions (e.g., compassion, love, gratitude, happy, calm, silly).

Materials: Feelings Finder board; Feelings Finder visuals (online appendices F–J), Types of Anger visual (appendix K), all available at http://www.newharbinger.com/49258.

Social-Emotional Competence: Emotion identification, emotion expression and communication, emotional awareness, emotional reactivity

Opportunity for Growth and Engagement: Grouchy attitude and bullying behavior

A child is frequently in a grouchy mood and says unkind words to others. They start fights with other children and often take their toys. The child doesn't seem to be aware that they are making angry facial expressions or using threatening body language.

Natural Learning Opportunity: Support the child to be able to identify and recognize emotions and express how they feel and how their face, body, and tone of voice may impact others.

Practice Modification: Feelings Finder—Story Time

Use the story The Grouchy Ladybug to help introduce the emotion of being grouchy, and how this attitude and threatening stance may make others feel. After reading the story, discuss how the ladybug felt, and pass around a mirror to have children make a grouchy face in the mirror. Then, have children make a cheerful face in the mirror. Next, have the children take turns using an angry tone of voice and then a cheerful tone of voice to say random phrases. Discuss how our faces and voices can affect others, and the importance of being aware of how our faces look and voices sound. As an optional extension, support children to do a ladybug craft in small groups to make grouchy and cheerful ladybugs for role-play.

Academic and Developmental Skills: Expressive and receptive language, listening, literacy, problem solving, categorization, decision making, fine motor skills, creative expression

Option 3: Feelings Finder—Teacher Model

Why: This practice involves modeling the use of the Feelings Finder board and/or picture cards (appendices F, G, H, I) in the rhythm of life to teach children about emotional awareness and perspective taking and also link emotions to self-regulation strategies.

When and where: As needed in the rhythm of life when you are feeling emotions, when you notice an emotion in others, or when a character in a story is experiencing emotions and makes a hurtful or kind choice that affects others.

How:

1. Model the use of the Feelings Finder board and visuals (appendices F–J) in the classroom as the need arises to share your personal emotional experiences; you can also link this to a strategy to address each emotion. For example, you might say, "I am feeling silly in my body, so I am going to do the down dog yoga pose to get some silly out. Does anyone want to join me?" or "This morning I broke my favorite coffee cup and I felt angry, so I did some birdie breathing and I felt better."

2. Use the Feelings Finder visuals if opportunities arise to discuss emotion during other classroom activities. For example, if you are reading a book and a character gets angry, use the Feelings Finder board to review this emotion, facial expressions, where the character may have felt emotion, and what the character did or could have done to manage the emotion in a way that did not harm others.

3. If children are having a difficult time identifying self-regulation or coping strategies, you can use the What Do I Need? board (appendix L) to show them different options.

Materials: Feelings Finder board; Feelings Finder visuals (appendices F–J), Types of Anger visual (appendix K), What Do I Need? board (appendix L), all available at http://www.newharbinger. com/492558.

Social-Emotional Competence: Emotion identification, emotion expression and communication, emotional awareness, emotional reactivity, emotion regulation

Option 4: Feelings Finder—"It's Okay to Feel Yucky Song"

Why: This song teaches about self-compassion by speaking about giving ourselves permission to have a tough day and to experience emotions such as anger and sadness, as these emotions are part of being human. It also teaches about the concept of impermanence, in that emotions come and go, and about practicing equanimity. It can be sung with the Feelings Finder board or visuals (appendices F, G, I) as props to illustrate emotions coming and going. It can also be a calming strategy for a child who is having a rough day.

When and where: Large group, small group, as needed as a calming strategy.

How:

1. Start by explaining the lesson of "It's okay to feel yucky" (e.g., "Some days we may feel mad or sad, but that's okay because those feelings don't stay—they go away. Even if we are feeling sad, we can still love ourselves and be kind to ourselves"). Use examples, questions, and prompts as needed to teach about self-kindness and impermanence.

2. After the lesson, play or sing the "It's Okay to Feel Yucky Song" while demonstrating the emotions coming and going on the Feelings Finder board and demonstrating the "sound effects" for the children to make along with the song.

3. Support children to sing the lyrics or hum to the melody, do sound effects, and make body or face movements to go with the sounds.

4. *As needed:* If a child is having a rough day, remind them that it is okay to feel yucky, and hum or sing the "It's Okay to Feel Yucky Song" if the child is receptive.

Materials: "It's Okay to Feel Yucky Song" audio download, OMPK song lyrics (appendix C), Feelings Finder visuals (appendices F–J) at http://www.newharbinger.com/49258.

Social-Emotional Competence: Emotion identification, emotion expression and communication, emotional awareness, emotional reactivity, emotion regulation

Daily Practice 6: Super Me Practices

These practice options involve noticing and expressing gratitude for prosocial behaviors, self-regulation, and social-emotional growth with supporting visual tools. The tools and practices serve as an anchor and reminder for both adults and children to notice, reinforce, and encourage prosocial behaviors, self-compassion, and acts of compassion and kindness. They also introduce new social-emotional vocabulary into the classroom setting. The visuals provide a reference for how to act with awareness, kindness, compassion, and respect and how to build resilience and make prosocial choices. You will find a visual and description of each of the twelve Super Me actions and characteristics in Super Me Superpower Small Cards in online appendix M, available at http://www.newharbinger.com/49258.

Option 1: Super Me—Noticing and Reinforcing

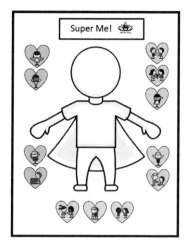

Why: This practice option involves using the Super Me Classroom Poster and/or Superpower Small Cards to notice and reinforce children or adults who have engaged in a positive behavioral action that benefits themselves and/or others. In addition, you may purchase Super Me magnets and outline for classroom use on a portable whiteboard or classroom whiteboard from https://www.littlelotustherapy.com, It can also be used to set a goal or intention for the day.

When and where: As needed in the rhythm of life when the opportunity arises; during small group, large group, or work time (art variation).

How:

1. When a child makes a positive behavioral choice (e.g., shares a toy instead of fighting for it, helps the teacher, asks nicely for help), recognize the act verbally, and reference the corresponding visual using the Super Me Superpower Small Cards (appendix M), Superpower of the Day Poster Cards (appendix N) or corresponding area of the Super Me Classroom Poster (appendix O).

2. Provide verbal recognition of the positive act and then express gratitude for the act (e.g., "You listened to Ms. Elliotte and followed her directions to line up for outside time! Thank you, Addison!").

3. *Target behavior or intention variation, AKA "Superpower of the Day":* This practice variation was named the "Superpower of the Day" by a brilliant OMPK Head Start teacher, Angela Asbury. Identify a prosocial behavior that you want to emphasize and place the corresponding Super Me magnet or small picture card (appendix M) in a visible place, or use the Super Me Superpower of the Day Poster Cards for a larger visual. Explain that this behavior is the "Superpower of the Day" and that you will be looking for people who are demonstrating this behavior, and using that superpower (e.g., "Today while we do work time and lessons, I will be watching for people who are trying hard"; "During story time, I will be noticing people who are being present").

4. *Art variation:* Use the Super Me clip art coloring and drawing pages (appendix P) to introduce and explain the Super Me prosocial behaviors

Materials: Super Me visuals (online appendices M–P, available at http://www.newharbinger.com/49258)

Social-Emotional Competence: Self-awareness, social awareness, prosocial behavior, relationship skills, responsible decision making, positive behavior vocabulary, self-concept

Option 2: Super Me—What Do I Need?

WHAT DO I NEED?

Why: Often when children are overwhelmed by difficult emotions or a problem, they have difficulty independently choosing a self-regulation or coping strategy. This activity provides a visual of different choices that a child can select to help them to calm themselves, feel safe, feel positive, and/or get through a difficult problem.

When and where: As needed when a child is having a difficult time. This can also be used as a lesson for teaching all of the different self-regulation options in a large-group or small-group format.

How:

1. Start by explaining the purpose of the What Do I Need? Board, and explain each of the strategies. This can also be paired with Daily Practice 5, Feelings Finder—Teacher Lesson (Option 2) or Teacher Model (Option 3).

2. Encourage discussion about which options children find to be most helpful.

3. *For individualized use:* When a child is having difficulty calming down or solving a problem, offer the What Do I Need? board as a menu of possible options. Support the child to access the chosen options.

Materials: What Do I Need board (online appendix L, at http://www.newharbinger.com/49258)

Social-Emotional Competence: Emotion identification, emotional awareness, emotional reactivity, emotion regulation, impermanence of emotions

Option 3: Super Me—Making an Apology

Why: This practice option helps children learn to make a meaningful apology to others.

When and where: As needed in the rhythm of life when a child engages in a behavior that hurts another person.

How:

1. When a child engages in a behavior that hurts another person, encourage the child they hurt to show how this made them feel using the Feelings Finder visuals (appendices F–K) as needed.

2. Discuss the feelings of the child who was hurt with the child who engaged in the hurtful behavior, and support the child to take the perspective of the child they hurt.

3. Support the child to identify a kind act to help to reduce the effects of the hurtful act, using the Super Me connection actions (color coded as green hearts) as choices if needed.

4. Support the child to select a social positive intention action (color coded as blue hearts), or an action to remember to do in the future to guide kind choices.

5. Support the child to make an apology to the child they hurt using the pictures (appendix M or O) or Super Me magnets and, if the child is verbal, words (e.g., "I'm sorry I hit you and you felt sad and scared. Now I can give you a high five. Next time I can ask nicely for the baby doll").

Materials: Feelings Finder visuals (appendices F–K), Super Me visuals (appendices M–O), all available at http://www.newharbinger.com/49258

Social-Emotional Competence: Self-awareness, social awareness, prosocial behavior, relationship skills, responsible decision making, positive behavior vocabulary, self-concept, empathy, compassion, kindness, compromise

Opportunity for Growth and Engagement: Arguing, fighting; difficulty sharing and seeing the other person's perspective; having empathy for a peer

Two children are arguing over who gets to play with a particular stuffed toy. Neither child wants to share, and one quickly grabs the toy from the other child's hands. The child becomes visibly upset, and their reaction is to hit the child who snatched the toy.

Natural Learning Opportunity: Support both children in learning to recognize the feelings of others, apologize for their hurtful behavior, and engage in prosocial behaviors such as sharing.

Practice Modification: Super Me—Finding Kindness

Introduce the Feelings Finder visuals (appendices F–J) to both children. Ask the child who had the toy taken from them how they feel, limiting the number of emotion visuals (appendices F and I) if necessary. Ask the child to place the cut-out emotions (appendix F) or emotion magnets that they feel on the Feelings Finder Outline (appendix G), or point to where they feel it in their own body. For example, the child may place the emotion for sad on the head of the board, indicating that having the toy taken makes them sad. Then, ask the child who took the toy how they felt during this act, and have them place the emotion on the board. The child may place the angry emotion on the hands of the board, for example, because they wanted the toy and didn't feel they could have it at that moment. Explain how both children made hurtful choices, but now is a chance to make helping choices. Use the Super Me visuals (appendices M–P) to show the children options for how to make the other person feel better. Support them to engage in their chosen acts and also in problem solving to make a plan for sharing the toy (e.g., alternating five-minute turns with the toy). Once they are sharing, show the children the Super Me sharing picture card or magnet to provide positive reinforcement for sharing.

Academic and Developmental Skills: Expressive and receptive language, listening, problem solving, decision making, turn taking.

Option 4: Super Me— Self-Kindness

Why: This practice option helps children learn to use self-kindness statements and engage in self-compassion.

When and where: As needed in the rhythm of life when a child engages in negative self-talk.

How:

1. When a child makes negative comments about themself, acknowledge how the child is feeling and gently remind them that they can be kind to themself (e.g., "Gabriella, it looks like you are feeling frustrated, but you can be kind to yourself! You are trying so hard! You have such cool ideas!).

2. Support the child to identify a self-kindness statement from the pink heart pictures on the Super Me Superpower Small Cards (appendix M). Then, support the child to use a self-kindness statement (e.g., *I love myself no matter what*).

Materials: Super Me visuals (appendices M–P)

Social-Emotional Competence: Self-awareness, self-kindness, self-concept, self-compassion, self-acceptance, self-forgiveness

Option 5: Super Me—"Super Me Song"

Why: This song teaches about self-kindness while also teaching rhythm, timing, and large body movements. It uses a cape made from recycled T-shirts, and decorated by the child, as an optional prop.

When and where: Outside (song), large group (song), small group (making the cape).

How:

1. *Making the cape (small group)*: Prepare the cape by cutting out the sleeves and either the front or back panel of a large t-shirt under the neckline so that the shirt can fit over the child's head and hang like a cape. During small-group time, children can paint and decorate their capes.

2. *Singing the song (large group):* Before singing the song, ask the children to select their capes and put them on with help as needed. Then, ask them to line up in a circle formation to march and do song movements.

Materials: Recycled T-shirt (light colored), paint pens, fabric paint, markers; "Super Me Song" audio download and OMPK Song Lyrics (appendix C), both available at http://www.newharbinger.com/49258.

Social-Emotional Competence: Self-awareness, self-kindness, self-concept, self-compassion, self-acceptance, self-forgiveness

Option 6: "Be Like a Tree Song"

Why: This is a song with associated body movements for teaching children that emotions and pain are impermanent and that while pain is inevitable, suffering is optional. Emotional storms come, and we can make these feelings worse when we try to stop them or run away from them. This is a metaphor for how to practice equanimity and to be resilient.

When and where: Large group, small group, before rest or quiet play, as needed as a calming strategy.

How:

1. Start by explaining the lesson of "being like a tree" (e.g., "When it is raining outside, and we want it to stop, what can we do? We can wait just like a tree. The tree doesn't try to run away or hit its friends because it knows that the rain will stop if it just waits"). Use examples, questions, and prompting as needed to teach related concepts, such as self-calming, patience, and impermanence.

2. After the lesson, play or sing the "Be Like a Tree Song" while demonstrating movements, and ask the children to imitate your movements.

3. Encourage children to sing the lyrics or hum to the melody as they perform the movements.

Materials: "Be Like a Tree Song" audio download, OMPK Song Lyrics (appendix C), both available at http://www.newharbinger.com/49258.

Social-Emotional Competence: Emotion identification, emotional awareness, emotional reactivity, emotion regulation, impermanence of emotions

Option 7: Be-Like-a-Tree Calm Down Jar

Why: This is a visual and hands-on tool to act as an extension of the Be Like a Tree lesson and song, and also to serve as a multisensory strategy for self-calming and acting with equanimity. The be-like-a-tree calm down jar can be used in the calm down or safe area.

When and where: Large group (teacher model), as needed as a calm down strategy in a quiet or safe space.

How:

1. *Making a be-like-a-tree calm down jar:* You can make a be-like-a-tree calm down jar by gluing a plastic tree on the bottom of a small plastic jar and filling the jar with water, glue, and glitter so that when the jar is shaken up, the glitter swirls around the tree like a storm.

2. *Teacher model:* Initially, explain and then model the use of the be-like-a-tree calm down jar in a large- or small-group setting. This can be done as needed until the children demonstrate understanding of the concept.

3. *As needed as a calm down strategy:* If a child is overwhelmed and appears to need help calming themself, offer the idea of using the be-like-a-tree calm down jar while sitting in the calm area. Support the child to use the strategy and supplement this activity with the "Be Like a Tree" song, birdie breathing, lotus breathing, or heartbeat meditation as needed (e.g., "Shake up the jar and feel your heartbeat while the glitter falls").

Materials: Be-like-a-tree calm down jar; "Be Like a Tree Song" audio download and OMPK Song Lyrics (appendix C), both available at http://www.newharbinger.com/49258.

Social-Emotional Competence: Emotion identification, emotional awareness, emotional reactivity, emotion regulation, impermanence of emotions

Opportunity for Growth and Engagement: A child is overwhelmed and upset during transitions

During transitions (e.g., lunch clean-up time, bathroom time, lining up to go outside), a child exhibits signs of distress (e.g., covers their ears, cries, tries to run out of the classroom), refuses to transition with the class, and hides under a table in the corner of the room. The classroom is noisy and busy with movement from other children. The teacher has observed that the child seems to startle easily and does not like to be a part of large groups.

Natural Learning Opportunity: Support the child to recognize difficult emotions, understand that the emotions are impermanent, and develop transition strategies and access to a safe space or other supports for self-regulation when they are feeling overwhelmed.

Practice Modification: Super Me—Be Like a Tree Timer

When the child is in a quiet and alert state, and the environment is calm, help the child to identify emotions that they feel during transitions that involve loud noise, movement, and stimuli. Explain that these feelings don't last and they are like a storm that comes. Tell the child that they can be strong like a tree until the storm is gone, and demonstrate using the be-like-a-tree calm down jar as a visual. Tell the child that when they are feeling overwhelmed, they can go to a safe space (e.g., under a table) and shake up the tree jar. They can notice the glitter settling, almost like a sand timer. Once the glitter settles, the child can notice if the feelings are also going away. The child can repeat as needed, and when they feel calm, they can join their friends. Provide support and reminders as needed in the rhythm of life *before the transition occurs* to remind them that they have this option.

Academic and Developmental Skills: Expressive and receptive language, transitions, cause and effect, problem solving

Option 8: "Talking Heart, Listening Ears Song"

Why: This song and role-play activity teaches children to be aware of how they talk to others, how tone and intention affect others, and ways to talk to others to make sure they are heard. Developmentally, preschoolers are driven largely by ego, so this song teaches that speaking nicely to others is not only kind to others, but can help children to get what they need because others will listen to kind voices.

When and where: Large group, as needed when children whine, yell, or use physical aggression to communicate.

How:

1. *Large group:* Introduce the listening ear (this can be a large photo of an ear, or the ear of a classroom toy or doll) and talk about listening and what it means. Present different ways to communicate and discuss which ways the listening ear can hear (e.g., listening ears can hear a kind voice, but yelling hurts and makes them close up).

2. Sing the "Talking Heart, Listening Ears Song" to present all of the different ways of communication.

3. Model and role-play situations for different means of communication, and support children to problem solve (e.g., "John wanted help, so he screamed and grabbed Ms. Amber's leg. What could he do to make sure her listening ears can hear him?").

4. *As needed:* The ear will serve as a visual reminder of the lesson in the classroom. During situations in which children are communicating unkindly, you can modify this activity to teach a better means of communication.

5. *Say it with a smile:* When a child is whining or talking in an unkind tone, ask the child if they can say it with a smile instead. Demonstrate by using a kind tone and a smile, and ask the child to give it a try.

Materials: "Talking Heart, Listening Ears Song" audio download, OMPK song lyrics (appendix C), available at http://www.newharbinger.com/49258.

Social-Emotional Competence: Attention, self-awareness, listening, mindful communication, awareness of impulses, environmental awareness, social awareness, impulse control, self-regulation, self-monitoring, emotion regulation, problem solving, cognitive flexibility

Helpful Hints for Implementing Daily Practices 5 and 6

The thing I love most about these practices is that they are so easy to integrate into the classroom day, because when you work with young children, opportunities to process and address emotions and coping skills so easily and naturally arise! All of the Feelings Finder and Super Me practices can be used both proactively, to teach about different emotions, self-regulation strategies, and prosocial choice making, and reactively in response to real-life situations. When you use them to teach and reinforce organic situations and needs that emerge, children receive the teaching in context, linked to something that is actually happening. However, you can also link these practices to books, videos, stories, and pretend play to address fictional or hypothetical situations. Here are some suggestions and strategies to remember for adding Daily Practices 5 and 6 into the rhythm of classroom life:

1. Whenever possible, when teaching about a new emotion, try to offer as much context as possible. This may include pictures, a storyline (e.g., a character in a book or video who is having the emotion), and opportunities to mimic the emotion with facial expressions and body language. You can use a mirror so that children can see themselves making each emotional expression, or have children mirror you or each other. This will help them integrate their perceptual understanding of the emotion with their somatic, or bodily, understanding of how the emotion is both felt and expressed.

2. Be sure to discuss not only painful or difficult emotions, such as anger, sadness, or fear, but also "positive" emotions, such as joy, gratitude, and compassion.

3. Pairing Feelings Finder and Super Me practices with books can not only help put the teachings into context, but can also help children retain key parts of the stories they hear and see. Characters' feelings and how they discuss problems and solutions are key story elements that can enhance comprehension.

4. You can use the Super Me Superpower of the Day (Option 1: Super Me—Noticing and Reinforcing) to create opportunities to grow positive behaviors in response to targeted or identified classroom challenges. For example, if children are having trouble with sharing, then the Super Me Superpower of the Day can be sharing. This will help you to notice, celebrate, and highlight the moments when children do share common materials and engage in turn taking, so that they can model these actions for others.

5. Remember that the Super Me practices are an alternative to saying something general, such as "Good job." Because they offer you a way to give specific reinforcement, they help children learn what exactly they have done that was "good."

6. One of the wonderful side effects of these practices is that children will start to reinforce and help each other. On so many occasions, I have witnessed one child see another child hurting or suffering, and bring them the be-like-a-tree calm down jar, or see a peer putting forth effort and say, "You are trying so hard—you can do it!"

7. If you look at the twelve Super Me Superpower Small Cards in online appendix M, you will notice that there are actions that relate to all of the OMPK Daily Practices and principles. You can use these visuals and language to reinforce engagement in the Daily Practices and to reinforce the concepts that go along with them. For example, there are Super Me visuals for being present and trying hard; you can use these to reinforce engagement in Daily Practices 1 and 2, and anytime you notice a child "showing up," being present, and putting forth effort.

CHAPTER 10

Daily Practices 7–10
Growing a Peaceful and Connected Classroom Environment

Daily Practice 7, Loving-kindness; Daily Practice 8, Gratitude; Daily Practice 9, Kindness Reporting; and Daily Practice 10, Soles of the Little Feet and Shifting, were designed to build upon and link to the other Daily Practices and to promote a classroom culture of kindness, connection, and consideration of others. Together, they serve to lay a foundation for acting with kindness and compassion for ourselves and for others, which can enrich the environment and add to a sense of felt safety, respect, and appreciation. They also work to build self-awareness, social awareness, responsible decision making, and meaningful relationships.

Daily Practice 7: Loving-Kindness Practices

These Daily Practice options offer children a means to extend loving-kindness to themselves and others. They are a modification of the Loving (red) REMIND practices. The words to the loving-kindness practice are "May you be happy, may you be healthy, may you be loved." Because this practice does not take much time, any of the options below can be done more than once during the day based on the children's needs, interests, and available time.

Option 1: Loving-Kindness Meditation as Greeting

Why: Teachers and children do this practice variation during classroom greeting time or when greeting a visitor; it serves to set the tone of the day and welcome another person with love and acceptance.

When and where: Large-group greeting time after all children have arrived, as a group when welcoming a visitor.

How:

1. Give a brief introduction to the practice and ask children to send each other and any visitors loving-kindness (e.g., "Good morning class, let's start the day by sending loving-kindness to each other").

2. Discuss how sometimes new visitors may feel shy or nervous, so it may make them feel safe and cared for to hear loving and welcoming words.

3. Ask the children to hold hands and say, "May you be happy, may you be healthy, may you be loved."

Materials: None

Social-Emotional Competence: Social greeting, kindness, empathy, compassion, unconditional acceptance

Option 2: Loving-Kindness Meditation as Farewell

Why: Teachers and children do this practice variation upon dismissal or when saying goodbye to one another, to caregivers, or to visitors. Offering kind words to someone who is leaving may make the person feel loved and appreciated.

When and where: During dismissal, when a child is leaving early, or when saying goodbye to a visitor or caregiver.

How:

1. Give a brief introduction to the practice and ask the children to send each other and any visitors loving-kindness (e.g., "Class, our visitors are leaving now; let's wish them and each other loving-kindness").

2. Discuss how sometimes when people leave somewhere, they may feel sad, or we may feel sad to see them go. Kind words may make someone who is leaving feel appreciated and loved.

3. Ask the children to hold hands and say, "May you be happy, may you be healthy, may you be loved."

Materials: None

Social-Emotional Competence: Social greeting, kindness, empathy, compassion, unconditional acceptance

Opportunity for Growth and Engagement: Difficulty separating from a caregiver

During morning drop-off, a child is crying, upset, and clinging to their grandmother because they don't want her to leave. The child has experienced chronic neglect in the past and was often left alone for long periods by their mother.

Natural Learning Opportunity: Support the child to develop a sense of safety, attachment, security, and comfort from sending and receiving love.

Practice Modification: Loving-Kindness Meditation—Connected by Love

Encourage the child to express their feelings (e.g., sadness, fear). Prompt the grandmother to recognize these feelings and to express feelings of love and compassion for the child. Ask the child to express love for the grandmother. Support the child to hold hands with her grandmother and say the Loving-Kindness Meditation. Provide two cut-out paper hearts, and have the child and grandmother draw or write positive pictures or comments on the hearts, and then exchange hearts. Explain to the child that even though their grandmother will be leaving, she will leave her love with the child, and take the child's love with her, and they will stay connected by love. Support the child to find a special safe place in the classroom to put the heart. If needed, throughout the day, connect with the child (e.g., get down on the child's level, smile warmly) and help them to go to the heart and send loving-kindness to their grandmother.

Academic and Developmental Skills: Expressive language, drawing and writing

Option 3: Loving-Kindness Meditation for Those Not in School

Why: Teachers and children do this practice variation to send loving-kindness to friends, teachers, and staff who are not in school that day. This is a way to think about others who may be feeling sick or having trouble, and offer an act of kindness.

When and where: After discussing who is not at school that day, or 1:1 when a child may be missing a particular peer, teacher, or family member.

How:

1. Give a brief introduction to the practice and ask the children to send loving-kindness to others who may not be in school that day (e.g., "Jessica, Hassan and Ms. Wendy are not here today. Let's send them loving-kindness").

2. Ask the children to say, "May you be happy, may you be healthy, may you be loved."

3. *For 1:1:* If a child is missing a loved one or peer, ask the child if they want to send this person loving-kindness. Support the child to say, "May you be happy, may you be healthy, may you be loved" and any other words of kindness to this person.

Materials: None

Social-Emotional Competence: Kindness, empathy, compassion, unconditional acceptance

Option 4: "Thank You for Being You Song"

Why: This song offers children a way to express unconditional love and appreciation to friends and recognize how each person is unique and special. It teaches children to express kind words and acceptance to others without the need for a specific reason.

When and where: Large group prior to dismissal, small groups after cooperative play or learning activities that require social interaction, transitions, outside.

How:

1. *In large-group or small-group setting:* Ask the children to pair up and sing the "Thank You for Being You Song" while holding hands and looking at their partners. Between each verse, ask the children to switch partners (three verses total).

2. *For transitions:* Introduce the song (e.g., "Wow, you guys all did different things at work time and you all worked so hard! All of our friends are so special in their own way. Let's sing the "Thank You for Being You Song" to show each other how much we care about each other"). Play the song and encourage the children to sing.

Materials: "Thank You for Being You Song" audio download, OMPK Song Lyrics (appendix C), at http://www.newharbinger.com/49258.

Social-Emotional Competence: Kindness, gratitude, unconditional acceptance

Option 5: Meditation for Sending Loving-Kindness

Why: This is a formal meditation practice that offers children a way to cultivate and send out unconditional love and kindness to themselves and others.

When and where: Large group, small groups prior to cooperative play or learning activities that require social interaction, small groups after conflict resolution

How:

1. *In large-group or small-group setting:* Ask the children sit up tall like a tree for any of the Daily Practice 1, Meditation, or practice options for breathing (options 2–7). Instruct children to "feel love grow" on the in-breath, and "send love to self" on the out-breath. Then repeat the practice by asking children to "feel love grow" on the in-breath, and "send love to others" on the out-breath.

2. *Group variation:* Ask children to take turns going around the group to send out loving-kindness as a group meditation. For example, one child breathes in (love grows) and exhales (sends out love) while looking at the child next to them. The next child repeats this and sends loving-kindness to the next child in the group, and so on until the loving-kindness has been passed all around the group.

3. *In a small group after conflict resolution:* Discuss the concept of forgiveness and how it is important to love others and ourselves no matter what, even if other people have made mistakes or hurt us. Ask children to face each other, and breathe in (peace grows) and breathe out (sends out love to the other child or children).

Materials: Meditation aids (e.g., Hoberman breathing ball) as needed

Social-Emotional Competence: Kindness, compassion, self-compassion, forgiveness, self-forgiveness, self-love, unconditional acceptance of self and others

Opportunity for Growth and Engagement: Name-calling and saying unkind words to others

Two children are arguing about playing a game and taking turns; one child has made up the rules of an outdoor game, and the other child has lost the game. The children are calling each other names, accusing each other of cheating, and beginning to become physically aggressive.

Natural Learning Opportunity: Support the children to engage in problem solving; to develop new collaborative game rules; and to express trust, forgiveness, and love to each other.

Practice Modification: Loving-Kindness Meditation—Fixing and Forgiving

Encourage each child to express their feelings using the Feelings Finder board (appendices F and G) as needed. Support the children to recognize each other's feelings and, once calm, to engage in problem solving to compromise and collaboratively create new game rules. Praise the children for working together and tell them that sometimes we may make choices that hurt others because we want to win. Explain the concept of forgiveness and ask the children to express forgiveness and love to each other by sending loving-kindness. Have the children touch fingers and do lotus breathing together by opening their fingers while breathing in and growing love, and then closing their fingers and breathing out while sending each other forgiveness. Teach children about trust and how they can decide to trust each other to play fair before starting a game.

Academic and Developmental Skills: Expressive language, problem solving, conflict resolution, compromise

Daily Practice 8: Gratitude and Interconnectedness Practices

These Daily Practice activities are designed to foster an attitude of gratitude—a way of living with appreciation for others and for what life has to offer, rather than for only what one wants or desires. This practice aligns with the Grateful (violet) REMIND practice. Expressing gratitude can be challenging for children at first, so it is helpful to model this practice often by giving specific examples. The more children practice, and the more attention they receive from adults, the better they get at noticing positive things and expressing gratitude. In addition, children with a history of trauma or neglect, and children who have a poor self-concept, can have a difficult time receiving compliments and praise, so expressing gratitude can help them to build a positive self-image and feel good about receiving recognition from others for positive acts and efforts.

Option 1: Mealtime Gratitude Practice

Why: This practice offers a way not only to foster feelings of gratitude, but also to teach the concept of interconnectedness and incorporate learning extensions for science and communication. It helps children to realize that even simple things, like a food such as carrots, are a cause for great feelings of gratitude because so many factors are responsible for the child's being able to eat the carrots at snack time (e.g., sun, rain, farmers, trucks, cashiers, school, cook, teacher).

When and where: Before mealtime or snacks; when discussing food or farming in a book, cooking, or science lesson

How:

1. Before lunch or snacks, support children to go around the table and list one thing they are grateful for. You can also encourage them to express gratitude to whom (mom, farmer) or what (sun, tomato plants) helped them receive their food. Initiate the activity by modeling the practice and sharing something that you are grateful for (e.g. "I am thankful for the rainwater that helped nourish and grow these carrots").

2. Ask for volunteers to share their thoughts of gratitude until each child who wants to share has had a turn. Call on children as needed, but do not force children to share.

3. Encourage those who are less verbal to point to or act out what they are grateful for.

4. Reflect on what the children have said by reviewing selected statements of gratitude, and also offer examples of interconnectedness (e.g., the farmer plants the carrot seeds, the rain helps the carrots grow, the shipping truck brings the carrots from the farm to the store).

Materials: Meal or snack

Social-Emotional Competence: Social awareness, cultural awareness, gratitude

Option 2: "Gratitude Flower Song"

Why: This is a song to increase awareness of gratitude for kind acts by others. This practice offers a hands-on experiential way of helping children learn how expressing gratitude to others causes gratitude to grow and spreads positive feelings. When people express gratitude for others, it not only helps generate positive feelings in others, but inspires others to also express gratitude. Expressing gratitude can be contagious!

When and where: Large group, small group for making materials (optional), outside; when children understand the concept of gratitude and want to engage in singing and movement

How:

1. Divide children into two groups. Give flowers to the children in one group and hearts to the children in the other group.

2. Have the children with flowers line up in one line and the children with hearts line up facing them.

3. Sing or play the "Gratitude Flower Song" to demonstrate the rhythm, and encourage the children to march in place to the song and imitate the movements (holding up the heart or flower at appropriate time) and sing the lyrics. Then, have the children with the hearts sing the first verse, and the children with the flowers say, "A flower grows inside my heart!"

4. For the second verse, ask the children to switch objects and then sing again, reversing their parts.

5. *Small group art extension:* Have the children make flowers and/or hearts out of paper or other craft materials to use during song.

Materials: "Gratitude Flower Song" audio download and OMPK Song Lyrics (appendix C), available at http://www.newharbinger.com/49258; silk flowers, paper or foam hearts, other craft supplies (optional)

Social-Emotional Competence: Self-awareness, social awareness, kindness, gratitude, relationship building

Option 3: Gratitude Flowers

Why: This is an "as needed" activity that uses flowers (artificial flowers or flowers the children have made) and a vase to represent the practice of gratitude ("When we are grateful, a flower grows in our hearts"). It provides a visual and physical way that a child can express gratitude to others (verbally or nonverbally) throughout the day by putting a flower in the vase. It also gives teachers a way to model the practice of gratitude for the children.

When and where: Large group, small group, rhythm of life as needed to express gratitude.

How:

1. *Presenting the activity (large group):* Show the class the basket, flowers, and vase; explain the activity; and give a demonstration. Use role-play to practice the activity with volunteers. For example, "Ms. Maria helped me carry my bags in this morning. A pink flower grew inside my heart!"

2. *Adding to the flower basket (small group):* Ask the children to make flowers to add to the gratitude basket as an art project.

3. *Using the gratitude flowers (as needed):* Model the practice of selecting a flower, stating the reason for gratitude, and putting a flower in the vase. Support children to do this as appropriate. Children can also make flowers to bring home to family members or friends to express gratitude.

Materials: Basket or tray, plastic vase, faux flowers; art supplies for making flowers (e.g., paper, craft foam, pipe cleaners, foam, egg cartons).

Social-Emotional Competence: Self-awareness, social awareness, kindness, gratitude, relationship building

Opportunity for Growth and Engagement: Difficulty accepting compliments and negative self-talk

Each time a teacher gives a child a compliment (e.g., "Great job, you are so smart!"), the child looks away and makes a self-deprecating comment (e.g., "No I'm not, I'm stupid"). The child seems to withdraw when given praise. The teacher has observed the father yelling at the child in the morning before drop-off.

Natural Learning Opportunity: Support the child to accept expressions of gratitude for their actions and to begin to cultivate self-acceptance and self-compassion.

Practice Modification: Gratitude Flowers—Reinforcing with Thanks

When the child engages in a positive or prosocial behavior or experiences success, thank the child using a gratitude flower and specific language that focuses on appreciation of the child's specific effort (e.g., listening and following directions for cleaning up) instead of recognition of a characteristic (e.g., being a great helper). For example, instead of saying, "Wow, you are a great artist; look at that rainbow"), present the child with a gratitude flower to put in the basket and say, "Thank you so much for trying so hard and for using every single color. You were smiling when you were making the rainbow, and I am so grateful that you seemed to like the art activity!")

Academic and Developmental Skills: Expressive and receptive language

Option 4: Gratitude Beads

Why: This activity is for practicing gratitude both in general and in response to a specific rhythm of life event (e.g., gratitude for a visitor who has come to class to share). To make the gratitude beads, string large wooden beads on a long cord or heavy string and securely tie the ends together. The beads offer a hands-on way to connect children in the gratitude practice and offer a prompt for waiting their turn. It also serves as a physical anchor to increase connection, turn taking, and engagement in children.

When and where: Large group, small group; when you want to model the practice of gratitude and give children an opportunity to share gratitude experiences.

How:

1. Present a lesson and an example of gratitude (e.g., "I am grateful for my sister because she cooked me dinner last night when I wasn't feeling well, even though she was really tired"). Then slide one of the beads over on the string.

2. Pass the gratitude beads around the circle and ask children to give an example of gratitude and slide a bead over. Use support and prompting as needed, but do not force children to share.

3. *Optional:* Extend the practice to include academic lessons such as phonetic awareness, preliteracy, and categorization (e.g., "What is an animal/word that starts with a "T"/word with an ooo sound...that you are grateful for?" This not only teaches academic concepts, but helps children identify new sources of feeling gratitude that they may not have previously considered.

Materials: String of large beads

Social-Emotional Competence: Self-awareness, social awareness, gratitude, relationship building, kindness

Option 5: Thank You Letter

Why: This activity is designed to teach children how to take the time to thank others for kind acts or gifts. It can be completed with drawing, stickers, and/or supported writing. This is a great activity to promote loving-kindness in relationships while teaching literacy skills, verbal communication, art, and phonetics. This also fosters relationship skills with peers.

When and where: Large group, small group, in the rhythm of life to give a written expression of thanks.

How:

1. *Teacher model (large group):* Provide an example of a situation in which someone performed a kind act. Introduce the concepts of giving thanks and gratitude. Model and support writing a thank you letter and/or drawing a picture.

2. *Small group:* During an appropriate time (e.g., after a visit by a volunteer or guest, or a cleanup from the custodian), ask the children to think about what the person has given.

3. Guide and assist them to write or draw something to show their thanks.

4. If the person is present (e.g., custodian), support the children to deliver the letters and/or pictures.

Materials: Paper, stickers, crayons, pencils, art supplies

Social-Emotional Competence: Self-awareness, social awareness, gratitude, relationship building, kindness

Daily Practice 9: Kindness and Compassion Reporting

This Daily Practice is designed to encourage children to notice and appreciate kind and compassionate acts by others, and to receive attention for noticing. It is a way of reporting and celebrating good news. I informally refer to this practice as the "anti-tattling practice," as it replaces the attention that children receive from tattling on a peer for a mistake or unkind choice with attention for reporting positive actions by a peer.

Option 1: Kindness and Compassion Discussion

Why: This activity option gives children and teachers an opportunity to share if they have noticed another person acting with compassion or kindness. A child can also report when they have done a kind or compassionate act. This option is also useful in the rhythm of life as opportunities naturally arise using the Super Me visuals.

When and where: Large group, at the end of an activity that required interaction or cooperation, rhythm of life as a spontaneous act.

How:

1. During the day, model the practice of noting a kind act by a child, teacher, or a classroom visitor or volunteer. Recognition of the kind or compassionate act should include as much specific detail as possible to model this for children (e.g., "Today I noticed that Omari picked up all the crayons that Stacey dropped because Stacey had a tummy ache. Thank you for being so compassionate, Omari!")

2. If a child shares an act of kindness that they have done, reinforce the child and then gently ask if they noticed *anyone else* who also did a kind act, with prompting as needed (e.g., "Thank you for being so kind! Did any of your friends do anything kind for you today?")

3. Ask other children to share any observations of others (e.g., parent, teacher, peer, visitor, cook) acting with kindness or compassion.

4. *As needed:* Model this practice during the day by using the Super Me materials to acknowledge and reinforce acts of kindness and compassion, and teach the difference between kindness and compassion.

Materials: Super Me materials (optional)

Social-Emotional Competence: Social awareness, self-awareness, attention, kindness, relationship skills, positive reinforcement of others, social responsibility

Option 2: Kindness Helper Job

Why: The purpose of this activity option is to give a child an opportunity to notice all the kindness that happens in the classroom and to report it on a daily basis at a designated time or as the opportunity arises as a classroom job (which can be very motivating!).

When and where: Large group, at the end of an activity that required interaction or cooperation, rhythm of life as a spontaneous act.

How:

1. Include a "Kindness Helper" picture (symbol such as a heart, or one of the Super Me Superpower Small Card images (appendix M)) as a choice among classroom "Super Me Helper" jobs.

2. Explain that the "Kindness Helper" is in charge of noticing all acts of kindness in the classroom and reporting them to teachers and friends.

3. *As needed:* Provide prompting as needed to the Kindness Helper if a kind act occurs and the child does not notice it (e.g., "Maya, did you see how Tokala gave Jin a hug after she fell down? That was so kind and compassionate!").

Materials: Kindness Helper Job image (see above)

Social-Emotional Competence: Social awareness, self-awareness, attention, kindness, relationship skills, positive reinforcement of others, social responsibility

Opportunity for Growth and Engagement: Tattling and complaining for attention

A child frequently approaches teachers to report negative or problem behaviors by others. The child complains about what other children have done and tattles when they have a conflict with another child.

Natural Learning Opportunity: Support the child to receive positive attention; shift focus from negative to positive occurrences, behaviors, and interactions; and build a sense of agency and awareness for reporting positive things that peers have done. Help the child to learn the difference between tattling to get others in trouble and reporting unsafe or hurtful behaviors that require teacher intervention.

Practice Modification: Kindness Reporter—Kindness Counter

Explain to the child that you have noticed how good they are at noticing and reporting the hurtful choices that their friends make, and that you are really interested to see if they can use those skills for reporting all the kind, compassionate, and helping choices that their friends make instead. Tell the child that they will be the Kindness Counter, and every time they notice someone doing a kind act, they'll report it and make a tally mark on the board to count the kind acts. To add interest and increase motivation, allow the child to ring the bell before reporting the kind act. Emphasize that the child can report if someone has made a hurtful choice that needs a teacher's help; give an example of a hurtful situation that requires teacher help.

Academic and Developmental Skills: Expressive and receptive language, problem solving, categorization, discrimination, decision making

Daily Practice 10: Soles of the Little Feet and Shifting Practices

These practices teach children to shift attention from a difficult emotion (e.g., anger, fear) to a neutral place to make space for a positive emotion. They are accompanying practices to, and adaptations of, the Soles of the Feet practice developed and extensively researched by Dr. Nirbhay Singh (Felver & Singh, 2020). I like to think of the little guy in the picture above as a young and wise Nirbhay!). When children are able to shift anger to a neutral place, they can process anger in a way that does not harm others, which is a beautiful practice of kindness in action.

Part 1: "Big Feelings, Small Bodies Song"

Why: This song offers a playful and upbeat way of teaching children how to manage difficult emotions that feel big, especially anger, by shifting attention to a neutral place.

When and where: Large group; small group; when children are showing interest in singing, music, and movement or may not be developmentally ready to learn the formal protocol.

How:

1. Start by explaining the lesson of "big feelings, small bodies" (e.g., "Sometimes we have big feelings, and we feel like we need to let them out! This is okay as long as we don't hurt ourselves or others"). Use examples, questions, and prompting as needed to teach about the way to release big emotions appropriately. You can also use the Feelings Finder visual tools (appendices F–J) as props for the lesson.

2. I like to give children this analogy: sometimes we can feel "full of angry" and it can seem hot. It is like we are carrying around hot water in a cup. It is okay if our angry feels hot, but we have to try our best not to spill it on other people!

3. After the lesson, play or sing the "Big Feelings, Small Bodies Song" while demonstrating movements and sounds (e.g., wiggling to get out big sillies) and responses to the call-and-response portion of the song (e.g., "Can I bite or spit?… NO!").

4. Encourage children to sing the lyrics or hum to the melody as they perform the movements and sounds.

Materials: "Big Feelings, Small Bodies Song" audio download, OMPK song lyrics (appendix C), Feelings Finder visuals (appendices F–K), Super Me visuals (appendices M–O)

Social-Emotional Competence: Emotion identification, emotional awareness, emotional reactivity, emotion regulation, impermanence of emotions, shifting attention

Part 2: Soles of the Little Feet Exercises

Option 1: Soles of the Little Feet—Practice Lesson

Why: Continued attention to a difficult emotion can make it grow and potentially cause suffering and unkind or disruptive behavioral reactions. Therefore, this practice teaches children to shift their attention away from the difficult emotion to a neutral place: the soles of their feet.

When and where: Large group, small group, 1:1 as needed if a child needs additional practice after initial presentation in group settings.

How:

1. Ask children to sit "like a tree" in a chair with their feet on the floor, or sit up on the floor with their legs out in front of them, knees bent, and feet on floor.

2. Instruct children to close their eyes and think about a happy place or happy time, and give examples as needed. Ask them to open their eyes and then discuss different "happy" places and moments.

3. Ask children to close their eyes and think about the happy time again, and to move their attention to notice their feet ("Now move to your feet"). Use prompts to help the children to bring attention and awareness to the soles of their feet (e.g., "Wiggle your toes, notice if your feet are cold or warm, notice how your socks feel, notice how the floor feels under your feet").

4. Discuss how the children were able to move from thinking about feeling happy to noticing their feet.

5. Repeat steps 2 and 3 but with an angry memory instead of a happy one.

6. Discuss how we have the superpower to switch from *thinking* about yucky feelings, like anger, to *noticing* something else, like our feet.

Materials: None

Social-Emotional Competence: Emotion identification, emotional awareness, emotional reactivity, emotion regulation, impermanence of emotions, shifting attention

Option 2: Soles of the Little Feet—Retrospective Practice

Why: This practice enables children to practice shifting attention from a recent difficult emotional experience that may have resulted in an unkind or disruptive behavioral reaction to a neutral place.

When and where: 1:1 following difficult emotional situation, small group following argument with physical or verbal aggression.

How:

1. Ask the child (or children) to stand, sit "like a tree," or sit up with their legs out in front of them.

2. Instruct the child to close their eyes and think about the recent difficult emotional experience or situation.

3. Then ask the child to move their attention to notice their feet. Use prompts to help the child to bring their attention and awareness to the soles of the feet (e.g., "Wiggle your toes, notice if your feet are cold or warm, notice how your socks feel, notice how the floor feels under your feet").

4. Discuss how the child has the superpower to switch from *thinking* about yucky feelings, like anger, to *noticing* something else, like their feet.

5. Support the child to think about different behavioral choices they could make if the situation happens again. Use the Super Me visuals and/or the What Do I Need? choices as needed to provide a visual of choices for self-kindness statements and positive behavior choices, and the Feelings Finder visuals as needed to further explore associated emotions.

Materials: Feelings Finder visuals (appendices F–K), What Do I Need? (appendix L), Super Me visuals (appendices M–O) (optional)

Social-Emotional Competence: Emotion identification, emotional awareness, emotional reactivity, emotion regulation, impermanence of emotions, shifting attention

Option 3: Soles of the Little Feet—Rhythm of Life Practice

Why: This practice is a way for children to experience shifting their attention from a difficult emotion to the soles of their feet as difficult emotions arise in the rhythm of life.

When and where: 1:1 as the child is demonstrating signs of anger or another difficult emotion, small group when children are showing signs of a pending altercation or argument.

How:

1. Ask a child or children to stop and notice the feelings in their bodies.

2. Instruct a child or children to "go to the soles of their feet." Use prompts as needed (e.g., "Wiggle your toes, notice if your feet are cold or warm, notice how your socks feel, notice how the floor feels under your feet").

3. Provide praise and prompts as needed using the Super Me visuals (appendix M, N, or O) to reinforce self-regulation of difficult emotions (e.g., You went to your feet and didn't throw the truck! Thank you for being like a tree!").

Materials: Super Me materials (appendices M–O) (optional)

Social-Emotional Competence: Emotion identification, emotional awareness, emotional reactivity, emotion regulation, impermanence of emotions, shifting attention

Option 4: Shifting Practice—Feelings Feeder

Why: This practice is a way for children to experience noticing a difficult emotion, shifting their attention from the difficult emotion, resisting the urge to "feed" the difficult emotion, and directing attention to a positive emotion. The item used for this practice is the Feelings Feeder.

When and where: 1:1 when a child is demonstrating signs of anger or another difficult emotion; small group when children are showing signs of a pending altercation or argument.

How:

1. *To make a Feelings Feeder:* Use the Feelings Finder Character Cards for love, compassion, calm, grateful, and happy/joy, and glue them onto a box or container. Cut a hole in each character's mouth and a corresponding hole in the box. Gather small items that can fit through the holes, like cotton, puff balls, or small paper balls, and place them in a small container by the box.

2. Explain that sometimes we have big feelings like anger and that these emotions can feel like monsters! When we make hurtful choices or we keep thinking about the feeling, it is like we are feeding it and it gets bigger and bigger until it might explode!

3. Tell children that we can make a choice to notice the hurting feeling and then to stop feeding it. When we stop feeding it, the feeling will get smaller and go away.

4. Present the Feelings Feeder, and explain that when we stop feeding a hurting feeling, like angry, sad, or scared, we can start to feed another feeling instead, like compassion, gratitude, calm, joy, or love. Provide an example and demonstrate the practice.

5. *Optional variation:* Open the box at the end of the day and count all of the times the class fed the positive feelings.

6. *Classroom helper job:* You can choose to make this a classroom helper job and assign one child to notice when friends calm down or shift from a challenging emotion.

Materials: Feelings Feeder box or container, small objects like puff balls, Feelings Finder Character Cards (appendix I, at http://www.newharbinger.com/49258)

Social-Emotional Competence: Emotion identification, emotional awareness, emotional reactivity, emotion regulation, impermanence of emotions, shifting attention to positive emotions

Opportunity for Growth and Engagement: Persistent fear and worry about the well-being of loved ones

A child who has experienced a recent loss of a family member through violence constantly verbalizes worry that something bad will happen to other family members or friends. The child repeatedly asks the teacher to call her mother and says she is scared that her mother will die.

Natural Learning Opportunity: Support the child to identify and evaluate their feelings and then shift from these feelings to a positive emotion, such as compassion, gratitude, calm, joy, or love.

Practice Modification: Feelings Feeder—Feeding Love and Gratitude Instead of Worry

Support the child to identify their feelings on the Feelings Finder board (appendix F and G) the Feelings Finder Size Strips (appendix J), or the Feelings Finder Character Cards (appendix I). Recognize and validate the child's feelings and teach the child that fear is an important emotion to help us know that we are in danger, but that sometimes it tricks us into thinking we are in danger when we are not, and this makes us worry. Explain that worrying can make us feel yucky and does not help protect us. Tell the child that when they feel scared or worried about their mother or friends, they can stop and choose to feed love (for mother and friends), compassion (for themself), gratitude (for all their friends and family who are okay), or calm. Support the child to choose a positive emotion to practice, and assist them to engage in a related OMPK practice (e.g., Loving-Kindness Meditation, Gratitude Flowers, Super Me—Self-Kindness, or Lotus Breathing). After the practice, ask the child to identify their feelings again and notice how they may have changed.

Academic and Developmental Skills: Expressive and receptive language, cause and effect, problem solving

Helpful Hints for Implementing Daily Practices 7–10

1. Start slow and introduce one or two of these practices at a time, and build as you feel more comfortable with leading the practices in context. You can plan the practices for an appropriate time in the schedule (such as Kindness Reporting during review and wrap-up at the end of the day) or in response to a need (for example, using Soles of the Little Feet when a child is showing signs of anger, giving a gratitude flower to a guest who has read a story to the class).

2. The loving-kindness, gratitude, and kindness reporter practices can all be modified to be used as classroom jobs. For example, you can have a kindness greeter to lead Loving-Kindness Meditation as a greeting for visitors or as children come into or leave class. In this way, all children are able to experience how it feels to lead these practices and receive authentic praise for doing so.

3. Continue your OpenMind REMIND practices throughout the school day. These will help you to model a present, patient, peaceful, and mindful state for your classroom and peers, and help you to be more aware of arising needs and opportunities.

Pause for Reflection...

The OMPK ten Daily Practices have been developed to teach and reinforce healthy prosocial habits and can be helpful for children, including those who are facing big obstacles, who have disabilities, and who experienced past trauma, which can lead to challenging behaviors. However, when difficult situations arise in daily life, it can be overwhelming for teachers and children, and you may find it necessary to bring in more tools and options to help. In part 4, you will learn about a structured process for using challenges as an opportunity to learn and grow, learn strategies for responding to five common classroom challenges, and discover ways to help even learners who struggle the most to experience enhanced quality of life and engagement.

Bringing the OMPK Program to All Learners to Promote Quality of Life and Engagement

CHAPTER 11

The 5P Process for Supporting Positive Behaviors

Imagine for a moment that you have just begun a lesson for which you have spent hours planning; you are excited to share the lesson with the children in your classroom. In addition, you are being observed by your supervisor for your annual review. Children are listening quietly and engaging in the activity you have prepared when all of a sudden a child screams, hits a peer, and starts to run around the room, knocking down chairs and crying loudly. Everyone stops and stares at the child, lesson and activity forgotten. What would you do in this situation? How would you feel? If you are thinking you may be feeling anxious, frustrated, and uncertain, you are not alone!

The 5P Process (Protect, be Present, Prepare; Process emotions; Problem solve; Practice Prosocial behavior; and Praise) is a framework for helping a child who is exhibiting challenging behaviors, distress, or intense emotional outbursts to build skills and remedy the underlying problems that are causing the behaviors. It serves as an alternative to another P—Punishment—which is so often a consequence of challenging behaviors for children. We live in a culture of punishment, in which we spend more resources to put and keep people in prison than we do to provide preventative services, such as mental health interventions and community supports. As we discussed in chapter 1, children living in poverty and minority children are more likely to be labeled as having behavior disorders than to be given an accurate and appropriate diagnosis such as ADHD or autism. In addition, children living in poverty are more likely to experience social and communication delays, and many children with learning disabilities and trauma history also exhibit behavioral challenges due to internal struggles and hardships. The resulting skill deficits can result in challenging behaviors, lead to perpetuated "bad kid" labels, and ultimately contribute to the continued cycle of poverty and institutionalization as children receive increasing levels of punishment rather than the skill support they need.

And yet, it can be difficult to break the tendency to use punishment or exclusively external behavioral modification practices because in the moment that a challenging behavior occurs, we often feel uncertain about how to respond and do not consider the whole picture, which includes both what is happening inside the child and what is happening inside of us.

When children engage in acts of aggression, destruction, disruption, or dangerous behaviors such as running away or harming themselves, it can be overwhelming, because our job as adults is to protect the children in our care and keep them safe and engaged. It can be easy for us to react strongly when a child has acted in an explosive or dangerous way, and it may be difficult to know exactly what to do in the moment. This is especially true if a child's behavior or intense emotions trigger us in some way, or remind us of a painful experience we have had. While there are specialists such as occupational therapists, speech and language pathologists, counselors, and psychologists who can help children figure out and work through the internal challenges that may be driving the external behaviors, these professionals are not always available every time a child experiences a distressing situation and acts in a disruptive way.

The 5P Process was created for just these moments; it is structured as a consistent, stepwise method to help you support children who are struggling with behaviors that result in suffering, harm, or disruption to self, others, and/or the environment. It can not only help guide you and children through the tough times as they are happening, but also assist you in developing a plan to support children to learn, build new skills, address the underlying behavioral causes, and avoid repeating these behaviors in the future. *In the OMPK program, we view challenging behaviors not simply as problems to be managed and extinguished, but as red flags that indicate a need for social-emotional skill development and patience, support, nurturing, and connection.* Thus, rather than calling this aspect of the program a "behavior management program," I call it a "supportive teaching process." This process supports a child who is struggling to learn *what to do* instead of focusing on telling them *what not to do*. Although the 5P Process is based on an occupational therapy frame of reference—in that it is holistic, functional, contextualized, and considers the interplay of the child with their physical and social environments—it was designed to be used by anyone who wishes to help children become more independent and successful in navigating the difficult life situations that can result in challenging behaviors.

Skills and Abilities Required for Prosocial Behavior and Self-Regulation

As adults working with children, we often hold children to high standards for behavioral compliance with our perceived social norms. Most people tend to label socially acceptable and desirable behaviors as "good," though I have found that using strong judgment adjectives such as "good" and "bad" can make children feel failure or shame if they do not meet the standards of "good" behavior. For this reason, we use the word "prosocial" to describe actions, choices, and behaviors that are beneficial to themselves and others. For children to be consistently able to make prosocial choices and engage in prosocial behaviors, they must have the ability to self-regulate.

It is a common belief that self-control is something that can be done at will by children. However, many (actually, I would say most) adults have not yet perfected the art of self-regulation of emotional responses, peaceful conflict resolution, and inhibitory control, as it tends to be a life-long process. Think about the phenomenon of road rage, the content of reality television shows, the hoarding of supplies during pandemics and natural disasters, and the way that adults can be cruel and reactive on social media. And to take it a step further, some adults have difficulty exhibiting self-regulation when they are reacting to children who are struggling with a lack of control. Have you ever witnessed an adult yelling at a child for screaming? Or spanking a child for hitting? Yet, we often expect young children to exhibit self-regulation skills at an age before they have fully developed.

For a child to follow social rules and demonstrate prosocial choices, behaviors, and actions, they must develop many important self-regulation skills. Some of the skills necessary for self-regulation in preschool children include self-awareness, emotional competence, inhibitory control of impulses and behaviors, social awareness, and theory of mind. *When children are lacking these skills, they may be unable to follow classroom rules or expectations for behavior no matter how much they want to, or how big the reward or punishment.* This is why, no matter how good the intentions, sticker and reward charts often do not work, or work only on a short-term basis. There is no sticker big or sparkly enough to bridge a skill gap. Each part of the 5P Process has been developed to target these developmental skills to help children build the abilities they need for self-regulation and quality of life. Let's review a few of these skills and abilities before we move on to the 5P Process itself. For your reference, supporting studies are cited in case you wish to learn more about these developmental concepts.

Self-Awareness

Self-awareness involves a child's understanding of their physical bodies and their emotions. By age three, children are able to form an understanding of the dimension of time and the concept of an enduring self, and they can express primary emotions (sadness, anger) and social emotions (guilt, embarrassment) (Rochat, 2003). Awareness of our bodies requires moment-to-moment integration of sensory information, including interoceptive (heart rate, temperature, pain, gut sensations), somatosensory (touch input), proprioceptive and kinesthetic (joint and muscle input, body movement), vestibular (position of head in relation to gravity), and special sense (vision, hearing, taste, olfaction) information.

If that wasn't enough, there is also the ever-changing interface and communication between our bodies and the physical and social environment. Decreased physical awareness can impact a child's ability to be safe (such as noticing and avoiding injury due to environmental obstacles) and to follow social norms (such as maintaining appropriate personal space during social conversations, working in small groups, and waiting in line). Additionally, when young children are coping with a developmental delay, trauma history, or other disability, it can hinder typical development of these emerging body and emotional awareness skills. For example, a child who has decreased awareness of joints and muscles may find it difficult to sit up and sit still on the carpet, and may be physically unable to sit still without full concentration on their body, which would in turn affect their ability to simultaneously listen to the teacher. A child who has increased sensitivity to sounds or being touched may have anxiety during transition times when noise levels rise and children are closer together and moving unpredictably.

Body sensations and emotions have commonly been regarded and studied as separate phenomena; however, there has also been longstanding interest in the theory of *embodied emotion*—meaning a connection between the physiological sensations we perceive and the identification of emotions—and a growing body of research supports this connection (Craig, 2009; Critchley & Garfinkel, 2017; Damasio, 1999; James, 1890; Seth, 2013; Zaki et al., 2012). In other words, we experience physiological sensations prior to and along with our awareness of an emotional state. For example, we may feel nausea along with fear, feel a lump in our throat with sadness, feel burning cheeks with embarrassment.

Young children may identify emotions by the way they feel the emotions in their bodies, and this is often the foundation of developing three important emotional skills: emotional awareness, affect labeling, and emotional granularity. *Emotional awareness* is the ability to notice and be conscious of feelings and emotions. *Affect labeling* is the ability to name a feeling state. This basic process of just naming what emotion you are feeling has been found to decrease response in the amygdala (one of the main areas of the brain responsible for emotional reactions) to negative affective images (Lieberman et al., 2007). Have you ever noticed that some young children have only one or two words to describe their emotions—usually "happy" or "sad"? This can be due to decreased vocabulary and awareness of different emotions and different words for similar emotions, such as sad, disappointed, discouraged, depressed; or anger, frustration, envy. Having a rich emotional vocabulary and being able to identify specific feeling states leads to *emotional granularity,* or the ability to represent and communicate our discrete emotional state with precision and specificity (Barrett, 2006; Tugade et al., 2004). People who have increased emotional granularity and the ability to communicate emotions have been shown to demonstrate improved emotional coping skills (Barrett et al., 2001; Gentzler et al., 2005; Salovey et al., 1993). One final note is that many children who have language or cognitive delays can struggle more than typically developing peers with emotional awareness, affect labeling, and emotional granularity, especially when they are experiencing distress. To sum up this whole section, being aware of and able to name and describe our emotions can decrease how intensely we experience and respond to these emotions and positively affect how we cope with them.

Environmental and Social Awareness

Self-regulation does not just happen in a vacuum of our own self-awareness. The regulation of our bodies and emotions can affect the physical and social environments with which we are interconnected, and our social awareness can in turn help us to further develop self-regulation. However, young children are just beginning to develop social awareness. They may need assistance understanding that their emotions affect not only their actions and words, but also their nonverbal means of expression—such as body language, facial expression, and voice tone—which can also have helpful or harmful consequences. When children are feeling an emotion such as shame or fear, they may unintentionally present to others as someone who is withdrawn, detached, or cold; if children are angry at themselves and experiencing regret, they may use an aggressive tone when responding to a teacher's question, even though they may not feel angry at the teacher. Furthermore, young children are just beginning to develop *theory of mind,* which is necessary for them to engage in perspective taking. Theory of mind is the awareness of the perspective and emotional states of others and of their own experience and expression of empathy. These skills are essential for a child to be able to understand how their actions impact others, and also to make a meaningful apology. For example, if a child has cut in front of another child in line because they want to take the next turn, they may not be able to understand how the other child feels because they can only understand their own perspective of not wanting to wait. In this case, if the child is forced to apologize, they may not understand why and therefore may not make a sincere and meaningful apology.

In addition, to exhibit prosocial behaviors and follow classroom rules, children must have awareness of their surrounding physical and social environments. Often, young children are focused so much on moving their own bodies or thinking their own thoughts that they fail to notice objects or people around them. For instance, a child may be concentrating so intently on carrying a wet picture they have painted, in order to show a teacher, that they step on and ruin a friend's artwork. Self-awareness, emotional competence, and social awareness are essential for effortful and inhibitory control of one's actions.

Inhibitory Control, Working Memory, and Flexibility

A full review of executive function and executive control is beyond the scope of this chapter, but it is helpful to have an overview of these important skills that underlie self-regulation. Inhibitory control can be simply viewed as the self-control we have over our impulses, such as the ability to wait for a delicious, piping hot French fry to cool down when we are very hungry so that we do not burn our mouths, to refrain from honking at the person in front of us the second a light turns green, or to not overly scratch an itchy bug bite. Inhibitory control in the rhythm of life enables a child to balance impulse and motivation with external expectations and social rules so that they may suppress a preferred or reflexive response and execute a nondominant response (Rhoades et al., 2009). In other words, children are able to hold themselves back from doing something for immediate gratification because they know there are rules for the greater good, or for the long term, or because there may be negative consequences. Children who have developed inhibitory control are able to wait for a reasonable amount of time with their hands raised to be called on instead of shouting out a response to a teacher's question; they are able to refrain from striking a child who has just screamed angry words in their face; they are able to sit in their seats instead of running around. Inhibitory control involves a spectrum of skills including waiting for a preferred item or activity, slowing down movements, go/no-go response to signals, effortful attention, and controlling voice volume (Kochanska et al., 1997; Kochanska et al., 2000; Kochanska et al., 1996). If you remember from chapter 8, these are the very categories that make up the inhibitory control bell exercises. Not only is inhibitory control vital to prosocial behaviors and choices, but it has also been linked to improved executive function and academic performance in early and later childhood (Bull et al., 2008; Diamond, 2002 Kirkham et al., 2003). But inhibitory control is not just about having good intentions for self-control; it also requires our ability to remember social rules, goals, and strategies.

Working memory is our ability to hold relevant information in our minds long enough to use it. Research has shown that working memory foundations are in place by age four (Alloway et al., 2006; Gathercole et al., 2004). Working memory includes the ability to remember the rules and expectations of a given task or social situation as well as our goals. Think back to the "closing the tabs" visual in chapter 5; working memory can be viewed as the computer screen in our minds, with open tabs of relevant information that we are using in any given moment. We may have tabs open for our goals, plans, and strategies and for new tasks; emerging ideas; and prior information—our working memory is the ability to manipulate all of that information in a given moment. You can see how this function would be vital to a child's abilities to remember rules, the different steps of a task, and information necessary to solve a problem, and how it can link to inhibitory control. In fact, it has been shown that working memory and inhibitory control are difficult to differentiate before age seven, as they are so interconnected (Shing et al., 2010). Simply stated, if children are expected to follow rules, they must be able to keep the rules in their memory. If a child has too many "windows" open, they may not be able to see and access the "rule" tab. For example, consider a child who is learning a new skill of writing their name and becomes so excited that they forget to modulate their own voice volume—the child may know they are not supposed to talk loudly, but that tab has been "minimized" so that they can access windows for new and emerging skills of fine motor coordination, visual motor integration, and orthographic recall. To take the metaphor a step further, a child may be so focused on certain tabs and windows that they are resistant to opening up new ideas or ways to solve a problem.

Flexibility refers to the ability to shift from one idea, task, choice, or response to another as situations, task demands, and circumstances change. This skill is necessary for resilience and adaptability. As with working memory, studies have found that this ability emerges during the preschool years, between the age of four and five (Buttelmann & Karbach, 2017; Doebel & Zelazo, 2015; Moriguchi & Hiraki, 2011). Given that this skill of seeing different solutions, choices, and perspectives is just developing during early childhood, it makes sense that preschool children often do not listen to reason when their minds are made up or when they are set on getting their way!

Many of the OMPK Daily Practices, such as the meditation practices, bell practices, Feelings Finder practices, and yoga practices work on building a child's self-awareness, emotional awareness, inhibitory control, working memory, and flexibility in problem solving. This is because these skills are essential to self-regulation, learning, and engagement, and are often not yet developed in young children. This can be especially true when a child is experiencing a developmental delay, has a history or trauma or stress, lives in an unpredictable environment, or is around adults or other children who do not demonstrate and model functional inhibitory control. Repeated practice can help a child to build foundational self-regulation skills, but some children require more specialized and targeted support to learn self-regulation in daily life. The 5P Process is intended to help you guide a child through a challenging situation; to build existing or emerging skills, such as self-awareness, emotion regulation, inhibitory control, and working memory; and to gain new skills, such as flexibility and perspective taking, that we as adults often take for granted and assume that preschool children have already developed.

The 5P Process

Often, when children are having meltdowns and big feelings, it can make us feel uncomfortable and can result in our reacting in a way to try to make the child's actions and feelings stop. When children are acting aggressively or engage in hurtful or disruptive behaviors, we may take these actions personally or see the child as deliberately ignoring rules or trying to manipulate the situation. When children exhibit challenging behaviors, adults often respond by ignoring the behavior, giving a time-out, or using punishment. However, these consequences can send a message to the child that they are not loved and accepted when they are having a rough time or having difficult emotions. These types of consequences also do not provide a means to teach a child the skills they are lacking, and so often these behaviors recur.

I developed the 5P Process to meet three primary goals: (1) to frame challenging behaviors as a sign that the child is lacking or has not yet adequately developed coping, self-regulation, and/or social-emotional skills, and to notice any unconscious bias that may impact how we respond to the child; (2) to give the child time and support to experience, process, and cope with difficult feelings and life challenges, and solve problems as they arise in context; and (3) to empower the child with a sense of competency, resilience, and autonomy when facing life's challenges. The 5P Process involves the following five steps that promote a milieu of attachment and supported social-emotional learning in distressing situations:

1. **P**rotect, be Present, Prepare

2. **P**rocess emotions

3. **P**roblem solve

4. **P**ractice prosocial behavior

5. **P**raise

These steps have been ordered to help you to support a child from the beginning of a problem to the end of a new learning opportunity. We will now examine each of these steps in the recommended sequence. All examples given are actual examples with names changed to protect privacy.

Step 1: **P**rotect, be Present, Prepare

This first P is actually made up of three interconnected P's: Protect, be Present, Prepare. The reason these are grouped together is that they collectively help a child to feel safe and supported during vulnerable and challenging moments, when children are often admonished or pushed away. Children who are exhibiting challenging behaviors are frequently in a flight-fright-fight-freeze state, and may need to feel protected by a trusted adult who is present for and focused on them, rather than on their behaviors. Once the child feels safe and connected, they can prepare to engage in the rest of the 5P process.

PROTECT

When a child is exhibiting a behavior that may be harmful to themself or others, the first part of the 5P Process—protect, be present, prepare—is to ensure that the child and others are safe and to protect those involved from harm. *No matter how motivated a child is to follow behavioral expectations and rules, a child's desire for safety and self-preservation will often win out, as humans are wired to escape from pain and threats (real or perceived) and to seek protection.* This is true not only when faced with a real threat, but also when faced with a perceived threat. For example, if one child loudly bumps against another child accidentally, and this child has had a history of physical abuse, is sensitive to being touched, or has an increased startle response, the child may react with aggression due to a fight-or-flight response and hit the other child in self-defense. In these instances, many adults react with the impulse to admonish, raise their voice to, or punish the child who has engaged in the hitting behavior, especially if the adult did not see the accidental bump that triggered the reaction. This can serve to increase the child's fight-or-flight response and add shame or anger toward themselves to the feelings of fear the child was already experiencing.

In contrast, the first part of step 1 is to initiate actions to make children feel safe and protected. It is important to designate a secure area of the classroom early on so that children are aware that there is a place they can feel safe when they are in distress. In addition, having a designated area prevents other people from watching the child, which can often trigger additional embarrassment or shame. When you observe a child or children engaging in harmful or unsafe behaviors, it is essential to calmly take action to protect the children involved by moving children to a safe and quiet area, separating them as needed. Once they are in a secure place, you can quietly reassure the child that they are safe and protected. Finally, it is important to note that some children send out a silent alarm of distress; this point was brilliantly shared with me by a teacher at an OpenMind 5P training for Navajo Head Start teachers. While some children may scream, cry, or act out with aggression, others may withdraw and shut down when in severe emotional distress. Especially for these children, it is vital to be present and notice signals that the child has shut town or is in a state of "freeze."

BE PRESENT

A primary foundation of the OMPK 5P Process for supportive teaching is nonjudgmental acceptance in the present moment and the state of *equanimity* that we discussed in chapter 4. Part of the practice of equanimity involves being able to mindfully respond to a child who is exhibiting challenging behaviors or distress. Instead of taking behaviors personally, making a premature cognitive judgment based on the child's past actions, or blaming the child for the difficult behavior, we can try to view the challenging behavior as an opportunity to practice and build social-emotional skills in times of authentic rhythm-of-life challenges. Often as humans we experience something called *a fundamental attribution error,* in which we make a judgment that a person's actions have occurred because of their personality traits instead of the situation that may have triggered their response. For example, if someone cuts us off in traffic, we judge that the person did this because they are rude and inpatient, when actually, the person may be rushing to the hospital to see a loved one who is in critical condition. Part of being present for a child who is struggling with a challenging behavior is staying open to the idea that the child is reacting to a situation the best way that they can in that moment.

Finally, you may remember from chapter 1 and from earlier in this chapter that according to research, minority children have been more likely to be labeled as having "behavior problems" and more likely to receive punishment than therapeutic intervention when compared to white peers. As a school-based therapist, I have witnessed BIPOC children being suspended or punished for behaviors and actions that white children have engaged in and have received less severe or often no consequences for. It is vital that we take note of our own potential unconscious implicit biases in the present moment when we are helping children to ensure that these biases do not result in disparity, unequal treatment, or unfair consequences. Furthermore, we often make assumptions about people's emotional states based on not only their facial expressions, but also their body postures. Even more fascinating, our body postures can influence our perceptions of other people's emotions (Dael et al., 2012). Consider how children who have experienced trauma, often generational trauma, may exhibit, even unknowingly, a posture of fear, tension, or self-preservation. When this happens, we may unconsciously make judgments that a child is aggressive or threatening, when they may just have developed a protective body posture; this assumption could even be further impacted if we are carrying trauma in our own bodies.

Witnessing events such as extreme distress and aggression in young children can be painful and can often make us as teachers, therapists, and parents feel helpless, triggered, and overwhelmed, especially because these behaviors can impact other children in the classroom. Thus, after the child is in a safe area, the second part of step 1 is to recognize the opportunity to help the child, and to be fully present for the child while assessing the situation without judgment of the child, dwelling on the past, or worrying about what will happen in the future. Letting the child know that you are there for them and present for them no matter what can be the most powerful part of this entire process. In my field, we refer to this as *therapeutic use of self*, which I have always felt is a wonderful way to express the power of just being there for someone else. It is vital that you are aware of your own emotional and physical state, as a child will often follow your lead; if you can cultivate a calm and peaceful state, the child is more likely to feel calm as well.

Remember that your responsibility is not to make a child's feelings stop or go away, but to offer support and your presence as the child works through these feelings and they naturally begin to change. When you are present for the child, you can give the child time to calm down and move from a fight, flight, or freeze state to a state of feeling safe and connected. *It is important to remember that being calm does not necessarily mean being still.* While calm = still may be true for many neurotypical children, many neurodiverse children use movement such as pacing, rocking, or hand flapping for self-soothing. When a child cannot self-calm or self-soothe, you can help the child to feel safe by providing co-regulation, which means helping the child to self-regulate with modeling and support. Strategies for helping a child to deescalate can include, but are not limited to, encouraging deep breathing, offering comforting words or gestures, gently rocking alongside the child, and giving the child time and space in a quiet and safe area. I often tell a child in distress something like "You are safe. I am here, sending you love."

PREPARE

A child in distress who is having an extreme emotional reaction cannot simultaneously use the part of the brain responsible for logical thinking and problem solving (Siegal & Bryson, 2012). The practice of offering the child protection and your presence will help to prepare the child to engage in the next steps of the learning process. When you notice that the child has calmed down, you can assess their readiness to initiate the next step of the 5P Process. You can prepare the child for the next step by asking them if they feel safe, feel better, or are ready to explore how they are feeling.

Following are suggestions for ways to help a child to feel safe and connected through the first step of the 5P Process:

- Help the child access a designated safe area. If the child cannot transition to the safe area, ensure that the environment is secure and other children are out of harm's way.

- Once the child is in the safe area, if they continue to scream, cry, or exhibit signs of distress or aggressive behavior (e.g., throwing, kicking, pushing), offer compassionate reassurance: "It looks like you are feeling upset. I have compassion for you. I am here with you. You are safe."

- Take care to breathe calmly, show a positive or neutral emotional expression, and use a calm tone of voice. Remind the child that they are safe and that you will wait there with them until they feel better.

- Try to use as few words as possible when the child is showing distress, as additional stimulation can add to the child's stress, especially if the child struggles with language.

- Provide co-regulation strategies as needed to help the child become calm (e.g., offer a hug, offer to breathe with the child). You can also use the What Do I Need board (see online appendix L at http://www.newharbinger.com/49258) to help the child decide what they need to feel safe and calm.

- Give the child time and space, and when they are calm, thank them for being brave and for trusting you to help.

Step 1: Protect, be Present, Prepare—Example

A group of preschool children was doing puzzles on the carpet and the noise level was getting loud. Jason, who was having difficulty with the noise and with putting the puzzle together, stopped to cover his ears. Jamal came over and, trying to be helpful, took the puzzle piece away from Jason and placed it in the puzzle board, saying loudly, "That is where it goes!" Jason screamed, threw the puzzle at Jamal, and began to scratch his own face, while other children stared. Using step 1 of the 5P Process, Ms. Martinez came over to Jamal and asked if he was okay. Then Ms. Martinez checked on Jason and gently removed his hands from his face so he could not harm himself. She told Jason that they would go to the quiet and safe space together. Once in the safe space, Ms. Martinez asked Jason if he would like a hug or to do some breathing. He screamed "No!" and continued to cry. She said, "I will sit with you, be calm for you, and be here when you need me." After a few minutes, he tapped her shoulder and opened his arms. Ms. Martinez opened her arms and Jason leaned in for a hug. She asked him if he would like to do ten birdie breaths (see chapter 5) together. After breathing, she thanked him for being brave and calming down.

Step 2: *Process Emotions*

Once the child has become calmer and is no longer in distress, the next step of the 5P Process—process emotions—is to support the child's processing of emotions, first in the present moment, and then in the time prior to, during, and after the behavioral or distressing incident. *This is important because humans, especially small humans, are emotional beings, and our emotions are typically the biggest factor driving our actions and reactions.* Before helping the child to process their own emotions, it can be beneficial to share your own emotions and to model the process. When I support children during this step, I avoid sharing emotions that could make a child feel shame or increase negative self-concept, such as saying, "I felt sad when you spit at your friend." Instead, I share less triggering but still authentic feelings, such as, "I feel compassion because I see that you are hurting and I want to help you," or "I feel confused because I don't know why you are hurting." Once you have shared your feelings, help the child to identify their own feelings—first those that are happening in the present moment, then those that occurred just before the incident, and finally those experienced during the incident. Given the relationship between body sensations and emotions, and the fluctuating and impermanent nature of emotions, it is helpful to support children to identify

- which emotions they are feeling,

- where they are feeling the emotions in their bodies, and

- the intensity of their emotions.

You can use the Feelings Finder materials (made or purchased board, appendices F–J) presented in chapter 9 to help children to identify emotions. These tools can be especially beneficial for children who have a language disorder, speak a different primary language, or may be experiencing residual emotional distress that prevents clear verbal labeling and expression of emotions. This second step of the 5P Process involves the processes of *affect identification* (ability to identify emotions in oneself and others) and *expression* (ability to communicate emotions), which, along with perspective taking, are key aspects of self-regulation and trauma-sensitive intervention. It also helps to build *emotional competence.* This includes emotional expressiveness, emotion knowledge and understanding, and emotion regulation (Denham et al., 2003). Children require emotional competence to be able to control behavioral responses, engage in positive relationships with others, feel empathy and compassion, and focus on active learning (Brackett et al., 2011; Denham et al., 2003).

Following are suggestions for carrying out the second step of the 5P Process, which can help children to develop the emotional insight they will need to progress to the next steps of the 5P process:

- Start by sharing with the child how you are feeling and modeling the process of identifying which emotions you feel, where you feel them in your body, and the intensity of the emotions. Then ask the child to share, giving them time to respond if needed.

- If the child does not want to share, you can describe how their face or body language looks, and ask if you can guess how they felt. Often children may engage in emotional processing at this point, especially if you are wrong!

- Next, help the child to identify feelings prior to and during the emotional outburst or incident.

- Remind the child about impermanence and how no feelings last forever, but all feelings change. Demonstrate as needed by using the Feelings Finder board or other visuals in appendices F–J to illustrate how feelings can come and go and move around on the body or ask the child to show or tell you how their feelings changed throughout the process (e.g., during the incident the child felt 100 angry feelings and now feels only one).

- If another child was involved in the situation, support the child to identify how the other child may have felt to build perspective taking and empathy. If the other child is willing, you can ask the other child to express their feelings for the child you are working with.

- Thank the child for sharing their feelings and growing their brains, and reassure them that everyone has big feelings sometimes, and that we can make kind choices even when we have big feelings.

Step 2: Process Emotions—Example

A five-year old kindergarten child named Mohamed was standing beside his classmate Jessica, who was crying on the floor in the hallway after lunch. A teacher who was not their classroom teacher saw Jessica on the floor and assumed that Mohamed had been aggressive with her. The teacher reported to the child's primary teacher, Ms. Simpson, that Mohamed made a "bad choice" and should go to the principal's office. Mohamed began to cry and clench his fists. After ensuring Jessica was not hurt, Ms. Simpson took Mohamed to a quiet area of the classroom and gave him reassurance and time to calm down. Once he stopped crying, Ms. Simpson showed him the Feelings Finder board (see chapter 9) and demonstrated her own feelings, saying that she felt confused because she didn't see what happened, and felt love because she cared about both children. She asked Mohamed to share his feelings, and Mohamed indicated feeling embarrassed and sorry (remorseful). Ms. Simpson then asked how Mohamed felt before the incident, and he indicated that he felt silly before the incident. Even though Mohamed was able to speak, he needed to express his emotions visually with the Feelings Finder pictures before verbally describing what happened. Once he showed his feelings using the visual images, and Ms. Simpson repeated the feelings back him, Mohamed told Ms. Simpson what happened as follows: "We were being silly and we tickled each other. It was funny. Then I tripped and crashed into Jessica and she fell down. She was crying. I felt embarrassed and sorry." The teacher then asked if it was okay to ask Jessica how she felt. Jessica said she felt silly too and then scared because she fell. She shared the same sequence of events as Mohamed and said she knew it was an accident. Ms. Simpson thanked both children for sharing their feelings, and she reflected on the possibility of unconscious bias on the part of the original teacher, who had assumed that Mohamed had committed an aggressive act.

Step 3: **P**roblem Solve

When a child engages in an act of aggression, self-harm, disruptive behavior, or intense emotional meltdown, there is typically a reason, or a trigger that stems from a problem, which brings us to step 3 of the 5P Process—problem solve. The problem may be related to an environmental challenge (e.g., a small play area with limited toys for sharing, high noise levels); a physical challenge (e.g., a child with poor body awareness, decreased coordination, frequent fatigue from poor nutrition); a communication challenge (e.g., difficulty with expressive language); an executive function challenge (e.g., decreased inhibitory control, working memory, flexibility); or a social-emotional challenge (e.g., feeling a lack of control over one's situation, experiencing grief and loss, having low self-efficacy). Often, the problem is multifactorial in nature and can involve the interplay of challenges from our self and the physical and social environment. One thing I have noticed is that some children use negative statements about themselves (*I am bad, I am stupid*) to avoid the problem-solving process because it is difficult for them. In these cases, you can reassure the child that they are kind and smart, and that you are there to help them solve a new problem. The problem solving step of the 5P Process is about working with the child to identify the possible problem, exploring the possible causes and solutions to prevent the problem from happening again, and more importantly, making the child feel safer and more successful in the future. For this part of the process it is essential to motivate the child to engage in problem solving by explaining or reminding the child that mistakes and problems give our brains a chance to grow and learn new things and to make new choices for how to act.

It is important to get the child's input and use guided exploration and discovery to brainstorm possible causes of the problem and potential solutions for the future, especially given that young children most likely have not yet developed the flexibility to do this independently. Support the child to identify alternatives to engaging in a challenging behavior (for example, instead of ripping up a paper with a mistake on it, screaming, and banging on the table, you can crumple the paper into a tight ball and shoot it into the trash can to make a basket, and then ask for a new piece of paper to try again). You can also use the OpenMind Super Me visuals, materials, and/or practices (see chapter 9, online appendices L–O) as needed to help the child to learn to generalize these strategies in the academic environment. If you need additional suggestions for brainstorming potential strategies for problem solving, see chapter 13 on the CREATE framework. In addition, the modules in the next chapter can provide strategies for commonly experienced preschool problems.

Following are suggestions for the third step of the 5P Process, which can help children to feel empowered and to develop autonomy and a sense of competency for encountering problems or challenges in the future:

- Tell the child that when we make a mistake or experience something that hurts us it is a chance to grow and solve new problems.

- Invite the child to solve the problem: "Let's grow our brains and solve the problem!"

- Support the child to put on a problem-solving hat (real or imaginary) to solve the problem peacefully and identify calming and coping strategies. It may sound silly, but I have used paper problem-solving hats for this purpose—the simple uniform seems to give children an official shift to the role of problem solvers.

- Use humor as needed to motivate problem solving; for example, suggest a ridiculous solution to the problem first.

- Support the child to identify alternatives to engaging in a challenging behavior (e.g., take turns with a peer using a timer instead of snatching a toy away; give themself a big hug instead of saying mean things to themself).

- Avoid using judgment words like "good" and "bad," and use alternative words for positive behavioral choices (e.g., "kind choices," "nice asking voice," "waiting patiently") and negative behavioral choices (e.g., "hurtful choices").

- Thank the child for growing their brain and helping to solve the problem.

Step 3: Problem Solve—Example

A four-year old neurodiverse child named Alexis was observed yelling and then hitting a friend named Jeffrey, who was climbing up a slide, and then Alexis began to scream and cry. Their teacher, Teacher Mai, led Alexis through the first two steps of the 5P Process and discovered that she was feeling scared that Jeffrey would get hurt because he was breaking a rule. When Jeffrey didn't listen and continued to climb, Alexis hit him to make him stop. Teacher Mai worked with Alexis to identify an alternative solution, and they decided to use her strength of following the rules and give her the classroom job as the playground safety monitor. Whenever Alexis would see another child breaking a rule and doing something unsafe, she would say, "Stop, be safe!" and report it to the teacher instead of physically trying to stop the child.

Step 4: Practice Prosocial Behavior

The fourth step of the 5P Process—practice prosocial behavior—teaches children that even when they make a mistake or a hurtful choice, they can do something positive to help repair the damage. This step involves supporting the child to recognize and experience the opportunity to practice compassion for those who may have been hurt in the behavioral incident. Too often, adults try to demand that children apologize while they are still upset, and the apology may not be authentic, or even worse, the child may feel resentment about being forced to apologize before they understand what they are apologizing for! The first three steps of the 5P Process help the child calm and settle (step 1), process emotions (step 2), and engage in problem solving (step 3). Once they've done that, they are much better equipped to engage in a prosocial act to make amends for a hurtful choice or disruptive behavior. It is important to note that even though this is a five-step sequence, the steps do not have to occur together in a short time frame—children may need more time to move to step 4.

Following are suggestions for the fourth step of the 5P process, practice prosocial behavior, which can help children to express compassion and remorse with a meaningful prosocial action:

- Model feeling empathy and compassion for the child and for other people who may have been hurt in the behavioral incident.

- Give the child options for making amends for hurtful or disruptive behavioral choices by choosing to engage in a helping or prosocial behavior; often these are natural consequences, such as cleaning up a mess their behavior contributed to. You may choose to use the same supported problem solving as you did in step 3 to brainstorm ideas for prosocial actions.

- Provide the child with choices for how they can help the other person feel better after a behavioral incident. Use the Super Me Superpower of the Day Poster Cards (online appendix N) or Classroom Poster (appendix O) to help the child choose if needed.

- If the child chooses to make an apology, you can use the OpenMind "I'm sorry" format (chapter 9 for brief Super Me practice; or module G, at http://www. newharbinger.com/49258, for the full version) to help the child include the parts of a meaningful and kind apology.

- Thank the child for helping their community and friends.

- Help the child show compassion for themselves for making a mistake and feel proud of themselves for doing a kind act.

Step 4: Practice Prosocial Behavior—Examples

In this section, we will explore examples of step 4 prosocial actions chosen by children in the examples for steps 1, 2, and 3 above.

Jason (Step 1 Example). *Once Jason calmed down (step 1), he was able to process his emotions (step 2) and communicate that he felt sad because he could not figure out how to complete his puzzle, felt angry at Jamal for snatching it away and doing it for him, and felt overwhelmed by the noise in the play area. For step 3, Jason and Ms. Martinez engaged in problem solving and came up with a strategy for Jason to get up and ring the bell for the bell exercise (see chapter 8) when the noise level got* *too loud. This would cause the class to pause and be quiet and allow Jason to have a reset. Jason then apologized (step 4) to Jamal for throwing the puzzle at him, and Ms. Martinez worked with Jamal to thank him for trying to help, while reminding him not to touch a friend's puzzle unless the friend asked for help. Jason decided to help Ms. Martinez clean up and organize the puzzle area as a prosocial act.*

Mohammed and Jessica (Step 2 Example). *Mohamed and Jessica worked with Ms. Simpson to problem solve a strategy for walking in line safely if they were feeling silly (step 3). They decided to each walk with their arms hugging themselves so they wouldn't be tempted to play or tickle each other in line because they were such good friends and liked to be silly. Mohamed got Jessica an ice pack from the school nurse for her knee and gave her a hug as a prosocial act (step 4).*

Alexis and Jeffrey (Step 3 Example). *With Teacher Mai's assistance, Alexis drew a picture for Jeffrey of the safe way to go down the slide and added a heart to it to express love. Because Alexis was stuck on the idea that Jeffrey had broken a rule, this was a way for her to do a kind act (step 4) that also included the ability to teach Jeffrey the rule that she valued.*

Step 5: Praise

When correcting a child who has not followed a rule or expectation, we as adults often focus on *what not to do* (e.g., "Don't run in the hallway"; "Don't dump out the toy bin"; "Don't kick your friends"; "Don't pick your nose"). This can be confusing for the child because it does not tell the child *what to do*. Steps 3 (problem solve) and 4 (prosocial practice) help to teach a child *what to do*. Step 5—praise—reinforces those actions with authentic and specific praise or expressions of gratitude. In this step, you provide verbal praise, gratitude, or recognition for a positive behavioral choice or effort that the child has demonstrated during the 5P Process. Remember that the more specific the praise is, the more the child will understand exactly what did work and which behaviors were positive and beneficial to the developmental, social, or academic situation. A simple "good job" is a kind gesture, but it does not give the child information about what specifically they did that was "good."

It is important to remember that if the child has broken a rule that calls for a specific consequence, the child will still receive the consequence. For instance, if the child engages in an aggressive action that breaks a classroom code of conduct and the child must be sent home, this will still occur. The difference is that the discipline doesn't end with the child receiving the consequence, feeling upset about their actions, and being sent home. Rather, it ends after the child has gone through the 5P Process and has received authentic praise for engaging in the learning opportunity working toward building skills and strategies to prevent recurrence of the behavior in the future.

Following are suggestions for step 5 of the 5P process, praise, which allows children to receive reinforcement and recognition of their effort, their willingness to learn, and the prosocial choices they made during the 5P Process:

- Provide verbal praise, gratitude, and recognition for positive behavioral choices. If a child feels uncomfortable receiving compliments in public, you can quietly praise the child.

- Use the Super Me materials (appendices M–O) as needed to give the child specific attention for the kind choices they made following the hurtful choice or disruptive action.

- Show gratitude for the child's positive choices and actions by thanking the child for specific behaviors (e.g., "Thank you so much for cleaning up the crayons and for working so hard on the beautiful picture for Mr. Li").

- Support children to praise themselves for their effort(s).

Step 5: Praise—Examples

In this section, we will look at examples of authentic praise given to the children in the examples for steps 1 through 3 above.

Jason (Step 1 Example). *Ms. Martinez praised Jason for staying in the quiet area, for trusting her, and for doing breathing practices to calm down. She was also able to thank him for sharing his feelings, thinking of a great idea for ringing the bell, and cleaning up the puzzle area.*

Mohammed and Jessica (Step 2 Example). *Ms. Simpson praised Mohamed and Jessica for sharing their feelings and working together to think of a safe strategy for walking in line. She thanked Mohamed for getting Jessica an ice pack to make her knee feel better.*

Alexis (Step 3 Example). *Teacher Mai offered praise to Alexis for respecting the rules, sharing her feelings, keeping her peers safe by being the playground safety monitor, and engaging in a kind action for making an apology.*

Putting It All Together: A 5P Process Case Study

The following case study was written by Emilee Schaumann, an OMPK trainer. The names of the children have been changed, but the case study illustrates an actual use of the 5P Process in a Head Start classroom.

Ollie was building with wooden blocks, when Devi came over and asked if she could build with him. Ollie said, "No, I'm building this. You can build your own, over there" (Ollie had exceptional verbal skills). Devi persisted and tried to build onto Ollie's structure and in doing so knocked part of it down. Ollie became very upset, knocked down the rest of his own structure, and began to leave the area, then turned around, stomped his foot, and screamed, "You're not my friend!" He then ran to the quiet area, fell on a pillow, and began to cry.

Step 1: Protect, Be Present, Prepare. I followed Ollie to the quiet area, sat near him on the floor, and let him know that I was there when he was ready. He at first told me to go away and stated, "I don't like you!" I offered to move a bit away from the area if that would make him more comfortable, and he quickly changed his mind and said, "No, stay there." I thanked him for allowing me to sit next to him and said that he could sit in my lap if he would like. After a few minutes, he did climb into my lap and stopped crying.

Step 2: Process Emotions. I asked Ollie how he was feeling. We used the Feelings Finder board (i.e., the faces cut out of the Feelings Finder Faces Key, and the Feelings Finder Outline, available at http://www.newharbinger.com/49258) to supplement the conversation, and he said he was feeling "sad and a little angry." He placed the sad face on the figure's face and the angry face on the figure's hand of Feelings Finder Outline (see chapter 9). We talked about how he felt when he was playing alone (calm and happy), how he felt when Devi asked to play (shy and nervous), and how he felt when Devi didn't respect his request to play by himself (angry). We also discussed how Devi might have felt when she was not allowed to play (sad), how she might be feeling for damaging his structure (at first he said happy, then changed his mind and said sorry), and how she may have felt when he yelled at her (scared and sad).

Step 3: Problem Solve. We then began to talk about what we could do in a similar situation in the future. At first Ollie said, "Well, I told her she couldn't play with me. She just didn't listen." I assured him that it was okay to want to play by ourselves sometimes; he was working so hard on his block structure. We agreed that if he needed help explaining to a friend that he wants to build by himself, he could ask a teacher for help. We also tried to come up with ideas that would make it okay for Devi to build with him; maybe she could build a separate structure that could be part of the same "village." He also said that it would have been "so easy" to fix the part of his structure that Devi knocked down. After this reflection, he said, "That would have been so easy. Now I have to redo the whole thing."

Step 4: Prosocial Practice. Ollie decided that he was going to rebuild the structure but ask Devi if she would like to help. He went back over to the block area and told her that he was sorry for yelling at her. Then he said, "I'm gonna build a new house and this time you can build with me. You can build your house there and be my neighbor."

Step 5: Praise. I thanked Ollie for working so hard to make it right and allowing Devi to play with him. I also commented that I noticed that he seemed very proud and excited to be the "leader" as he and Devi built the new block house neighborhood.

Pause for Reflection…

The 5P Process—Protect, be present, protect; Process emotions; Problem solve; Prosocial practice; Praise—was designed to give children a comprehensive learning experience when faced with a challenge or difficulty that results in a behavior that is disruptive or harmful to themselves or others. While it may seem like it requires a lot of time, it is a time investment that will result in learning, skill building, connection, and improved quality of life in the future. When you first begin the process, it may take time, especially if you are also new at learning how to use the Daily Practices from chapters 7 through 10, which can accompany the 5P Process steps. It works best when one teacher, paraprofessional, counselor, or therapist is able to stay with the child through the whole process for comfort and continuity, though this may not be possible due to teacher resources and ratios. Remember that it is not your job to make a child's feelings stop or to control the child's actions. Rather, you can help the child to feel loved, connected, and supported unconditionally, and to learn new skills for coping when difficult emotions and situations arise. Use the OpenMind REMIND practices (see chapters 4–5) to help you maintain a state of equanimity and nonjudgmental presence throughout the 5P Process.

In chapter 12, we will explore five common challenges experienced by preschool and kindergarten classroom teachers. We will also learn strategies, involving several modules, for each challenge to support children's positive engagement and enhance the problem-solving aspect of the 5P Process.

Strategies for Responding to Common Classroom Challenges:
The Positive Engagement Support Modules

The 5P Process we covered in chapter 11 was designed so that it could be modified for children of all abilities, though some children may not be able to fully engage in all steps, especially step 3, problem solve, due to differences in chronological and developmental age and cognitive, executive function, and/or language abilities. The positive engagement support (PES) modules were developed to offer you a means for applying general strategies to aid in problem solving and to support learning opportunities and engagement for five common challenging classroom situations that can act as barriers to teaching and learning if not addressed, or if addressed with punishment.

These common problems have been identified by teachers throughout the country in different preschool and kindergarten settings and reflect situations that can occur often in this population, as young children are just learning to build social-emotional skills. The modules were developed to provide extra strategies that complement the OpenMind program to help teachers navigate these challenges and support children where they need it most. Another purpose of these modules is to help you shift your perspective from viewing these challenges as negative "behaviors" to seeing them as a less functional method of social and academic engagement due to a deficit in foundational skills. The following table lists the name of each module, the skills it supports, and the challenging actions it can help to address.

Positive Engagement Support Modules	Skills to Build and Develop	Challenging Actions to Decrease
Module 1: Receiving attention and increasing social connections	Attachment and bonding, relationship building, self-efficacy	Seeking attention through disruptive behaviors, yelling out, or talking during quiet time or while others are talking
Module 2: Engaging in teacher-directed activities and cooperating with teacher requests	Cognitive flexibility, acceptance, nonjudgment, emotion regulation	Difficulty with or refusing to engage in a teacher-directed activity, refusing or ignoring teacher requests
Module 3: Staying present in the learning and/or eating area	Inhibitory control, self-awareness, self-regulation	Difficulty staying in one place, running around, wandering around, leaving the area without asking
Module 4: Making transitions within a routine and coping with changes	Anticipating and coping with changes, autonomy, emotion regulation	Difficulty with transitioning appropriately to or from an activity or area or shifting from one task to the next
Module 5: Sharing and working with others	Cognitive flexibility, compromising, emotion regulation	Difficulty sharing with peers, refusing to collaborate or cooperate with peers

What Is Common to All of These Classroom Challenges?

If you look closely at the five different common challenges, you will see that they are all related to a child's need to feel safe and connected and to have some autonomy and control in their physical and social environments. In other words, these challenges result from children trying to make sure their most basic needs are met, even if they are using means that may be disruptive, aggressive, or against social and classroom rules. As you may remember from the previous chapter, there are many prerequisite skills that enable a child to follow classroom rules and expectations, including self-awareness and emotional competence; environmental and social awareness; and inhibitory control, working memory, and flexibility. Much like the 5P Process, the PES Modules provide a means to stimulate learning and emergence of new skills or development and refinement of lacking skills as an alternative to providing negative consequences or punishment, which can often result in shame or feelings of helplessness.

An Overview of the Positive Engagement Support Modules

Each of the following sections provides a description of the common classroom challenge along with strategies to help support children to overcome the challenge, to feel more socially and academically engaged, and to increase self-efficacy and a sense of competence. Each section will contain strategies to help you to:

- act before a challenging action occurs to help prevent the difficult situation or problem from occurring or escalating

- teach a child to build skills to make them feel more autonomy and success

- increase a child's social and academic engagement

- foster and build quality of life and positive learning experiences for the child

Module 1: Receiving Attention and Increasing Social Connections

Children often seek attention from adults and peers to feel acknowledged, validated, seen, and heard. This drive to be noticed and accepted by others can be stronger if a child highly values social connections and attention, or if a child has not experienced consistent attention or connection from family, friends, and others. You may have found that some children tend to call out, get up, run around, or "perform" to make people notice, laugh, or respond. While it is understandable that this may happen in a preschool or kindergarten class from time to time as kids are learning social rules and self-control, or in the context of having fun, when it happens often or with increased intensity it can be very disruptive and make teaching a challenge! When children are struggling with foundational skills of attachment and bonding, social awareness, self-awareness, inhibitory control, and/or self-efficacy, they may seek attention through methods such as talking out of turn, saying inappropriate things or using materials inappropriately, or acting overly silly. In addition, children who feel overwhelmed or have a history of trauma may be seeking attention to get help to escape a situation they may find uncomfortable, even if they are not aware of it. This module will guide you through some strategies to help you to support children through these challenges and to build more functional methods for receiving attention, connection, recognition, and a feeling of autonomy and positive self-concept.

Things you can do *before* a child engages in the challenging action:

1. Before starting an activity, tell the class or small group some specific things that you will be paying attention to (e.g., sitting up tall like a tree, using a kind voice, trying hard); this will tell the child exactly how to earn extra positive attention by engaging in positive actions.

2. Before and leading up to group activities, give specific praise for positive interactions and actions (e.g., "You are walking so slowly and carefully to circle— thank you!").

3. If it appears that the child's actions are escalating, such as moving from picking up materials at an inappropriate time to reaching an arm back to throw items across the room, provide an opportunity for connection so that the child feels safe, loved, and accepted before the action starts to escalate. Once they are calm, support the child in using a Feelings Finder practice to show you how they felt and where, then offer support in problem solving. For example, if a child reports his hands were feeling "silly," you could offer to let the child try to demonstrate to the class how to throw a paper ball into the bin while making a funny face after the lesson is over.

4. Prior to activities and situations in which the child may seek attention, offer the child an opportunity to have a helping, sharing, or leadership role. For the example above, you could offer to let the child to hold a special clicker and click every time someone raises their hand. In this way, the child can have something to do with their hands when feeling "silly" and receive attention for helping the teacher track hand raising.

5. Offer the child an opportunity for choice making in front of peers to receive attention and feel autonomy. For example, before large-group circle, ask the

child to select the morning meditation option (if the child is nonverbal or shy, they can point or demonstrate; if the child has the language skills, they can explain how to do it to the class).

6. Offer the child opportunities to have a peer "buddy" to play with during free play time.

7. Make frequent and positive contact with the child during the day, and thank the child regularly for positive behavioral choices and actions, for effort, and for engagement.

8. Model being present for the child (e.g., make eye contact, get down at the child's level, listen mindfully), thank the child for being present, and talk to the child about how others feel when we are present for them.

Things you can *teach* a child to do to take care of their own needs:

1. Support the child to request attention by asking others, "Are you present for me?" and teach the child to look for signals that it is time to engage in conversation, speak out, or get up and be silly.

2. Teach the child how to know whether someone can be present for them (e.g., the other person is not engaged in talking to or helping someone else).

3. Teach the child what they can do if they have to wait for someone to be present for them.

4. Teach the child to seek help from an adult if they do not feel safe by asking or using a signal.

5. Teach the child the meaning of positive social emotions, such as love, compassion, and gratitude, and how to express these feelings to others in the rhythm of life using the Feelings Finder practices.

Things you can do to *increase* the child's attention and social connection:

1. Provide specific praise when the child is being present and/or asks if another person is present for them; use the Super Me Classroom Poster as an extra visual for reinforcing kind actions and effort.

2. Use the Super Me Classroom Poster and/or Kindness and Compassion Reporting practices to help the child receive attention for noticing the kind choices of others (e.g., asking nicely, sitting nicely in group).

3. Offer gratitude flowers and/or gestures of thanks (e.g., hug, high five) through-out the day when the child has put forth effort, used kind actions, helped others, or requested attention appropriately.

Quality-of-life factors these strategies *strengthen* in the child:

1. Increased awareness of their own emotions, other people's emotions, and the effects of their actions on others

2. Increased ability to request attention in a positive and nondisruptive manner

3. Increased tendency to feel safe, connected, seen, recognized, and valued

Module 2: Engaging in Teacher-Directed Activities and Cooperating with Teacher Requests

Despite our best efforts at planning to make social, play, and academic learning opportunities exciting and engaging, there are times when children do not cooperate with planned activities and our requests. Sometimes children may refuse a request or activity by directly saying no, and sometimes the child may engage in a nonverbal no and leave a work area, ignore a request, or reject classroom learning or play materials. To many adults, these behaviors can look like a child is being noncompliant or disrespect-ful. However, many children who do not cooperate with a teacher request or activity are missing or have decreased foundational skills in the areas of task initiation (the ability to get started), sequencing, working memory, flexibility (being able to do a task in more than one way, or wanting to do something else), acceptance and nonjudgment (being able to do a task that is not their favorite or that they think will not be fun), language (understanding task directions or requests), fine motor skills, gross motor skills, and/or sensory processing skills. Often when children feel like a task's demands exceed their ability, they can't remember the steps, they are fearful that they will not like the task or it will be uncomfortable, they do not fully understand what they are being asked, or they do not find the task meaningful, they may not want to engage in the task, and adults will often label these tasks as "nonpreferred" tasks. An important note to remember is that it is easy to develop an "ableist" mindset and expect all children to find meaning in "typical" play and learning tasks. It can be difficult to discern whether a child is refusing to do a task because they are lacking skills or because they do not find meaning in it (especially for neurodiverse children). This module will provide you with strategies to help you support children to feel more competent, safe, and willing to put forth effort to engage in teacher-directed activities and cooperate with teacher requests, or self-advocate for an alternative and more meaningful activity.

Things you can do *before* a child engages in the challenging action:

1. Before asking a child to engage in a "nonpreferred" activity, give the child choices about the activity (e.g., "We are going to walk to circle time now; do you want to walk like a bear or like a puppy?").

2. Before asking a child to engage in a nonpreferred activity, ask the child for help with a task that may be motivating or simple (e.g., "Oops, I dropped my pen, can you please pick it up for me? Thank you!"). This way, the child enters the nonpreferred task feeling helpful and competent.

3. When supporting a child to engage in a nonpreferred task, consider the child's interests and find ways to integrate these into the task to increase motivation (e.g., "It would be so cool if you could trace letters using a race car!").

4. When a child is faced with a situation that requires cooperation and may be difficult, use OpenMind intrinsic motivation language and visuals (see Learning Activities Module D, http://www.newharbinger.com/49258) as needed to support an attitude of growth (e.g., "Wow! You are waiting so patiently; you are really growing your heart and brain! Your hands are getting really strong when you use those scissors!").

5. Support the child to use the "Is it difficult? Is it fun?" scale (see Learning Activities Module D) to learn about judgment and nonjudgment of activities the child typically avoids because they perceive them as difficult or boring.

6. If you believe a child may need assistance because a task is too difficult in terms of initiation or execution, ask the child if you can try it together.

7. If you believe a child is struggling with understanding what you have asked or has misinterpreted what you have asked, offer to show the child what you mean or explain it in a different way.

8. Before asking a child to engage in a task or request that they have refused in the past, take time to explain the reason behind the activity or request.

Things you can _teach_ a child to do to take care of their own needs:

1. Teach the child to cope with difficult emotions that may arise when they are asked to engage in a nonpreferred task, and reinforce how these feelings are impermanent and do not last forever.

2. Teach the child to ask for help when having difficulty engaging in a teacher-directed activity and to ask for a break as needed.

3. If you feel that an activity is not meaningful for a child because the child has prioritized a self-soothing activity such as pacing, teach the child to self-advocate to engage in the preferred activity.

4. Teach the child to ask for help to get started or to remember what to do next.

5. Teach the child the definition of a compromise, and how to ask for a compromise if a task is too difficult.

6. Using the Feelings Finder practices (Daily Practice 5, chapter 9), teach the child to understand how _teachers_ feel during situations that require a child to engage in nonpreferred tasks (e.g., the teacher feels compassion for the child who has difficulty using scissors and wants to help them learn).

7. Support the child to notice and reinforce when other people are listening to the teacher and engaging in activities; this can be done as a teacher helper job.

Things you can do to _increase_ the child's engagement:

1. Provide praise when the child cooperates with teacher requests and engages in classroom activities. Use the Super Me actions (e.g., cooperating, effort, listening, encouragement) as needed.

2. Provide praise for effort over performance (e.g., "Wow, I love how hard you are trying; you are so brave for trying something new!").

3. Allow the child time to calm down in a safe space with the be-like-a-tree calm down jar (chapter 9) or other preferred item if they become upset about making an effort to engage in a nonpreferred activity.

4. Offer for the child to do a part of the activity instead of the whole activity.

5. Help the child to break down the nonpreferred activity into steps and include a break midway through.

6. If the child makes an attempt to use appropriate and kind strategies, praise their effort and support them in problem solving what to do differently next time.

Quality-of-life factors these strategies *strengthen* in the child:

1. Increased ability to calm down when upset about the need to cooperate with teacher-directed activities and requests

2. Increased willingness to try new or challenging activities or stay engaged in activities perceived as "boring" or "too difficult"

3. Increased engagement in teacher directed activities

4. Increased sense of autonomy and control in situations that require cooperation with teacher requests and the classroom schedule

Module 3: Staying Present in the Learning and/or Eating Area

One of the biggest challenges of teaching and working with young children is that young children are hardwired to move! They learn by moving during play and exploration. However, sometimes learning experiences require children to stay in one place so that they can be present to receive new lessons and engage in activities, including those that require a degree of stillness for safety, such as during eating. Many young children in a classroom setting have not yet developed the foundational skills to be able to stay in one place because they have limited awareness or control of their body movements, they do not have the strength or endurance to sit unsupported to sit for long periods of time, they use movement for self-regulation, or they have limited attention that prevents them from staying in one place. As adults who work with preschool and kindergarten children, we realize that young children need frequent opportunities to move and that sitting completely still for more than several minutes is not realistic. However, when children are struggling to the degree that they are running, rolling, and jumping around during times for eating and instruction, it can be very disruptive to the whole classroom environment. This module will share strategies for helping children to stay present in the learning and/or eating area for a reasonable and developmentally appropriate amount of time.

Things you can do *before* a child engages in the challenging action:

1. Before circle time, meal time, small group, or table-based activities, provide the child with a choice between two positions for working (e.g., kneeling on a chair, standing, sitting on special cushion, sitting on a stool, sitting on teacher's lap).

2. Give the child specific instructions for each position option. Support the child to make a choice before transitioning to the learning or eating area. Allow the child to move or alternate between these two positions during table-based, small group, or circle time activities. The child may benefit from an option to sit against a wall or a bookshelf when in large group to get extra body input and support.

3. Give the child a finite amount of time to stay present in the learning and/or eating area, and emphasize that *being present does not have to involve sitting still*. This is especially important for children who may engage in self-regulation strategies such as rocking or hand flapping; just because a behavior is not neurotypical does not mean it should be discouraged if it makes the child feel more comfortable and more engaged.

4. If the child must sit and listen in a circle setting, or wait for a turn, they may benefit from holding a waiting object that is grounding, nonstimulating, and not distracting (e.g., weighted stuffed animal).

5. Provide the child with opportunities to move that are functional to the sitting or circle activity (e.g., pointing to specific items in a book every few minutes or so; holding a pointer to point to the letter as a helper).

6. If you notice the child is showing signs that they want to move, ask them if they want to have a movement break (e.g., weight-bearing yoga poses), and support them to practice self-advocating for and taking a timed movement break.

7. Give the child their own special sitting spot if they enjoy sensory input or need a visual cue for personal space. This will help them to understand where their body should be. Some ideas to try include a textured sitting spot, a weighted rice bag, or an inflatable cushion to sit on that gives some movement input.

Things you can _teach_ a child to do to take care of their own needs:

1. Teach the child to use words or other means to let you know when they need to leave the working, eating, or learning area (e.g., raise their hand or hold up a popsicle stick sign to ask to be excused). Prompt the child as needed to ask to obtain a sensory item or movement break.

2. Teach the child where to access sensory items for waiting and sitting time, and encourage them to independently request and select an item to use as a fidget toy for self-regulation as needed.

3. Teach the child physical movement options that they can use when they need to move (e.g., push-ups, planks, weight-bearing yoga poses, qi-gong shaking, rocking on a peanut ball in a designated area).

4. Teach the child safe and appropriate ways to use sensory items and movement items.

Things you can do to _increase_ the child's engagement:

1. Give the child a helping task that involves movement input (e.g., "Will you please get the box of markers for Ms. Yolanda?").

2. If a child's attention begins to shift, prompt them to be present by asking, "Are you present for me?"

3. Provide praise while the child is sitting patiently, staying in the learning area, or using sitting and working positions appropriately, and when they ask before leaving the learning area. Use the Super Me actions (e.g., being present, trying hard, being like a tree) as needed.

4. Provide opportunities for comforting and/or grounding body input (e.g., high five, bear hugs) if the child enjoys this.

Quality-of-life factors these strategies _strengthen_ in the child:

1. Greater awareness of what they need to help them to focus and stay present during large-group circle time, table-based work tasks, small groups, eating, and snacks

2. Increased social engagement with peers during eating and learning activities

3. Tendency to be more present for large group lessons and table-based activities

4. Increased ability to tell you their needs more quickly

5. Increased choice and control over what they do each day

Module 4: Making Transitions Within a Routine and Coping with Changes

Transitions can be challenging for young children, as they involve shifting from one activity or place to another. Children may have difficulty making a transition because they do not want to stop what they are doing, they do not want to move to the next place or activity, or they are uncertain or fearful about the next place or activity (especially if it is an unplanned transition or change, or an activity associated with a trauma). In addition, many children struggle with the waiting involved in transitions; for example, waiting in line to use the bathroom, waiting in circle for the teacher to get ready, and so on. Finally, transitions can often be times of increased noise, movement, and overall sensory stimulation—think about how chaotic, unpredictable, and noisy clean-up time can be after small-group activities! For children who struggle with the foundational skills of anticipating and coping with changes, with flexibility, and with emotional and sensory regulation, transition times can be particularly difficult and even unpleasant. They may use disruptive or nonfunctional coping actions, such as running away, screaming, or refusing to transition; being aggressive with others or materials; or shutting down and withdrawing. This module will offer you strategies for helping to support children to anticipate and cope with expected and unexpected changes and to feel a sense of safety and autonomy with transitions.

Things you can do *before* a child engages in the challenging action:

1. Before transitions, provide the child with a choice between two transition objects to carry to and from an activity or area; the objects may be related to the nature of the activity (e.g., carry special hand soap to the bathroom, carry a recess ball back inside to a designated area) or can be a comforting or preferred item.

2. If the child must wait in line for a transition, provide them with specific "waiting challenges" to engage in while waiting (e.g., "back in my body challenges" [see Learning Activity Module A; http://www.newharbinger.com/49258], yoga posture, Simon Says).

3. Give the child their own spot in line for transitions, such as line leader if they want to be a leader, or "caboose" if they need extra personal space in line.

4. Give the child a transitioning movement strategy for transitions; for example, ask the child to walk slowly and meow quietly like a cat to move to the toy area for cleanup (if the child likes cats!).

5. Give the child—and the entire class—a prompt before a transition (e.g., "We have two more minutes before we will line up to go inside"). The child may also benefit from having the opportunity to provide the prompt to their peers; this may be a classroom job to announce the two-minute warning.

Things you can *teach* a child to do to take care of their own needs:

1. Teach the child to express emotions about difficulties with transitions. For example, a child may feel fear at the idea of going to the bathroom if there are traumatic memories associated with the experience or shame due to frequent accidents; a child may feel sadness if recess is over. Provide support and modeling to help them express these feelings using Feelings Finder practices as needed (chapter 9), and reassure the child that they are safe and that the emotion will go away.

2. Teach the child strategies they can use independently if they have to wait in line during a transition, as well as the difference between appropriate and safe strategies and disruptive or noisy strategies. For example, they can practice holding a favorite yoga pose for 10 seconds, hold a fidget item, or do five birdie breaths.

3. Teach the child to reference a visual schedule or a "first-then" board so that they will know what activity is coming next during the day.

4. Teach the child about the daily schedule and transitions, and develop strategies for difficult transitions by using supported problem solving. For example, if a child is nervous about transitioning to the bathroom, you can offer for them to go last so it is calmer and they have more privacy.

5. Teach the child the reasons for the daily schedule and for transitions.

Things you can do to *increase* the child's engagement:

1. Provide praise when the child transitions to or from an activity or area or engages in a transition helping task. Use the Super Me actions (e.g., helping, listening) as needed.

2. Provide opportunities for choice making after the transition (e.g., "Thank you for coming in from recess so nicely. What small group would you like to start in first?").

3. Before whole-class transitions, ask the child to "announce" to the class what the class will do next (verbally, or by signaling a transition with a bell); this could be a special job ("schedule helper") to help them to be more engaged in transitions. The child can also have a special job such as "door holder" or "friend counter" (counting friends as they transition in or out of an area).

Quality-of-life factors these strategies *strengthen* in the child:

1. Increased social engagement with peers during transitions

2. Tendency to be more *present* for and aware of time and the daily schedule

3. Likelihood of feeling safer and more prepared during transitions

4. Increased choice and control over what they do each day

Module 5: Sharing and Working with Others

A primary drive in humans is self-preservation, which, particularly for young children, can sometimes seem incongruous with our ability to work with and give to others—skills we develop as we learn about social dynamics and begin to cultivate empathy and compassion. We also have drives to avoid pain and discomfort; to seek pleasure, purpose, and competence; and to feel empowered by a sense of autonomy. These drives, paired with the emerging development of social decision making, perspective taking, a sense of equity and justice, and the simple fact that resources in preschool and kindergarten classes are finite, can result in classroom challenges when it comes to sharing and cooperating with others. This can be especially true when certain classroom items or activities are new or interesting and everyone wants to play with them at once!

Children who lack the foundational skills of theory of mind and social perspective taking, being flexible, deferring gratification until their turn comes, and understanding how to compromise and cooperate may use actions such as aggression, or they may become overwhelmed with emotion in situations that require them to share. There is that old expression "You get what you get and you don't get upset"; I have always thought that wasn't really fair to kids who are genuinely feeling disappointed. It is unrealistic for young children who have difficulty with sharing and working with others to not have emotional outbursts when they are required to share, cooperate with someone else's rules for a game, or take turns. The key is to (1) prevent children from hurting themselves and others and (2) help them grow new skills for coping with these emotions and for sharing and playing fairly with others. This module will offer some strategies for this very common classroom challenge.

Things you can do *before* a child engages in the challenging action:

1. Prior to work time, set rules for the whole class with regard to the amount of time each child may use a classroom resource, toy, or material when others also want a turn with it. This can be especially helpful when introducing a new activity, set of learning materials, or toy or if there are not enough of a certain material for the whole class. It may be helpful to time turns with a visual timer.

2. Before social situations that involve sharing or cooperative learning, give the child an opportunity to pick out a waiting toy that they may engage with in case another toy is being used by a peer.

3. Before games and activities that have rules to follow, allow the child to make choices about aspects of the game or activity that can be controlled (e.g., decide which friend will go first, decide which letter of their name to practice first).

4. Before unstructured play or small-group time, help the child plan what they could do if they have to share something.

5. If the child must take a turn, wait to select an activity, or share materials with a peer, allow the child to experience some autonomy and control (e.g., by setting the timer or deciding where they will wait).

Things you can *teach* a child to do to take care of their own needs:

1. Teach the child to cope with difficult emotions that may arise when they are asked to share or cooperate with others, and reinforce that these feelings are impermanent and do not last forever.

2. Teach the child to ask for help when having difficulty sharing or cooperating with others.

3. Using the Feelings Finder practices, teach the child to understand how others feel during situations that require cooperation and sharing (e.g., another child is happy about taking a turn in a game or playing with a toy pizza set).

4. Using the Super Me—Making an Apology (chapter 9, Daily Practice 6) or the "I'm Sorry" practice (Learning Activity Module G), teach the child how to apologize when they engage in a hurtful behavior instead of cooperating or sharing.

5. Teach the child the meaning of a compromise and how to make a compromise when engaged in an argument or a situation that requires flexibility and sharing. *Give examples of compromise when you see them in books and stories and model examples of compromise in real-life situations.*

Things you can do to *increase* the child's engagement:

1. Provide praise when the child shares and cooperates with peers. Use the Super Me actions (e.g., sharing, cooperating) as needed.

2. Allow the child time to calm down in a safe space with the be-like-a-tree calm down jar or other preferred item if they become upset about cooperating with others.

3. Reinforce the child for noticing when others share and cooperate.

4. If the child makes an attempt to use appropriate and kind strategies, praise their effort and support them in problem solving what to do next time if needed.

5. Support the child to notice and reinforce when other people are waiting, cooperating, or sharing; this can be done as a teacher helper job.

Quality-of-life factors these strategies *strengthen* in the child:

1. Increased social engagement with peers during cooperative learning activities

2. Increased ability to calm down when upset about the need to share and cooperate with others

3. Increased patience when working with other children

4. Increased sense of autonomy and control in situations that require cooperation with others

Pause for Reflection...

The strategies in these five modules have been designed to provide a means to address five common classroom challenges and situations. You may already use many of these strategies, but hopefully you have gained a few more tools or, at the very least, some new insight into the types of foundational skill difficulties that may be causing children to engage in these challenging actions or nonfunctional coping methods. Much like the 5P Process covered in chapter 11, the Positive Engagement Support modules help to transform challenging actions and situations into opportunities for learning and skill development and increased engagement. The Daily Practices, 5P Process, and these modules can enable most children to engage in social and academic learning, yet there will be some children who require even more modification and adaptation of supports due to challenges and disabilities. The 5P Process and corresponding modules also provide an excellent opportunity to collaborate with other professionals, such as occupational therapists, speech and language pathologists, physical therapists, counselors, and social workers. In the next chapter, you will discover a framework for creating opportunities for mindful engagement in children who may need even more support.

CHAPTER 13

How to C.R.E.A.T.E. Engagement and Provide Mindful Engagement Support for Struggling Learners

Humans are occupational beings, which means that our health, wellness, and identity, or how we define ourselves, are shaped by our ability to engage in activities that we find meaningful and purposeful and that occupy our time—in other words, occupations. We are also driven by the roles, habits, and routines that support these occupations. Our occupations are not simply tasks that occur in a vacuum; they involve a unique interplay between ourselves, others, the physical environment, the social environment, our resources, materials, and the time we have available. The way we interface with our occupations and our environment and our drive to do, experience, create, and learn make us uniquely human and contribute not only to our quality of life and purpose, but also to our most basic needs for health and wellness. While modern capitalist society—which values the earning of money—tends to define an "occupation" as a job that we do for pay, this chapter will refer to any purposeful activity that gives our lives meaning as an occupation.

Reflecting on survival in brutal living conditions in the Nazi concentration camps, psychiatrist and Holocaust survivor Victor Frankl said, "Those who knew there was a task waiting for them to fulfill were most apt to survive" (Frankl, 1985). Research has shown us that when people are deprived of engagement in occupations, their health and wellness decline; this is exemplified in prison environments that are designed to highly restrict people from engaging in occupational freedom as a primary form of punishment (Molineux & Whiteford, 1999). This culture of punishment by taking away freedom to engage in meaningful activities is seen even in preschool and kindergarten classrooms: young children who struggle with coping and following classroom guidelines are given consequences such as losing recess time or sitting in time-out. In my field of occupational therapy, we refer to the taking away of one's ability (either by consequence or limited opportunity) to do tasks that add to one's health, wellness, and/or identity as *occupational deprivation*. When people do not have the opportunity to engage in meaningful activities and occupations due to social, economic, physical, and environmental barriers or factors, this is called *occupational injustice.* Conversely, when people are able to engage in meaningful occupations, their wellness and health increase. Our very identity is shaped by what we do, and it can be argued that our quality of life is influenced by the degree to which we invest in what we do.

You may be asking yourself what this whole topic has to do with teaching preschool and kindergarten children! While young children's primary occupation is play, they are also learning the occupations of self-care, helping, cleaning up, solving problems, developing relationships, advocating for themselves, creating and building, communicating, and self-regulating. When children experience decreased academic and social engagement due to factors such as developmental disability, physical disability, learning disability, social injustice and poverty, inequity, trauma, and neurodiversity, they may not be able to engage fully in meaningful childhood occupations. This is because they face barriers to their understanding, their interests, or their particular method of learning, which may stem from rigid or inflexible programming and curricula. When they cannot access meaningful occupational engagement, they may feel disconnected and experience frustration, loss, or a decline in well-being, just as we adults do.

One of the most important challenges we face as educators, therapy practitioners, and caregivers is how to help those children who miss out on important opportunities to learn and engage in childhood occupations due to behavioral difficulties, disabilities, decreased motivation, language and communication difficulties, limited resources, and many other factors. This is because we want to maximize, and not waste, human potential. For years, I worked as a consultant helping health care teams figure out how to help nonverbal individuals who had severe and profound mental and physical disabilities, along with multiple medical challenges, to engage more fully in life and experience a better quality of life. This amazing group of people were just surviving, being medically managed and cared for, and very few of them showed signs that they were enjoying life. I remember talking with a caregiver who said that one woman she was caring for had never smiled in over twenty years!

These individuals had their health care providers stumped, and my team and I would go in and spend time with them, complete evaluations and preference assessments, talk to caregivers, and come up with strategies that their caregivers could use to support them to be more engaged in daily life so that they would be able to enjoy a better quality of life. As I worked with people who were facing so many barriers and struggles, who were living in institutions, many of them their whole lives, I learned that the best thing I could do was to be present with them, to listen, to be open to new ways of doing things, and to consider all the factors that could affect their ability to engage in activities that made their lives worth really living, instead of just helping them make it through the day. When we worked with people and saw them immersing themselves in life and feeling connected to others instead of just tolerating activities and passing time each day, we called this mindful engagement. They were more aware, active, and present, and their caregivers were doing tasks *with them* instead of just *for* or *to* them. I designed the framework presented in this chapter to help teachers, caregivers, and therapy professionals consider some basic human factors that can often get overlooked but that can be essential to supporting mindful engagement in our life's occupations.

This chapter will help you to look holistically at a child or classroom situation and consider new and multifaceted ways to help those children who struggle to engage in and access classroom activities that may be easy for other children. It may help you to problem solve and discover novel ways of supporting your students who face the biggest challenges and barriers to learning, or even give you inspiration for how to modify a learning situation to deepen understanding and experience for other students. First, we will examine the concept of mindful occupational engagement a little further and learn why it is so important to quality of life in the classroom and beyond.

Mindful Occupational Engagement

Mindful occupational engagement involves the active investment of ourselves into daily activities. It is the "moment-by-moment awareness and nonjudgmental engagement in an activity, without expectation of specific outcomes" (Jackman, 2014, p. 243). Mindful occupational engagement is a state of being while doing that offers a richness of experience—one that might be missed when we feel pressured to do something because we have to; when we are not equipped to do something; or when our awareness is dimmed because we are overworked, pressed for time, or pressured to multitask. Mindful engagement is a way of living and interacting with our physical and social environment that we can experience naturally or can learn through formal and informal mindfulness practices. In fact, the practices in chapter 5 were designed to build your capacity for mindful occupational engagement. Similarly, the Daily Practices, 5P Process, and Positive Engagement Support (PES) Modules that we discussed in chapters 11, 12, and 13 were developed to help children experience mindful occupational engagement and the benefits that accompany this state of being present while doing.

Engagement requires us to be fully immersed in the present and doing a task not only for the outcome, reward, or avoidance of consequence, but also (and most importantly) for the benefit of the experience itself. In contrast, *participation* is commonly tied to an external obligation or contingency or can become automatic in nature, resulting in one's "going through the motions" in a mindless manner, either because it is a familiar habit, or just to complete a task because it is required. Take for example the expectation for children to engage in activities that target preset academic standards in a "one size fits all" approach that doesn't account for diversity and differences in learning, development, culture, and neurological processing. Just because we as educators and therapists create learning activities and opportunities for children, this doesn't mean that all children will experience meaningful occupational engagement in the activities. This may be due to differences in interest, skills, abilities, or the availability of necessary resources. Thus, no matter how comprehensive and flexible the Daily Practices, 5P Process, and PES Modules may be, some children may require additional support to experience mindful engagement. The purpose of this chapter is to provide a framework, called the C.R.E.A.T.E. framework, to help you to become an architect and design experiences for engagement to more naturally occur in children of all backgrounds, abilities, and interests. Before we learn more about this framework, let's take a look at exactly how mindful engagement experiences occur in daily life.

How Does Mindful Engagement Occur?

Many factors can work together to create an opportunity for mindful engagement to spontaneously occur. Have you ever been so immersed in what you were doing that you lost all track of time and place? This experience is very similar to mindful engagement and is called a *flow state*—a state in which we become completely absorbed in what we are doing. This can happen when we are doing things such as running, playing music, making art, reading, or playing games. Researchers have theorized that many factors are needed for a flow state to occur, such as challenge-skill balance, merging of action and awareness, clear goals, clear feedback, high concentration, sense of control, loss of self-consciousness, and transformation of time (Csikszentmihalyi & Csikszentmihalyi, 1990).

The difference between a flow state and mindful engagement is that while a flow state requires a degree of skill challenge (for example, creating a masterpiece by painting with a toothbrush), a mindful engagement state can be experienced during a more routine, seemingly low-challenge activity, such as just brushing our teeth (Jackman, 2014). In the latter case, while the task demands may appear to be rather simple, the active investment in brushing our teeth— without the mind wandering or multitasking—can be quite difficult unless we are practicing mindfulness. As discussed in chapters 4 and 5, much of what we adults do in daily life is done on autopilot, and often out of a sense of obligation. Children, on the other hand, are more likely to become absorbed in what they are doing, as so much of what they experience is new and exciting.

For many children with differences in learning, social skills, development, neurological processing, motor control, cultures, and interests, daily activities and occupations at school that may seem easy to other children may present big challenges that exceed their skill or attention levels. This can make it difficult for a child to fully engage in the activity, or to even try it at all. However, if the child (1) is motivated to try the activity because it aligns with their interests, (2) feels like it is possible, (3) has the right level of energy (not too much, not too little), (4) is in a state of alertness appropriate for the task, (5) feels adequately challenged but not overwhelmed by the task, and (6) is motivated and curious about the task, they are more likely to experience mindful engagement, without much coercion or extrinsic motivation such as rewards. These factors can unite to create an experience in which the child values the process more than the outcome; in other words, the focus is on the journey rather than the destination.

Think of a child who becomes completely immersed in making a card for their mother; it may have a bottle of glue poured on it, the drawing may be off center, and it may be utterly illegible, but the child works away, tongue hanging out in concentration, beaming with pride at the beautiful mess they have created! The joy and learning were in the engagement of creating, motivated by love for their mother. For many children, these experiences just happen spontaneously, but for some children, we can help to create them by setting the right stage—I call this *mindful engagement support*. In the following section, we will explore some of the core concepts underlying mindful engagement support and how it differs from more traditional methods of social and academic curriculum delivery.

Core Concepts of the C.R.E.A.T.E. Model of Mindful Engagement Support

The mindful engagement support model is a flexible method for increasing children's engagement and quality-of-life factors, which will naturally create a setting more likely to lead to learning and enjoyment. The C.R.E.A.T.E. framework—which stands for Choice, Remembrance, Environment, Awareness, Task demands, and Energy—offers a road map to help guide teachers and therapists through the problem-solving process for identifying barriers and potential solutions to children's learning and engagement. While the more traditional education model can be referred to as child centered and child driven, it typically involves daily activities that are selected and planned by adults based on preprogrammed academic and social standards. As teachers and those who work in the education setting, we rarely have any control over these standards. In contrast, the C.R.E.A.T.E. framework and the mindful engagement support model are rooted in using compassionate and mindful adult awareness to support quality-of-life outcomes for children who are not typical learners or who are facing barriers due to injustice or inequity. It is designed to accompany or supplement your current process for differentiation and scaffolding of learning and provide you with another tool to add to your current ones. Before learning the specific elements that make up the C.R.E.A.T.E. acronym, it's important to understand how the mindful engagement support model is unique and different. The following sections will contrast the core features of this model with a more customary model of encouraging participation and outcomes in learning.

Supporting vs. Assisting

The act of assisting a child is typically inspired and driven by the desire to help the child succeed in or complete an activity that everyone else is doing. Think of the well-intentioned parents who "help" their children with at-home projects that end up looking like they were completed by college-level design students. Assisting tends to result in the child's being a passive and often an unwilling or reluctant participant; this defeats the purpose of learning, which is really focused on the process more than the outcome. For example, consider a child who does not have prewriting or fine motor skills to hold a crayon and receives hand-over-hand assistance to write their name while crying and trying to leave the table. In contrast, supporting means that we follow the child's lead, ensure that a task is aligned with their abilities and interests, and provide just enough support so that the child remains an active and primary participant in the activity. In terms of the example above, the child may be more engaged using small blocks to form prewriting lines on the table or carpet, or using large chalk to write lines on a blackboard or sidewalk and then "erasing" them with a large wet paintbrush.

Autonomy vs. Independence

Some children with disabilities, developmental delays, and differences in learning may be unable to perform standard daily tasks independently and require support, modification of the task, specialized equipment, and/or modification of the environment to maximize performance and independence. However, working toward independence (i.e., being able to do a task without the help from others or specialized supports) does not necessarily contribute to enhanced engagement or quality of life. On the other hand, autonomy speaks to the child's ability to have control and choice over daily activities, which may or may not involve independence. For example, a child may be physically able to walk independently, but they may choose to use a walker or power chair to conserve energy so that they may engage in other activities they enjoy, such as coloring, dancing to music, and transferring into a standard chair to eat lunch at the table with friends.

Mindful Engagement vs. Participation

Mindful engagement is a state of being that requires active presence. In contrast, participation can be passive and is typically focused on a goal-directed task or avoidance of a consequence or attainment of a reward. There is a qualitative, observable difference between a child who is participating or doing something without awareness, or with a goal-directed focus, and a child who is mindfully engaged. For example, think of child who is listening intently to a story, leaning forward, laughing joyfully, pointing at the colorful illustrations...this is engagement. Now think of a child who may have limited social language and listening comprehension, hindering their ability to fully understand the story, and also has difficulty sitting still. This child may try to participate in story time and stay in the circle, but only because they know they are supposed to stay put, not because of enjoyment. This child is just participating, and often just waiting for something to be over. Participation can be even more unpleasant when a child feels a press for time, big feelings, physical discomfort, or boredom or frustration because the task is too easy, not interesting, too hard, or not meaningful. With participation, a child may do a task just because they are worried about what will happen if they don't, or because they want to get it done to meet an expectation or reward. However, in the process of mindful engagement, there is enjoyment and reinforcement in the act of just being in the middle of the activity; the reward is in the engagement and the experience itself and not only dependent on the outcome of the activity or achievement of an objective. So, the child above who has difficulty with listening comprehension and being still during story time may be more engaged by standing, being the page turner for the teacher, and being close enough to really visualize the bright images on the pages. As a teacher, you can tell when your students are truly engaged in a learning experience; you can see it in their faces and hear it in their voices; you don't have to prompt them or persuade them, they are just right there in the middle of the experience. These moments tend to be the most fulfilling for us as adults too.

Relaxing vs. Rushing

As a teacher of young children, you are expected to achieve so much in the relatively short span of a school day. If you remember back to chapter 4, this can feel like you are required to empty out an ocean using only a teaspoon! The resulting tendency is to rush or to multitask. Mindful pause and mindful pace are essential to having a more relaxed presence and preventing the "hurry up and wait" mentality that is consistent not only with educational culture, but also with the Western culture at large. When we can relax the human tendency to push forward and achieve as much as we can as quickly as possible, we can nurture and develop the patience to let things unfold. It may sound irrational, but often the best way to keep up the with the fast pace of a classroom is to slow down. When we rush, we can make mistakes, we can miss important cues, and we set the tone for others to rush too. Slowing the pace of teaching and assessing learning and understanding can require a lot of patience, which is a critical component of acceptance and present-moment awareness. Sumedho and Amaro (2007, p. 113) taught, "Patience is an essential ingredient. It means that we are willing to let something be what it is." Often when children have delays in processing, have difficulties with motor planning, or are just beginning to learn a skill, they may need to move very slowly. This can be especially true when children are responding to questions.

Answering questions requires children to use auditory processing, receptive language, working memory, word retrieval, filtering of ideas, expressive language, and the ability to verbalize and articulate what they want to say. Delays in any of these areas can result in a child being slow to answer; however, in typical adult conversation, there is usually not much of a pause. It can feel awkward to wait more than a few seconds for someone to respond. When children do not answer right away, this may be interpreted as ignoring, not listening, or not understanding the question, when in reality the child may just need more time to process and answer. I remember working with a very bright, gifted, neurodiverse kindergarten child with the highest verbal IQ our school psychologist had ever seen; he had so much knowledge and so many ideas, he actually took up to ten seconds to answer just so he could sift through it all. Ten seconds may not seem like long, but in the course of a conversation it can feel like an eternity! In addition to using mindful pauses during listening and conversations, just the practice of being relaxed and taking care not to hurry will model this pace for your students, and they will be more likely to follow your pace and feel less pressure to act quickly and more likely to engage mindfully.

Now that you are more familiar with the general concepts of the mindful engagement support model, we can examine the C.R.E.A.T.E. framework, which will help guide you in problem solving how to help all students feel more engaged.

The C.R.E.A.T.E. Framework for Mindful Engagement Support

As teachers and therapists, we know how often a one-size-fits-all lesson presentation does not work for all children, especially children who have differences in executive function, learning, language, culture, and cognition. This calls for moments of flexibility and creative problem solving. So many teachers and therapists do this intuitively, but it can sometimes be easy to get stuck, especially given how restricted our time and resources can be. The acronym C.R.E.A.T.E. (Choice, Remembrance, Environment, Awareness, Task demands, and Energy) provides a framework for developing and customizing practice and activity modifications for children who are struggling with engagement or access to meaningful occupations. Its purpose is to guide you through a list of factors to consider to help a child be intrinsically motivated to engage instead of just going through the motions. It can be an alternative to extrinsic motivators like bribes, rewards, or negative consequences.

The C.R.E.A.T.E. framework has six domains representing various aspects that contribute to mindful engagement. Manipulation of these domains can empower us to modify and individualize OpenMind practice activities and standard academic and social activities to meet children where they are in terms of interests, motivation, and development. You will notice that some of these domains apply to how you as a teacher will provide support to facilitate engagement, and some will align more with considerations to make activities and practices more accessible to children who do not fully respond to the Daily Practices, the 5P Process, or the PES Modules due to differences in learning, processing, interests, motivation, or background.

C: Choice

Choice is central to an engagement experience, particularly in young children who may have little opportunity for autonomy or difficulty accessing preferred items and communicating wants and needs. *Control, curiosity,* and *culture* are all factors that relate to choices that a child can make. In a highly structured, curriculum-driven educational environment, children are often placed into situations in which they feel powerless, as schedules are often predetermined and activities might be rigid in design and plan.

The first factor related to the domain of choice—control—is well illustrated by a story a colleague told me about a three-year-old child who was struggling at bath time. His mother brought him in for an occupational therapy evaluation with the primary concern that every time she turned on the water for his bath, he would start screaming and banging his head. She was worried that he was sensitive to the noise or the feel of the bathwater and requested a comprehensive assessment of his sensory processing as part of the evaluation. As the therapist began to assess the child's independence with all steps of bathing, she asked him to turn on the water. He smiled and looked so happy as he turned it on; no screaming, no banging, just an expression of joy! The mystery was solved—he simply wanted to turn the water on himself! As this example shows, providing a sense of control to children who struggle to engage in a given situation may increase their intrinsic motivation to initiate or maintain engagement.

In determining which choices to provide a child to give them some control over their situation, it is helpful to start with interest, which can be the primary motivator. Giving the child a choice between a high-interest choice and a low-interest choice can be a good way to shape a child's investment in a given activity. For example, if a child does not like to practice counting objects and writing numbers but loves animals, you can give them a choice of doing a counting worksheet or counting all the plastic animals in the "zoo" for the zookeeper, and marking each animal group with the appropriate magnetic number. For children who have limitations in communication and cannot verbalize preferences, you can conduct a preference assessment by exposing them to different objects and experiences and observing how they respond. Other options for choices can include where and how to sit, where to stand in line, what types of breaks they need, which calm-down strategy to use, and how they want to be a "leader."

The second factor related to choice is curiosity, as we choose to engage in the things that capture our attention or inspire wonder. Attention research has shown us that novel or unexpected items tend to be more likely to capture attention. Making a child curious is more likely to lead to exploration and engagement and can also promote learning and memory (Gruber et al., 2014). Adding a new or interesting element like an object, puppet, mystery item, or book to an established practice can increase curiosity and engagement. You can also add on to existing preferences; for example, if a child is fascinated by zippers, you can provide new objects with different zippers for them to explore.

Finally, the third element of choice is culture. When one set or type of cultural ideals, books, traditions, and values guides classroom activities and lessons, many children find authentic engagement to be difficult. It is of vital importance to ensure that stories, dolls, puppets, and lessons represent a broad and diverse multicultural perspective, and that children are encouraged to share their own traditions, perspectives, and family structures. Even materials as simple as a spectrum of flesh-toned crayons can help children with tasks such as drawing themselves and loved ones.

R: Remembrance

If you will recall in one of our first chapters, we noted that the Pali word for mindfulness, *sati,* means remembrance. This means on a regular basis, when we are mindful, we remember to be present; we remember to respond instead of reacting quickly and possibly harmfully; we remember to be kind, to be grateful, to remember our intentions; *we remember what is most important to us and our students.* There are three essential aspects to the remembrance domain: *recognition with mindful responses, regret prevention,* and *reinforcement.*

When we are caught up in meeting outcomes for our students, for getting through required standards or planned activities, it is easy to forget those core quality-of-life factors that are at the heart of the very best learning experiences. When we—and our students—get too caught up in the pressure of achieving specific goals, or doing things in a certain way, we can emotionally react when things do not turn out the way we want them to, or we can avoid the tasks completely. On the other hand, when we remember to be present, flexible, and not tied too closely to expecting a specific outcome, we can ensure that we provide mindful responses for each child because we are able to recognize their specific motivations and struggles in the moment, before an extreme reaction to the situation occurs. Using the REMIND practices will help you remember to stay present to recognize what may be important to a child's most basic needs for learning and socialization and to cultivate the skill of careful responses over more quick and emotionally driven reactions.

The second element involved in remembrance is what I term "regret prevention." When we are mindful in our responses, we are more likely to be encouraging and patient, and less likely to react in a way that may result in a child's feeling ashamed, pressed for time, or angry at themselves for making a mistake while learning. In short, we avoid responding in ways that we will regret.

The final aspect of this domain is the provision of positive reinforcement of a child's effort and prosocial choices, which requires ongoing awareness and attention to the child's cues and behaviors. For example, a child who struggles with multiple aspects of a complex task—such as self-control, movement, memory, attention, sequencing, and coordination—may find a typical preschool or kindergarten task, like sorting and cleaning up materials, to be overwhelming. Instead of focusing on the outcome of sorting and putting away all the materials in a center, you can focus on reinforcing one aspect of the task, such as the effort to talk quietly during cleanup or to carry a basket of materials that a peer sorted. The more mindful we are, the more we can remember to reinforce elements such as effort and engagement as they occur, which may make it more likely for children to continue with these actions.

E: Environment

This domain involves an understanding of how our environment can support or act as a barrier to mindful engagement. This may include the physical environment (e.g., temperature, noise level); the social environment (e.g., the presence of an unfamiliar classroom volunteer); the embodied context (e.g., feeling anxiety in the pit of one's stomach, reexperiencing past trauma after being accidently shoved); and the temporal context (i.e., time of day). I will never forget working with an adult with profound developmental and intellectual disabilities who was unable to express himself verbally and was dependent on a wheelchair for ambulation and on physical assistance for transfers to and from his bed and wheelchair. He was so frequently pulling his arms and legs up into a ball that he was beginning to develop tightness in his limbs, and was so frequently digging his fingers into his head that he was developing dents in his skull. Because of the perceived risk, his residential treatment team had decided to put him in soft restraints to prevent contractures from developing. His treatment team said that he never used his hands for anything functional, though he seemed to enjoy music.

When I met this lovely man, he had just had his restraints removed and returned to the balled-up position. Being someone who gets cold easily, I immediately noticed that he had goosebumps on his arms, had very little body fat, and was positioned under an air vent. Review of his labs showed that he also had anemia, which can result in cold hands and feet. I asked a staff member to put a blanket in the dryer for a few minutes, and we put it on his lap. Immediately his whole body relaxed and he smiled. I placed a drum in his hands and he began to hit it, completely engaged. Everyone began to realize that he wasn't engaging in a difficult behavior or refusing to use his hands; he was simply trying to meet his most basic needs and make himself warm. Though this is an example of an adult in a residential facility and not a young child in a preschool or kindergarten classroom, I always think of this example when I consider whether a child's environment may be impacting their engagement. Often even the seemingly smallest factors in our environment can have a huge impact on our ability to feel safe and comfortable enough to be mindfully engaged.

The most important thing about a learning environment—even more important than its ability to provide enrichment and simulation—is its ability to provide security and felt safety. When children have a history of trauma, or have sensitivity to sensory information such as noises, they may develop hypervigilance or have a fear response to sudden noise, bright lights, being touched by others, and increased movement around them. They may benefit from being seated by a teacher or in a position where they can see what is happening around them and cannot be surprised by people coming up behind them unexpectedly. Modifying these environmental factors can help a child to feel more comfortable, secure, and safe.

Finally, awareness of the impact of the environment on each child also requires a broad awareness of child patterns, habits, and trends. OpenMind practices and activities are designed to be performed in the most appropriate environment to support learning (e.g., playground, snack area, large-group circle time). A child who is unwilling to engage in an activity in one environment may be more willing in an environment where they feel more secure or comfortable. For example, a child who has dyspraxia or poor motor planning may be more successful when doing yoga in an outside area, where there is more room to move and they are less likely to trip over equipment, carpets, or peers.

A: Awareness

Awareness is fundamental to mindful engagement because we must be able to notice what is happening inside us and around us to fully be present to navigate the challenges and experience the joys of learning and interaction. The domain of awareness involves *attention* and *attitude*. Attention helps us to filter our awareness and focus on the aspects that are necessary for the activity or task, and a positive and open-minded attitude is required for us to fully be present and engaged.

If a child cannot shift attention to a learning activity or is not aware of important aspects of a learning task, they cannot be fully aware of or engaged in learning. In this circumstance, it can be helpful to shift your attention to what the child *is* focusing on. This can help you to come into their world and figure out a way to integrate what they are interested in into what you are teaching. For example, if a child is focused on repeatedly cutting a piece of paper into tiny pieces, and the rest of the class is painting a picture of a rainbow to learn about colors and sequence, you can give the child the opportunity to cut small pieces of colored paper to then glue onto the outline of a rainbow.

This domain of awareness, which includes attention and an open-minded attitude, is closely linked to the domain of remembrance. They both involve an active ability to notice what is happening in the moment, to identify what barriers a child may be facing, and to be flexible and willing to adapt planned activities to meet the present-moment needs of a child. However, this domain relates specifically to a child's level of awareness and attention. For example, a child may not be able to sustain their focus and attention long enough to engage in certain advanced breathing and meditation practices, such as birdie breathing, rainbow breathing, or breathing with the bell. In these cases, it can be helpful to do a warm-up with a simpler practice, such as listening to the sound of the bell, before leading the class in the more advanced practice so that the child can experience engagement and success with a version of the task that has less attentional demands.

T: Task Demands

The example above shows how attentional demands of a task can be higher than the child's skill level, resulting in decreased engagement, but when modified, a task can be just right for the child. Engagement and learning are more likely to occur when challenge and skill levels are in balance—too much challenge can induce anxiety, and too little challenge can result in boredom. Kids tend to be most engaged when they are experiencing an optimal balance between skills and task demands—in my field of occupational therapy, we call this the "just right challenge," and teachers are often masters of providing just right challenges!

Ensuring meaningful engagement for children with differing abilities may require careful task analysis and task modification to match a child's abilities to what the task is requiring. This can mean simplifying a task or modifying equipment, such as pre-cutting shapes to help a child who struggles with fine motor skills to work on sorting, giving a child a lightbox to trace an image instead of drawing it freehand, allowing a child who has difficulty sitting to lie on the floor to do a puzzle or worksheet, using picture boards for choices for children who struggle with language, or giving a child who is hypersensitive to noise some noise-canceling headphones during loud transition times. It can also involve making a task more challenging or complex. For example, if a child has become bored or complacent because their interests and abilities exceed the task demands, adding extra steps or encouraging the child to help teach a concept to peers will likely enhance their engagement.

E: Energy

The last domain of the C.R.E.A.T.E. framework pertains to recognizing a child's energy level and its importance in creating an engagement experience. If a child is too tired or too excited for a planned activity, they may not engage in that activity. To complicate things even further, sometimes children compensate for fatigue by increasing their movements. As a teacher, when you recognize that a child is too tired or too energetic to complete a given activity, you have two options. You can modify the activity to fit the energy level of the child or classroom, or you can support the child or group to become more alert or relaxed to match the activity and allow for engagement to unfold.

For example, if children are jumping and rolling around the carpet before lesson time and do not seem ready to listen quietly, you can either modify the activity and incorporate movement into the listening experience (e.g., choose a book that calls for physical responses, ask children to model movements of characters in the book) or lead them through a series of mindful movements or yoga postures to release some of their energy. This can also involve changing the time of day of a planned activity to align best with the class's level of alertness. For instance, many teachers conduct meditation practices first thing in the morning, when young children may still be too sleepy to fully be present. Moving the meditation practice to a time of the day when children are calm but alert may result in more engagement.

Pause for Reflection...

So often in the academic environment, emphasis falls on persuading children to complete tasks or achieve outcomes, and these outcome or tasks may not be possible for all children. As a result, some children may tune out or disconnect, refuse to do a task, exhibit signs of distress, use nonfunctional behaviors or coping responses, or even just show a lack of interest. Children who experience barriers and struggles may be focused on just getting through their day, and they aren't able to experience quality engagement in classroom learning and occupations that are fun and meaningful to them. The C.R.E.A.T.E. framework was designed to help you to consider ways to modify tasks to help children become more mindfully engaged. When children are engaged, they are more likely not only to learn, but also to smile, grow, laugh, connect, and succeed.

The assumption of the mindful engagement support model is that engagement can be nurtured and can occur even in individuals with differences in learning and development given the right combination of physical, environmental, emotional, and motivational modifications and supports. Analysis of all six factors in the C.R.E.A.T.E. framework—choice, remembrance, environment, awareness, task demands, and energy—can supplement your ability to develop creative solutions and opportunities to help all children experience some degree of mindful social and academic engagement. In the next and final chapter, you will find an overview and some examples of additional supplemental learning activities that can be used as part of the OMPK program and the process of mindful engagement support.

CHAPTER 14

OMPK Supplemental Learning Activities

The OMPK Supplemental Learning Activities were created to enhance the OMPK program, which includes the ten Daily Practices, the 5P Process, the PES Modules, and the Mindful Engagement Support process. You can use the OMPK Supplemental Learning Activities in the natural course of the academic day to teach children how to live more mindfully; build self-regulation; connect socially; and act with equanimity, loving-kindness, compassion, and joy. The OMPK Supplemental Learning Activities are divided into eight downloadable modules that address a different functional social-emotional learning skill.

Much like the ten Daily Practices, the practices in each module are arranged to progress in level of difficulty so that you can match an activity to the child's developmental level and interests. Given that child learning, understanding, and retention of concepts can be enhanced by having the child teach them, each module also includes an option for giving children an opportunity to lead and teach the prosocial skills and practices. These practice options can also serve as classroom and teacher helper jobs, and can provide older or more developmentally ready children with additional opportunities to apply and embody OMPK practices.

The eight modules of the OMPK Supplemental Learning Activities are grouped in terms of how they support the development of the following specific functional social-emotional learning skills:

Module A: Self-awareness and self-control of movement

Module B: Attention and awareness in the present moment

Module C: Self-calming

Module D: Self-regulation of emotions for making positive behavioral choices

Module E: Social awareness and social connection

Module F: Social communication

Module G: Positive interaction with others (conflict resolution, sharing, helping)

Module H: Self-kindness and self-compassion

The following table provides a brief description of each functional social-emotional learning skill area.

Functional Social-Emotional Learning Skill Area	Description
Self-awareness and self-control of movement	The ability to be aware of what one's body is doing, concentrate on movement, and be in control of body movements within the classroom environment
Attention and awareness in the present moment	The ability to be aware of what is happening in the present moment, both inside one's own body and in the external environment
Self-calming	The ability to calm down after an emotional outburst, a meltdown, a feeling of disappointment, or a conflict with peers
Self-regulation of emotions for making positive behavioral choices	The ability to respond, rather than react, to challenging emotions and situations and to make decisions that do not hurt others
Social awareness and social connection	The ability to take the perspective of others and to act with nonjudgment and acceptance of others
Social communication	The ability to communicate respectfully and appropriately with others to express needs and opinions and engage in social interaction
Positive interaction with others (conflict resolution, sharing, helping)	The ability to resolve conflicts and arguments with others, share classroom materials, contribute to classroom chores and tasks, and help others
Self-kindness and self-compassion	The ability to love and accept one's self unconditionally and refrain from engaging in negative self-talk

You can use the OMPK Supplemental Learning Activities to help with your lesson planning; the activities support not only learning about mindfulness practice but also the social-emotional learning elements found in most preschool educational curricula. OMPK Supplemental Learning Activities can be incorporated into lesson plans to support individual and class goals. These activities are a guide, much like a recipe is a guide to cooking various dishes. The activities are dynamic in that you can pick and choose which activities are appropriate, not only during the lesson planning process in anticipation of children's needs, but also in the rhythm of life based on what children need in each unfolding moment. The activity instructions include enough information to guide you in how to complete the activity, but are flexible enough to enable you to use your creativity and insight to add extension lessons, and even modify the activities based on what the children are doing and responding to in the rhythm of the school day.

It is important to note that the Supplemental Learning Activities are optional and are designed to give you more choices to supplement the core OMPK program, especially if you are seeing a need for additional support for certain SEL skills. Including all of the practice instructions and corresponding visuals and reference tools for each of the eight modules within in this chapter would make this book quite lengthy and difficult to navigate. For this reason, I will instead provide an overview of each module and the practices and functions associated with each corresponding social-emotional learning skill. Each section includes a table listing the activities in that module, the types of skills and quality-of-life indicators that may increase with the implementation and integration of each activity, and challenging behaviors that may decrease with the use of each activity. The activity in italics represents a "child as teacher" practice that gives the child an opportunity to learn by teaching and helping others. The behaviors and skills targeted by these activities serve not only to enhance learning and development, but also improve quality of life.

Overview of the OMPK Supplemental Learning Activities Modules

The eight complete modules, along with corresponding practice instructions and full color visual tools, are available for download at http://www.newharbinger.com/49258.

Module A: Self-Awareness and Self-Control of Movement

These activity options help children to be aware of the parts of their bodies and the kinds of movements their bodies make, to build control of their body movements by focusing and concentrating, and to identify what types of movements their bodies need throughout the day.

Self-Awareness and Self-Control of Movement Activities	Skills and Quality-of-Life Indicators That May Increase in Children	Challenging Behaviors or Problems That May Decrease in Children
Back in My Body	Body awareness, concentration on body movements, balance, and control of speed and force of movements	Difficulty with controlling activity level (e.g., running around and being silly), poor awareness of body movement (e.g., hitting or running into others)
Sitting Spots and Waiting Hands, Ask Before ____, and How I Wait	Ability to wait for a turn without disturbing others, respect for property and classroom routine, ability to delay gratification and wait patiently	Being impulsive, fidgety, or upset when required to wait for a turn, for help, for an activity, or for an object; impulsively taking an object or leaving a designated area
Bloga Teacher	Creativity, balance, teaching of new movements, confidence	Shyness, decreased confidence

Module B: Attention and Awareness in the Present Moment

These activity options help children to be aware of what is happening inside their minds and bodies and all around them. They help to bring children back to the present moment.

Attention and Awareness in the Present Moment Activities	Skills and Quality-of-Life Indicators That May Increase in Children	Challenging Behaviors or Problems That May Decrease in Children
Heart Meditation	Body awareness, ability to sit quietly and listen, ability to notice other body sensations	Difficulty with staying present and listening, difficulty with focusing and being aware of one's body
Present Rocks, Present Monitoring	Ability to be present and aware in the present moment and to notice and appreciate what is happening	Talking out of turn, distractibility, difficulty listening, decreased awareness of degree of being present
Observation of thoughts, feelings, and body sensations	Ability to observe, decenter, and objectively name and/or rate thoughts, feelings, and sensations	Feeling overwhelmed by and identifying with thoughts, feelings, and body sensations
Present Reporter	Noticing and appreciating when peers and teachers are being present	Demanding or expecting attention and presence from others

Module C: Self-Calming

These activity options help children to calm down when they become overstimulated, overwhelmed, emotional, noisy, or hyperactive during quiet work time. Initially children may need teacher support to use these strategies for self-calming, but with practice they may be able to use them independently.

Self-Calming Activities	Skills and Quality-of-Life Indicators That May Increase in Children	Challenging Behaviors or Problems That May Decrease in Children
Pinwheel Breathing	Independent self-calming using a visual classroom object, preparing for quiet work or activity	Screaming, crying, whining, rapid shallow breathing, having a "meltdown"
Candle Calm Down (see also Lotus Breathing Daily Practice Activity), Heart Meditation for Calming	Independent self-calming using one's own body as a calming strategy	Screaming, crying, whining, having a "meltdown"
Before and After, Turning It Around	Ability to decenter from difficult emotions, ability to shift attention from negative emotions to positive emotions	Continued focus on negative emotions (e.g., sadness, anger), escalating negative emotions, identification with negative emotions
Calm Counselor	Empathy, compassion, helping others to calm down when upset	Antagonizing others, insensitivity to others who are upset

Module D: Self-Regulation of Emotions and Behavior

These activity options teach children to stop before acting out impulsively during times that they feel overwhelmed with difficult emotions. They help children learn how to shift from focusing and dwelling on difficult emotions to a neutral place or to a positive behavioral choice.

Self-Regulation of Emotions and Behavior Activities	Skills and Quality-of-Life Indicators That May Increase in Children	Challenging Behaviors or Problems That May Decrease in Children
Puppet Play for Self-Regulation	Noticing difficult emotions and the importance of pausing before reacting and hurting others	Verbal and physical aggression, property destruction following peer conflict, difficult emotions (e.g., anger)
Do New Plan, Stop-Breathe-Kind Choice, Lose and Choose, Choose Kindness!	Ability to stop during difficult emotional experiences or social situations and make a kind choice that does not hurt others, ability to be aware of the needs and feelings of others	Remorse and distress over emotional and behavioral reactions, verbal and physical aggression, property destruction, difficult emotions (e.g., anger)
I Can Scale	Attitude of nonjudgmental acceptance when faced with a challenging or nonpreferred task	Refusal or reluctance to engage in a task perceived as difficult or boring
Kind Choice Counselor	Understanding and communicating how to notice impulses and opt to make a kind choice	Difficulty describing and communicating how to notice impulses and opt to make a kind choice

Module E: Social Awareness and Social Connection

These activity options help children to be aware of others, notice what other children are doing, and accept and not judge others who may differ in looks or behavior. These practices help children realize that we all have a human connection, and all have similarities and differences.

Social Awareness and Social Connection Activities	Skills and Quality-of-Life Indicators That May Increase in Children	Challenging Behaviors or Problems That May Decrease in Children
Copy Cats, Listen Building	Noticing and valuing what others are doing, listening to and watching others	Resistance to listening to others' suggestions or ideas, exclusion of others, limited awareness of what others are doing
Laughter Yoga	Bonding socially with others through fun and laughter, experiencing empathetic joy	Laughing inappropriately at the expense of others, seeking "silliness" in an inappropriate way (e.g., using potty words)
Feel Better Letter, Stop-Ask for a Hug	Ability to notice when others may not be feeling well or may be going through a hard time, ability to notice the needs of others	Decreased awareness or compassion for others who may be facing challenges or illness, decreased awareness of signs of distress in others
Puppet Play for Acceptance and Nonjudgment, Same and Different	Acceptance, nonjudgment, and inclusion of others	Judgment of others, exclusion of others, making fun of others for being different
Super We Teacher Helper	Noticing and acknowledging prosocial acts by others	Focusing on and complaining about negative actions of others

Module F: Social Communication

These activity options help children to effectively and functionally communicate their needs, and to do so in a way that is respectful to others.

Social Communication Activities	Skills and Quality-of-Life Indicators That May Increase in Children	Challenging Behaviors or Problems That May Decrease in Children
Helping Hand	Ability to effectively communicate a need for help in a way that is respectful and kind to others	Whining, yelling, hitting, or engaging in tantrum behaviors to seek help, escape, or request items
Voice Volume Levels, Tone Zone Game	Ability to talk with appropriate, considerate, and respectful voice volume and tone	Yelling, using a disrespectful or hurtful tone, screaming and making silly loud noises during quiet time
Help Helper	Noticing when others are struggling and need help, offering to help or obtain help for others	Ignoring others who are struggling, thinking only of one's own needs

Module G: Positive Interaction with Others (Conflict Resolution, Sharing, Helping)

These activity options help children learn to work and play cooperatively, express a heartfelt apology, and engage in conflict resolution.

Positive Interaction with Others (Conflict Resolution, Sharing, Helping) Activities	Skills and Quality-of-Life Indicators That May Increase in Children	Challenging Behaviors or Problems That May Decrease in Children
I'm Sorry Letter (Teacher Model), I'm Sorry Letter (Rhythm of Life)	Ability to take another person's perspective, ability to make a meaningful apology, forgiveness	Difficulty taking another's perspective, problems with making a meaningful apology after hurting another person
Puppet Play for Conflict Resolution, Sharing, and Helping; Rainbow Sharing	Ability to notice when others need help and offer assistance, cooperation and sharing with others, problem solving	Refusing to help with classroom chores or responsibilities, reluctance or refusal to share with others
Peacemaker	Ability to help others shift to loving-kindness and reach a peaceful compromise after a conflict or disagreement	Becoming upset, antagonizing, or joining sides when a conflict is occurring between others

Module H: Self-Compassion

These activity options help children to use self-kindness, self-acceptance and self-compassion, and refrain from saying negative things about oneself.

Self-Compassion Activities	Skills and Quality-of-Life Indicators That May Increase in Children	Challenging Behaviors or Problems That May Decrease in Children
Try Hard Scale, Super Me Self-Compassion Letter (Teacher Model), Super Me Self-Compassion Letter (Rhythm of Life)	Ability to accept oneself no matter what, ability to be kind to oneself and identify with others who are experiencing similar emotions and problems, ability to recognize one's own effort, trying even when a task is difficult	Negative statements about self, poor self-concept, self-judgment, escape from tasks perceived as too difficult
Self-Kindness Coach	Recognizing suffering and negative self-talk in others, encouraging and supporting others	Negative statements about self, limited awareness and encouragement of others who are suffering

Final Thoughts to Remember as You Begin the OMPK Program

The OMPK Program is a very robust and comprehensive program for both you and the young children you support, comprising many tools—the OpenMind REMIND practices for you, the ten Daily Practices for the classroom, the 5P Process, the Positive Engagement Support Modules, the C.R.E.A.T.E. framework, and the optional Supplemental Learning Activities—each containing numerous options. The reason there are so many options is to ensure that there will be at least one practice, activity, or technique that can help every person, no matter their abilities, preferences, culture, or unique life situation. When you become familiar with the ten Daily Practices, with using the 5P Process, and with providing mindful engagement support to children, these practices and processes will become natural and intuitive; you will feel like you aren't adding anything additional, but rather embedding these tools into what you are already doing in life and in the classroom. As you use the practices and processes, they will become less effortful and more rooted in the culture of learning and interacting. It is my hope that you can take at least one new practice from this book and use it to help make a child's life better, to make your job less stressful, to shift your perspective, or to open up new possibilities and pathways for learning, connection, engagement, and growth. Remember that you have everything you need for this journey already inside of you.

Acknowledgments

Writing this book was much more difficult than I thought it would be. As a full-time therapist and mother to four kids, who is also living with chronic illness, there would have been no way to share these ideas with you if I hadn't had an amazing spectrum of supports. Using the rainbow metaphor that is central to so many of the teachings in this book, I would like to thank:

My beautiful mother, Sheryl; my husband, Jeffrey; my mother-in-law, Paula; and my dear friend Leann, who have shown me what it means to live with unconditional kindness, service, and thoughtfulness; and my dad, Richard, who has left a legacy of enduring love and connection for us and countless others [RED];

My mentor, Nirbhay, who has taught me about mindfulness, awareness, equanimity, and life itself, and set me on this path; Joan Halifax, Pema Chödrön, and all of the brilliant mindfulness teachers and researchers before me and around me; my first mentor, Edna; Jill, Stephanie, Kelly, Emilee, and Jenny, and everyone at JFCAC who opened the door to the OMPK research opportunity; and all of the problems, mistakes, conflicts, and uncertain times that have given me an education in open acceptance [ORANGE];

My sister, Melissa, the funniest person I know; my sunshine BFF, Nicole; my fun-loving family, including my bonus siblings Joe, Jason, Audrey, Dan, Debby, Sandy, and Carrie, my nieces and nephews, cousins, aunts and uncles; my amazing friends; Jess, Wendy, Alicia, Kelcee, Kristen, Lisa, Lizzette, Ramasamy, Suzzette, Rob, Daphna, and the Ya-yas (Kimmie and Jodi), who have brought me boundless joy and laughter [YELLOW];

All of the teachers, Head Start staff, nurses, clients, and caregivers I have worked with and been inspired by; and the brave hearts who have fought unimaginable battles (especially the brilliant lights, Emmanuel and Kyle), who have shown me what it means to stay grounded [GREEN];

The beaches, trees, moon, sky, rocks, and the words "be still and know that I am God," which have brought me peace [BLUE];

The pain, chronic illness, and loss I have experienced that have deepened my compassion [INDIGO]; and finally,

My four beautiful, wonderful, inspiring, perfect children, Gabriella, Maxim, Miles, and Paxton, and my magical grandson, Isaac, who have filled me with more gratitude, inspiration, and appreciation than I can put into words [VIOLET].

I also would like to thank New Harbinger for the opportunity to publish this book, and my editors, Tesilya, Caleb, Rona, and Michele for their patient and kind guidance and support, for their brilliant feedback, and for letting me have so much rainbow in a black and white book.

References

Abenavoli, R. M., Jennings, P. A., Greenberg, M. T., Harris, A. R., & Katz, D. A. (2013). The protective effects of mindfulness against burnout among educators. *Psychology of Education Review, 37*(2), 57–69.

Alloway, T. P., Gathercole, S. E., & Pickering, S. J. (2006). Verbal and visuospatial short-term and working memory in children: Are they separable? *Child Development, 77*(6), 1698–1716.

Anālayo, B. (2016). Early Buddhist mindfulness and memory, the body, and pain. *Mindfulness, 7*(6), 1271–1280.

Baglivio, M. T., Wolff, K. T., Piquero, A. R., Greenwald, M. A., & Epps, N. (2017). Racial/ethnic disproportionality in psychiatric diagnoses and treatment in a sample of serious juvenile offenders. *Journal of Youth and Adolescence, 46*(7), 1424–1451.

Barrett, L. F. (2006). Are emotions natural kinds? *Perspectives on Psychological Science, 1*(1), 28–58.

Barrett, L. F., Gross, J., Christensen, T. C., & Benvenuto, M. (2001). Knowing what you're feeling and knowing what to do about it: Mapping the relation between emotion differentiation and emotion regulation. *Cognition & Emotion, 15*(6), 713–724.

Barrett, L. F., Tugade, M. M., & Engle, R. W. (2004). Individual differences in working memory capacity and dual-process theories of the mind. *Psychological Bulletin, 130*(4), 553.

Battig, W. F. (1979). *The flexibility of human memory: Levels of processing and human memory.* Lawrence Erlbaum Associates, 23–44.

Baumeister, R. F., Bratslavsky, E., Finkenauer, C., & Vohs, K. D. (2001). Bad is stronger than good. *Review of General Psychology, 5*(4), 323.

Bechara, A., Damasio, A. R., Damasio, H., & Anderson, S. W. (1994). Insensitivity to future consequences following damage to human prefrontal cortex. *Cognition, 50*(1–3), 7–15.

Birch, S. H., & Ladd, G. W. (1997). The teacher-child relationship and children's early school adjustment. *Journal of School Psychology, 35*(1), 61–79.

Blair, C., Raver, C. C., Granger, D., Mills-Koonce, R., Hibel, L., & Family Life Project Key Investigators. (2011). Allostasis and allostatic load in the context of poverty in early childhood. *Development and Psychopathology, 23*(3), 845–857.

Brackett, M. A., Rivers, S. E., & Salovey, P. (2011). Emotional intelligence: Implications for personal, social, academic, and workplace success. *Social and Personality Psychology Compass, 5*(1), 88–103.

Bradley, R. H., & Corwyn, R. F. (2002). Socioeconomic status and child development. *Annual Review of Psychology, 53*(1), 371–399.

Bull, R., Espy, K. A., & Wiebe, S. A. (2008). Short-term memory, working memory, and executive functioning in preschoolers: Longitudinal predictors of mathematical achievement at age 7 years. *Developmental Neuropsychology, 33*(3), 205–228.

Buttelmann, F., & Karbach, J. (2017). Development and plasticity of cognitive flexibility in early and middle childhood. *Frontiers in Psychology, 8,* 1040.

Cacioppo, J. T., Hawkley, L. C., Crawford, L. E., Ernst, J. M., Burleson, M. H., Kowalewski, R. B., Malarkey, W. B., Van Cauter, E., & Berntson, G. G. (2002). Loneliness and health: Potential mechanisms. *Psychosomatic Medicine, 64*(3), 407–417.

Chambers, R., Lo, B. C. Y., & Allen, N. B. (2008). The impact of intensive mindfulness training on attentional control, cognitive style, and affect. *Cognitive Therapy and Research, 32*(3), 303–322.

Chiesa, A., Calati, R., & Serretti, A. (2011). Does mindfulness training improve cognitive abilities? A systematic review of neuropsychological findings. *Clinical Psychology Review, 31*(3), 449–464.

Chödrön, P. (2001). *Start where you are: A guide to compassionate living.* Shambhala Publications.

Cohn, M. A., Fredrickson, B. L., Brown, S. L., Mikels, J. A., & Conway, A. M. (2009). Happiness unpacked: Positive emotions increase life satisfaction by building resilience. *Emotion, 9*(3), 361.

Collaborative for Academic, Social, and Emotional Learning. (2013). *Effective social and emotional learning programs: Preschool and elementary school edition.*

Craig, A. D. (2009). Emotional moments across time: A possible neural basis for time perception in the anterior insula. *Philosophical Transactions of the Royal Society of London. Series B, Biological Sciences, 364*(1525), 1933–1942.

Critchley, H. D., & Garfinkel, S. N. (2017). Interoception and emotion. *Current Opinion in Psychology, 17,* 7–14.

Csikszentmihalyi, M., & Csikzentmihaly, M. (1990). *Flow: The psychology of optimal experience* (Vol. 1990). Harper & Row.

Dael, N., Mortillaro, M., & Scherer, K. R. (2012). Emotion expression in body action and posture. *Emotion, 12*(5), 1085.

Damasio, A. R. (1994). Descartes' Error. Emotion, reason, and the human brain. Grosset/Putnam.

Damasio, A. R. (1999). The feeling of what happens: Body and emotion in the making of consciousness. *New York Times Book Review, 104,* 8.

Damasio, A. R. (1996). The somatic marker hypothesis and the possible functions of the prefrontal cortex. *Philosophical Transactions of the Royal Society of London. Series B: Biological Sciences, 351*(1346), 1413-1420.

Denham, S. A., Blair, K. A., DeMulder, E., Levitas, J., Sawyer, K., Auerbach-Major, S., & Queenan, P. (2003). Preschool emotional competence: Pathway to social competence? *Child Development, 74*(1), 238–256.

Desbordes, G., Negi, L. T., Pace, T. W., Wallace, B. A., Raison, C. L., & Schwartz, E. L. (2012). Effects of mindful-attention and compassion meditation training on amygdala response to emotional stimuli in an ordinary, non-meditative state. *Frontiers in Human Neuroscience, 6,* 292.

Diamond, A. (2002). Normal development of prefrontal cortex from birth to young adulthood: Cognitive functions, anatomy, and biochemistry. *Principles of frontal lobe function,* 466–503.

Diamond, A., Barnett, W. S., Thomas, J., & Munro, S. (2007). Preschool program improves cognitive control. *Science* (New York, NY), *318*(5855), 1387.

Diamond, A., & Lee, K. (2011). Interventions shown to aid executive function development in children 4 to 12 years old. *Science, 333*(6045), 959–964.

Doebel, S., & Zelazo, P. D. (2015). A meta-analysis of the Dimensional Change Card Sort: Implications for developmental theories and the measurement of executive function in children. *Developmental Review, 38,* 241–268.

Duncan, G. J., & Brooks-Gunn, J. (2000). Family poverty, welfare reform, and child development. *Child Development, 71*(1), 188–196.

Durlak, J. A., Weissberg, R. P., Dymnicki, A. B., Taylor, R. D., & Schellinger, K. B. (2011). The impact of enhancing students' social and emotional learning: A meta-analysis of school-based universal interventions. *Child Development, 82*(1), 405–432.

Egeth, H. E., & Yantis, S. (1997). Visual attention: Control, representation, and time course. *Annual Review of Psychology, 48*(1), 269–297.

Emmons, R. A., & Mishra, A. (2011). Why gratitude enhances well-being: What we know, what we need to know. *Designing Positive Psychology: Taking Stock and Moving Forward,* 248–262.

Ertel, K. A., Glymour, M. M., & Berkman, L. F. (2009). Social networks and health: A life course perspective integrating observational and experimental evidence. *Journal of Social and Personal Relationships, 26*(1), 73.

Everson-Rose, S. A., & Lewis, T. T. (2005). Psychosocial factors and cardiovascular diseases. *Annual Review of Public Health, 26,* 469–500.

Farb, N. A., Segal, Z. V., & Anderson, A. K. (2012). Mindfulness meditation training alters cortical representations of interoceptive attention. *Social Cognitive and Affective Neuroscience,* nss066.

Felver, J. C., & Singh, N. N. (2020). *Mindfulness in the classroom: An evidence-based program to reduce disruptive behavior and increase academic engagement.* New Harbinger Publications.

Finn, J. D., & Rock, D. A. (1997). Academic success among students at risk for school failure. *Journal of Applied Psychology, 82*(2), 221.

Fiske, S. T., & Taylor, S. E. (2017). *Social cognition: From brains to culture* (3rd edition). Sage.

Frankl, V. E. (1985). *Man's search for meaning.* Simon and Schuster.

Gathercole, S. E., Pickering, S. J., Ambridge, B., & Wearing, H. (2004). The structure of working memory from 4 to 15 years of age. *Developmental Psychology, 40*(2), 177.

Gentzler, A. L., Contreras-Grau, J. M., Kerns, K. A., & Weimer, B. L. (2005). Parent-child emotional communication and children's coping in middle childhood. *Social Development, 14*(4), 591–612.

Gilovich, T. (1983). Biased evaluation and persistence in gambling. *Journal of Personality and Social Psychology, 44*(6), 1110.

Greenberg, M. T., Katz, D. A., & Klein, L. C. (2015). The potential effects of SEL on biomarkers and health outcomes: A promissory note. In J. A. Durlak, C. E. Domitrovich, R. P. Weissberg, & T. P. Gullotta (Eds.), *Handbook of social and emotional learning: Research and practice* (pp. 81–96). The Guildford Press.

Gruber, M. J., Gelman, B. D., & Ranganath, C. (2014). States of curiosity modulate hippocampus-dependent learning via the dopaminergic circuit. *Neuron, 84*(2), 486–496.

Halifax, J. (2008). *Being with dying: Cultivating compassion and fearlessness in the presence of death.* Shambhala Publications.

Hamilton, D. M. (2013). *Everything is workable: A Zen approach to conflict resolution.* Shambhala Publications.

Hasselkus, B. R. (2006). The world of everyday occupation: Real people, real lives. *American Journal of Occupational Therapy, 60*(6), 627–640.

Hofmann, S. G., Grossman, P., & Hinton, D. E. (2011). Loving-kindness and compassion meditation: Potential for psychological interventions. *Clinical Psychology Review, 31*(7), 1126–1132.

House, J. S., Landis, K. R., & Umberson, D. (1988). Social relationships and health. *Science, 241*(4865), 540–545.

Holzel, B., Lazar, S.W., Gard, T., Shuman, Z., Vago, D.R. & Ott, U. (2011). How does mindfulness meditation work? Proposing mechanisms of action from a conceptual and neural perspective. *Perspectives on Psychological Science, 6*(6) 537–559.

Hutcherson, C. A., Seppala, E. M., & Gross, J. J. (2008). Loving-kindness meditation increases social connectedness. *Emotion, 8*(5), 720.

Jackman, M. M. (2014). Mindful occupational engagement. In N. N. Singh (Ed.), *Psychology of meditation* (pp. 241–277). Nova Science Publishers.

Jackman, M. M., Nabors, L. A., McPherson, C. L., Quaid, J. D., & Singh, N. N. (2019). Feasibility, acceptability, and preliminary effectiveness of the OpenMind (OM) Program for Pre-School Children. *Journal of Child and Family Studies, 28*(10), 2910–2921.

James, W. (1890). Principles of Psychology 2 vols. New York: Henry Holt. 1992-94. *Collected Correspondence of William James, 8.*

Jazaieri, H., McGonigal, K., Jinpa, T., Doty, J. R., Gross, J. J., & Goldin, P. R. (2014). A randomized controlled trial of compassion cultivation training: Effects on mindfulness, affect, and emotion regulation. *Motivation and Emotion, 38(1),* 23–35.

Jennings, P. A., & Greenberg, M. T. (2009). The prosocial classroom: Teacher social and emotional competence in relation to student and classroom outcomes. *Review of Educational Research, 79(1),* 491-525.

Jinpa, T. (2010). Buddhism and science: How far can the dialogue proceed?. *Zygon, 45(4),* 871–882.

Kabat-Zinn, J. (1990). University of Massachusetts Medical Center/Worcester. Stress Reduction Clinic. Full catastrophe living: using the wisdom of your body and mind to face stress, pain, and illness. *Delta, New York.*

Kabat-Zinn, J. (1994). *Wherever you go, there you are: Mindfulness meditation in everyday life.* Hyperion.

Kaiser, A. P., Hancock, T. B., Cai, X., Michael, E., & Hester, P. P. (2000). Parent-reported behavioral problems and language delays in boys and girls enrolled in Head Start classrooms. *Behavioral Disorders, 26(1),* 26–41.

Kang, Y., Gray, J. R., & Dovidio, J. F. (2014). The nondiscriminating heart: Lovingkindness meditation training decreases implicit intergroup bias. *Journal of Experimental Psychology: General, 143(3),* 1306.

Kaplan, S. (1995). The restorative benefits of nature: Toward an integrative framework. *Journal of Environmental Psychology, 15,* 169–182.

Kaplan, S., & Berman, M. G. (2010). Directed attention as a common resource for executive functioning and self-regulation. Perspectives on Psychological Science, 5(1), 43–57.

Kerr, C. E., Sacchet, M. D., Lazar, S. W., Moore, C. I., & Jones, S. R. (2013). Mindfulness starts with the body: Somatosensory attention and top-down modulation of cortical alpha rhythms in mindfulness meditation. *Frontiers in Human Neuroscience, 7,* 12.

Kiecolt-Glaser, J. K., McGuire, L., Robles, T. F., & Glaser, R. (2002). Emotions, morbidity, and mortality: New perspectives from psychoneuroimmunology. *Annual Review of Psychology, 53(1),* 83–107.

Kiken, L. G., & Shook, N. J. (2011). Looking up: Mindfulness increases positive judgments and reduces negativity bias. *Social Psychological and Personality Science, 2(4),* 425–431.

Kim, E., Jackman, M. M., Jo, S. H., Oh, J., Ko, S. Y., McPherson, C. L., Hwang, Y-S., & Singh, N. N. (2020). Effectiveness of the mindfulness-based OpenMind-Korea (OM-K) preschool program. *Mindfulness, 11(4),* 1062–1072.

Kim, E., Jackman, M. M., Jo, S. H., Oh, J., Ko, S. Y., McPherson, C. L., & Singh, N. N. (2019a). Feasibility and Acceptability of the Mindfulness-Based OpenMind-Korea (OM-K) Preschool Program. *Journal of Child and Family Studies,* 1–12.

Kim, E., Jackman, M. M., Jo, S. H., Oh, J., Ko, S. Y., McPherson, C. L., & Singh, N. N. (2019b). Parental Social Validity of the Mindfulness-Based OpenMind-Korea (OM-K) Preschool Program. *Journal of Child and Family Studies,* 1–5.

Kirkham, N. Z., Cruess, L., & Diamond, A. (2003). Helping children apply their knowledge to their behavior on a dimension-switching task. *Developmental Science, 6(5),* 449–467.

Klimecki, O. M., Leiberg, S., Lamm, C., & Singer, T. (2012). Functional neural plasticity and associated changes in positive affect after compassion training. *Cerebral Cortex, 23(7),* 1552–1561.

Kochanska, G., Murray, K., & Coy, K. C. (1997). Inhibitory control as a contributor to conscience in childhood: From toddler to early school age. *Child Development, 68(2),* 263–277.

Kochanska, G., Murray, K. T., & Harlan, E. T. (2000). Effortful control in early childhood: continuity and change, antecedents, and implications for social development. Developmental Psychology, 36(2), 220.

Kochanska, G., Murray, K., Jacques, T. Y., Koenig, A. L., & Vandegeest, K. A. (1996). Inhibitory control in young children and its role in emerging internalization. *Child Development, 67*(2), 490–507.

Kok, B. E., Coffey, K. A., Cohn, M. A., Catalino, L. I., Vacharkulksemsuk, T., Algoe, S. B., Brantley, M., & Fredrickson, B. L. (2013). How positive emotions build physical health: Perceived positive social connections account for the upward spiral between positive emotions and vagal tone. *Psychological Science, 24*(7), 1123–1132.

Kok, B. E., & Singer, T. (2017). Phenomenological fingerprints of four meditations: Differential state changes in affect, mind-wandering, meta-cognition, and interoception before and after daily practice across 9 months of training. *Mindfulness, 8*(1), 218–231.

Krishnamurti, J. (1972). *The flight of the eagle.* Harper & Row.

Kyabgon, T. (2007). *The practice of lojong: Cultivating compassion through training the mind.* Shambhala.

Lai, S. T., & O'Carroll, R. E. (2017). 'The Three Good Things' – the effects of gratitude practice on wellbeing: A randomised controlled trial. *Health Psychology Update, 26*(1), 11.

Lama, D., Tutu, D., & Abrams, D. C. (2016). *The book of joy: Lasting happiness in a changing world.* Penguin.

Lieberman, M. D. (2013). *Social: Why our brains are wired to connect.* Crown Publishers/Random House.

Lieberman, M. D., Eisenberger, N. I., Crockett, M. J., Tom, S. M., Pfeifer, J. H., & Way, B. M. (2007). Putting feelings into words. *Psychological Science, 18*(5), 421–428.

Lutz, A., Slagter, H. A., Dunne, J. D., & Davidson, R. J. (2008). Attention regulation and monitoring in meditation. *Trends in Cognitive Sciences, 12*(4), 163–169.

Magill, R. A. (2001). *Motor learning: Concepts and applications* (6th ed.). Brown & Benchmark.

Magill, R. A., & Hall, K. G. (1990). A review of the contextual interference effect in motor skill acquisition. *Human Movement Science, 9*(3–5), 241–289.

McCown, D., Reibel, D., & Micozzi, M. S. (2010). *Teaching mindfulness: A practical guide for clinicians and educators.* Springer.

Mistry, R. S., Benner, A. D., Biesanz, J. C., Clark, S. L., & Howes, C. (2010). Family and social risk, and parental investments during the early childhood years as predictors of low-income children's school readiness outcomes. *Early Childhood Research Quarterly, 25*(4), 432–449.

Moffitt, T. E., Arseneault, L., Belsky, D., Dickson, N., Hancox, R. J., Harrington, H., Houts, R., Poulton, R., Roberts, B. W., Ross, S., Sears, M. R., Thompson, W. M., & Caspi, A. (2011). A gradient of childhood self-control predicts health, wealth, and public safety. *Proceedings of the National Academy of Sciences,* 108(7), 2693–2698.

Molineux, M. L., & Whiteford, G. E. (1999). Prisons: From occupational deprivation to occupational enrichment. *Journal of Occupational Science, 6*(3), 124–130.

Morgan, P. L., Hillemeier, M. M., Farkas, G., & Maczuga, S. (2014). Racial/ethnic disparities in ADHD diagnosis by kindergarten entry. *Journal of Child Psychology and Psychiatry, 55*(8), 905–913.

Moriguchi, Y., & Hiraki, K. (2011). Longitudinal development of prefrontal function during early childhood. *Developmental Cognitive Neuroscience, 1*(2), 153–162.

National Center for Children in Poverty (2018). *United States demographics of young, poor children.* https://www.nccp.org/demographic/?state=US&id=9.

Öhman, A., Lundqvist, D., & Esteves, F. (2001). The face in the crowd revisited: A threat advantage with schematic stimuli. *Journal of Personality and Social Psychology, 80*(3), 381.

Osterman, K. F. (2000). Students' need for belonging in the school community. *Review of Educational Research, 70*(3), 323–367.

Peeters, G., & Czapinski, J. (1990). Positive-negative asymmetry in evaluations: The distinction between affective and informational negativity effects. *European Review of Social Psychology, 1*(1), 33–60.

Pratto, F., & John, O. P. (1991). Automatic vigilance: The attention-grabbing power of negative social information. *Journal of Personality and Social Psychology, 61*(3), 380.

Raver, C. C., Blair, C., & Willoughby, M. (2013). Poverty as a predictor of 4-year-olds' executive function: New perspectives on models of differential susceptibility. *Developmental Psychology, 49*(2), 292.

Raver, C. C., Jones, S. M., Li-Grining, C., Zhai, F., Bub, K., & Pressler, E. (2011). CSRP's impact on low-income preschoolers' preacademic skills: Self-regulation as a mediating mechanism. *Child Development, 82*(1), 362–378.

Rhoades, B. L., Greenberg, M. T., & Domitrovich, C. E. (2009). The contribution of inhibitory control to preschoolers' social-emotional competence. *Journal of Applied Developmental Psychology, 30*(3), 310–320.

Robles, T. F., & Kiecolt-Glaser, J. K. (2003). The physiology of marriage: Pathways to health. *Physiology, 79*(3), 409–16.

Rochat, P. (2003). Five levels of self-awareness as they unfold early in life. *Consciousness and Cognition, 12*(4), 717–731.

Rozin, P., & Royzman, E. B. (2001). Negativity bias, negativity dominance, and contagion. *Personality and Social Psychology Review, 5*(4), 296–320.

Salovey, P., Hsee, C. K., & Mayer, J. D. (1993). Emotional intelligence and the self-regulation of affect. In D. M. Wegner & J. W. Pennebaker (Eds.), *Handbook of mental control* (pp. 258–277). Prentice-Hall, Inc.

Santoro, D. A. (2011). Good teaching in difficult times: Demoralization in the pursuit of good work. *American Journal of Education, 118*(1), 1–23.

Santos, R. M., Fettig, A., & Shaffer, L. (2012). Helping families connect early literacy with social-emotional development. *Young Children, 67*(2), 88–93.

Schofield, T. P., Creswell, J. D., & Denson, T. F. (2015). Brief mindfulness induction reduces inattentional blindness. *Consciousness, 37*, 63–70.

Schoenewolf, G. (1990). Emotional contagion: Behavioral induction in individuals and groups. *Modern Psychoanalysis, 15*(1), 49–61.

Seth, A. K. (2013). Interoceptive inference, emotion, and the embodied self. *Trends in Cognitive Sciences, 17*(11), 565–573.

Shing, Y. L., Lindenberger, U., Diamond, A., Li, S. C., & Davidson, M. C. (2010). Memory maintenance and inhibitory control differentiate from early childhood to adolescence. *Developmental Neuropsychology, 35*(6), 679–697.

Singh, N. N., Lancioni, G. E., Karazsia, B. T., Chan, J., & Winton, A. S. W. (2016b). Effectiveness of caregiver training in mindfulness-based positive behavior support (MBPBS) vs. training-as-usual (TAU): A randomized controlled trial. *Frontiers in Psychology, 7*, 1549.

Singh, N. N., Lancioni, G. E., Karazsia, B. T., & Myers, R. E. (2016a). Caregiver training in Mindfulness-Based Positive Behavior Supports (MBPBS): Effects on caregivers and adults with intellectual and developmental disabilities. *Frontiers in Psychology, 7*, 98.

Singh, N. N., Lancioni, G. E., Karazsia, B. T., Myers, R. E., Winton, A. S., Latham, L. L., & Nugent, K. (2015). Effects of training staff in MBPBS on the use of physical restraints, staff stress and turnover, staff and peer injuries, and cost effectiveness in developmental disabilities. *Mindfulness, 6*(4), 926-937.

Singh, N. N., Lancioni, G. E., Karazsia, B. T., Winton, A. S., Myers, R. E., Singh, A. N., Singh, D. A., & Singh, J. (2013). Mindfulness-based treatment of aggression in individuals with mild intellectual disabilities: A waiting list control study. *Mindfulness, 4,* 158–167.

Singh, N. N., Lancioni, G. E., Winton, A. S., Karazsia, B. T., Myers, R. E., Latham, L. L., & Singh, J. (2014). Mindfulness-based positive behavior support (MBPBS) for mothers of adolescents with autism spectrum disorder: Effects on adolescents' behavior and parental stress. *Mindfulness, 5*(6), 646–657.

Singh, N. N., Lancioni, G. E., Winton, A. S., Singh, A. N., Adkins, A. D., & Singh, J. (2009). Mindful staff can reduce the use of physical restraints when providing care to individuals with intellectual disabilities. *Journal of Applied Research in Intellectual Disabilities, 22*(2), 194–202.

Singh, N. N., Singh, A. N., Lancioni, G. E., Singh, J., Winton, A. S., & Adkins, A. D. (2010). Mindfulness training for parents and their children with ADHD increases the children's compliance. *Journal of Child and Family Studies, 19*(2), 157–166.

Sumedho, A. (1990). *Teachings of a Buddhist monk.* Buddhist Publishing Group.

Sumedho, A., & Amaro, A. (2007). The sound of silence: The selected teachings of Ajahn Sumedho. Simon and Schuster.

Suzuki, K., Garfinkel, S. N., Critchley, H. D., & Seth, A. K. (2013). Multisensory integration across exteroceptive and interoceptive domains modulates self-experience in the rubber-hand illusion. *Neuropsychologia, 51*(13), 2909–2917.

Tang, Y. Y., Hölzel, B. K., & Posner, M. I. (2015). The neuroscience of mindfulness meditation. *Nature Reviews Neuroscience, 16*(4), 213–225.

Thanissaro Bhikkhu. (1996). *Wings to awakening: An anthology from the Pali canon.* Dhamma Dana Publications.

Tsang, K. K., & Liu, D. (2016). Teacher demoralization, disempowerment and school administration. *Qualitative Research in Education, 5*(2), 200–225.

Tugade, M. M., Fredrickson, B. L., & Feldman Barrett, L. (2004). Psychological resilience and positive emotional granularity: Examining the benefits of positive emotions on coping and health. *Journal of Personality, 72*(6), 1161–1190.

Uchino, B. N. (2006). Social support and health: a review of physiological processes potentially underlying links to disease outcomes. *Journal of behavioral medicine, 29*(4), 377–387.

Vago, D. R., & Silbersweig, D. A. (2012). Self-awareness, self-regulation, and self-transcendence (S-ART): A framework for understanding the neurobiological mechanisms of mindfulness. *Frontiers in Human Neuroscience, 6,* 296.

Wanless, S. B., McClelland, M. M., Tominey, S. L., & Acock, A. C. (2011). The influence of demographic risk factors on children's behavioral regulation in prekindergarten and kindergarten. *Early Education & Development, 22*(3), 461–488.

Waters, L. (2012). Predicting job satisfaction: Contributions of individual gratitude and institutionalized gratitude. *Psychology, 3*(12A special issue), 1174.

Willis, J., & Todorov, A. (2006). First impressions: Making up your mind after a 100-ms exposure to a face. *Psychological Science, 17*(7), 592–598.

Zaki, J., Davis, J. I., & Ochsner, K. N. (2012). Overlapping activity in anterior insula during interoception and emotional experience. *Neuroimage, 62*(1), 493–499.

Zeidan, F., Johnson, S. K., Diamond, B. J., David, Z., & Goolkasian, P. (2010). Mindfulness meditation improves cognition: Evidence of brief mental training. *Consciousness and Cognition, 19*(2), 597–605.

Monica Moore Jackman, OTD, MHS, OTR/L, is an occupational therapist, and owner of Little Lotus Therapy. She has a doctorate in occupational therapy from Chatham University, and undergraduate and master of health sciences degrees from the University of Florida. Monica has authored book chapters and research papers on mindful engagement, the mindful engagement support model, and mindfulness interventions, and has developed and implemented mindfulness-based training programs for adults, caregivers, preschoolers, and school-aged children. As an occupational therapist, she is dedicated to making mindfulness-based interventions inclusive and accessible to all learners, and supporting people to experience meaning, connection, and engagement in life. She has presented nationally and internationally on mindfulness-based programs and interventions. She has practiced for over twenty years in a variety of clinical settings, and served as an expert consultant to the Department of Justice for cases under the Civil Rights of Institutionalized Persons Act. Finally, she is a mother of four who uses these practices with her own family.

Foreword writer **Nirbhay N. Singh**, PhD, BCBA-D, is clinical professor of psychiatry and health behavior at the Medical College of Georgia at Augusta University, a certified behavior analyst, and developer of the Mindfulness-Based Positive Behavior Support (MBPBS) and Soles of the Feet programs. His research focuses on assistive technology, health and wellness interventions, and mindfulness-based programs across the life span that reduce suffering and enhance quality of life. He is editor in chief of *Mindfulness* and *Advances in Neurodevelopmental Disorders*.

Index

Hoberman sphere, 100, 120, 121
How Can I Help? practice, 83
humor, sharing, 68

I

implicit bias, 23, 52, 58–59
inattention blindness, 57
inattentional bias, 43
independence vs. autonomy, 227
indigo color, 16, 46, 80
informal mindfulness practices, 16, 49; being present and open, 62–64; compassion in action, 82–83; gratitude in action, 85–86; grounded in action, 73–75; joy in action, 67–68; loving-kindness, 54–55; peaceful in action, 79
inhibitory control, 119, 185–186
interconnectedness practices, 21, 161. *See also* gratitude practices
interoceptive awareness, 69–70
"It's Okay to Feel Yucky Song," 139

J

jokes, sharing, 68
joy practices, 65–68; active forms of, 67–68; characteristics of, 16, 46, 66; empathetic joy and, 32, 66, 68; formal meditations as, 66–67; PAUSE practices as, 68; when they're helpful, 66
judgments: biases and, 58–59; noticing your own, 64

K

Kabat-Zinn, Jon, 47, 71, 124
kindness: acting with, 55; discussion about noticing, 168; helper job activity, 169, 170; practice of reporting, 21, 168–170; self-kindness as, 145; Super Me practice of, 144
kinesthetic awareness, 69
King, Martin Luther, viii
Krishnamurti, J., 41

L

laughter, 66, 68
learning readiness, 4–5
Letting It All Settle practice, 79
Listen to the Pain practice, 75
Listening for Your Own Bell practice, 63
listening mindfully, 57–58, 60–61
lotus breathing, 86, 102

lotus flower metaphor, 84
loving-kindness practices, 51–55, 154–160; active forms of, 54–55; benefits corresponding to, 21; characteristics of, 16, 32, 46; Connected by Love activity, 156; Fixing and Forgiving activity, 160; greetings/farewells based on, 154–155; meditations as, 53–54, 154–155, 157, 159; PAUSE practices as, 55; sending loving-kindness, 159; "Thank You for Being You Song," 158; for those not in school, 157; when they're helpful, 52

M

mealtime gratitude practice, 162
meditation: body scan, 71–72, 126–127, 129; breathing and, 47–48; context and location of, 48; Daily Practices of, 20, 98–110; felt safety related to, 49; habit and routine of, 49; loving-kindness, 53–54, 154–155, 157, 159; rainbow practice of, 86–87; REMIND practices of, 16, 74, 86–87; sitting, 20, 98–108; skills and behaviors served by, 20; stable postures for, 47; walking, 20, 74, 109–110, 127. *See also* mindfulness
meta-awareness, 30
mindful eating, 124–125
mindful engagement: C.R.E.A.T.E. model supporting, 225–236; in human occupations, 25–26, 223–225; participation vs., 25, 224, 227–228
mindful movement, 73, 127–128
mindfulness: ability to teach, 40–41; benefits to practicing, 39–43; caregiver training in, 42–43; children's practice of, 10, 13; classroom management and, 35; definition and description of, 8–10; five parts in practice of, 29–32; formal practice of, 16, 47–49; informal practice of, 16, 49; link between SEL and, 34–35; listening with, 57–58; rainbow practice of, 86–87; secular vs. religious practice of, 28–29; teacher practice of, 15–17, 38, 39–43. *See also* meditation
Mindfulness-Based Stress Reduction, 71, 124
minority children, 23–24, 180, 190
mirror neuron system, 69
monkey mind, 30, 55
movement: guided, 20, 109–110; large group, 127–128; matching sound and, 121–122;

mindful, 73, 127–128; self-control of, 238, 240; slow, 120
multitasking: mindfulness vs., 9–10; practicing serial, 79

N

negativity bias, 59, 68
Ninja Tower activity, 110
nonjudgment, 31, 58–59
Noticing Joy in Self practice, 67
Noticing Thoughts practice, 61
Noticing Your Own Judgment, Perception, and Bias practice, 64

O

observational learning, 15
occupational deprivation, 221
occupational injustice, 222
occupations: definition of, 16, 25, 221; human importance of, 221–222; mindful engagement in, 25–26, 223–225; OMPK format based on, 17
open heart practices, 31–32
open monitoring meditation, 16, 46, 61. *See also* present and open practices
Opening Up a Window practice, 62
OpenMind Preschool and Kindergarten (OMPK) program, vii–viii, 2–3; accessibility and learning readiness, 4–5; equanimity developed through, 7–8; five foundations of, 14–26; format of, 26–27; learning modalities within, 93; mindfulness practice and, 8–10, 13; overarching strengths of, viii; practices associated with, 5–7; reasons for using, 13; REMIND practices, 15–16; research supporting, 10–12
OpenMind-Korea (OM-K) program, 11–12
orange color, 16, 46, 55
Orange Elephant Meditation, 61

P

pain: meditation on noticing, 72; practices for working with, 74–75; suffering distinguished from, 70–71
participation vs. engagement, 25, 224, 227–228
"Pass the Water Song," 126
patience, 228
PAUSE practices, 16–17, 49–50; compassion, 83; gratitude, 86; grounded, 75; joy, 68;

loving-kindness, 55; peaceful, 79–80; present and open, 65
peaceful practices, 76–80; active forms of, 79; focused attention and, 76–77; formal meditations as, 78; PAUSE practices as, 79–80; when they're helpful, 77
pleasure vs. joy, 66
positive behaviors, 23–24
positive engagement support (PES) modules, 204–220; Module 1: Receiving Attention and Increasing Social Connection, 206–209; Module 2: Engaging in Teacher-Directed Activities and Cooperating with Teacher Requests, 209–212; Module 3: Staying Present in the Learning and/or Eating Area, 212–215; Module 4: Making Transitions Within a Routine and Coping with Changes, 215–217; Module 5: Sharing and Working with Others, 217–220; overview table describing, 205; reasons for development of, 204; reflection on implementing, 220
positive interactions, 238, 246
posture for meditation, 47
poverty, children living in, 24, 180
practices, 5–7; planned lessons and, 22–23; rhythm of life and, 17–21; teacher mindfulness, 15–17. *See also* Daily Practices
praising children, 199–201
preparing children to learn, 191–192
present and open practices, 55–65; active forms of, 62–64; characteristics of, 16, 46, 56–60; formal meditations as, 60–61; PAUSE practices as, 65; when they're helpful, 60
present-moment awareness, 228, 241
problem solving, 195–197
proprioceptive awareness, 69
prosocial behaviors, 182, 197–199
protecting children, 188–189
punishment, 180–181, 221

Q

qi-gong practice, 73
quality-of-life factors, 209, 212, 214–215, 217, 220
Quiet Bell activity, 118

R

racism, systemic, 23–24
rainbow breathing, 103

rainbow meditation practice, 86–87

red color, 16, 46, 51

regret prevention, 231–232

reinforcement, 232

relationship skills, 34

relaxing vs. rushing, 228–229

religious/spiritual practices, 28–29

remembrance, 231–232

REMIND practices, 15–16, 51–86; benefits of, 43–45; compassion practices, 80–83; formal vs. informal, 47–49; gratitude practices, 84–86; grounded and embodied practices, 69–76; joy practices, 65–68; loving-kindness practices, 51–55; peaceful practices, 76–80; present and open practices, 55–65; purpose of, 39, 40–41; rainbow meditation and, 86–87; SOS strategy and, 87–88; suggestions for using, 89; wellness states corresponding to, 16, 46

reporting kindness and compassion, 21, 168–170

research supporting OMPK program, 10–12

responsible decision making, 34

restlessness, sitting with, 62

rhythm of life practice, 17–21, 174

"right" mindfulness, 9, 13

rushing vs. relaxing, 228–229

S

samatha meditation, 98

Schairer, Sara, 82

Seeing with My Hands exercise, 124

self: loving-kindness to, 53; noticing joy in, 67; therapeutic use of, 190

self-awareness, 33, 183–184, 238, 240

self-calming, 238, 242

self-compassion, 82, 238, 247

self-control, 119, 238, 240

self-kindness, 145, 238, 247

self-management, 33

self-preservation, 217

self-regulation, 4, 182, 184, 187, 243

self-serving attributional bias, 59

Serial Multitasking practice, 79

sharing: gratitude, 86; helping children with, 217–220, 246; joy and humor, 68

shifting practices, 171–176; "Big Feelings, Small Bodies Song," 171; Feelings Feeder activities, 175, 176; rhythm of life practice,

174; skills and behaviors served by, 21; Soles of the Little Feet exercises, 172–174

Singh, Nirbhay, vii–ix, 42, 171

sinking ship metaphor, 39, 87

sitting meditation, 98–108; bell exercises, 99, 104; breathing exercises, 100, 102–104, 106–107; daily practice instructions, 108; skills and behaviors served by, 20

Sitting with Boredom or Restlessness practice, 62

skills: generalization and retention of, 17–18; targeted in 5P Process, 182–187

slow movement exercises, 120

social awareness, 33, 184–185, 238, 244

social communication, 238, 245

social connections, 208–209, 238, 244

social-emotional learning (SEL) programs, vii, 3; five domains of, 32–34; link between mindfulness and, 34–35

Soles of the Little Feet practices, 171–176; "Big Feelings, Small Bodies Song," 171; exercises for teaching, 172–174; rhythm of life practice, 174; skills and behaviors served by, 21

somatosensory awareness, 69

SOS strategy, 87–88

sound, movement matched with, 121–122

special sense awareness, 69

spiritual/religious practices, 28–29

staying present, 212–215

stereognosis, sense of, 124

stop and go exercises, 120–121

stress, mindfulness practice and, 40

suffering: compassion practices for, 82–83; pain distinguished from, 70–71

Super Me practices, 140–146; Be Like a Tree Timer, 149; helpful hints for implementing, 151–152; making an apology, 143; noticing and reinforcing, 141; self-kindness, 145; skills and behaviors served by, 21; What Do I Need? activity, 142

"Super Me Song," 146

Superpower Small Cards, 140, 141, 145, 152

Supplemental Learning Activities, 22–23, 237–247; overview and explanation of, 237–239; on positive interaction with others, 246; on present-moment awareness and attention, 241; on self-awareness and self-control of movement, 240; on self-calming, 242; on self-kindness and

self-compassion, 247; on self-regulation of emotions and behavior, 243; on social awareness and social connection, 244; on social communication, 245
supporting vs. assisting, 226
Suzuki Roshi, Shunryu, 39

T

"Talking Heart, Listening Ears Song," 150
task demands, 234–235
teachers: burnout or demoralization of, 38–39; connection with children, 41–42; cooperation with requests made by, 209–212; engagement in activities directed by, 209–212; mindfulness practice of, 15–17, 38, 39–43; REMIND practices for, 15–16, 38–89
"Thank You for Being You Song," 158
thank you letter activity, 167
Thanking Others practice, 85
theory of mind, 184–185
thoughts, noticing, 61
Thoughts, Emotions, and Sensations Self-Monitoring Tool, 75
top-down practices, 35, 87–88
transitions: making within a routine, 215–217; walking meditations for making, 127

Tsoknyi Rinpoche, 65

V

vestibular awareness, 69
violet color, 16, 46, 84
visual tools/prompts: breathing with, 100, 103; Feelings Finder practice, 133–134
voice volume control, 122

W

waiting: bell exercises related to, 119–120; practicing the skill of, 6, 113, 119–120
walking meditation: guided movement and, 109–110; informal practice of, 74; skills and behaviors served by, 20; stop and go exercise of, 120; transitions utilizing, 127
Watching the Sky practice, 61
website for book, 23, 27
What Do I Need? activity, 142
working memory, 57–58, 186
working with others, 217–220

Y

yellow color, 16, 46, 65
yoga postures: bell exercise with, 120; body awareness and, 73, 123; skills and behaviors served by, 20

Real change *is* possible

For more than forty-five years, New Harbinger has published proven-effective self-help books and pioneering workbooks to help readers of all ages and backgrounds improve mental health and well-being, and achieve lasting personal growth. In addition, our spirituality books offer profound guidance for deepening awareness and cultivating healing, self-discovery, and fulfillment.

Founded by psychologist Matthew McKay and Patrick Fanning, New Harbinger is proud to be an independent, employee-owned company. Our books reflect our core values of integrity, innovation, commitment, sustainability, compassion, and trust. Written by leaders in the field and recommended by therapists worldwide, New Harbinger books are practical, accessible, and provide real tools for real change.

 **newharbinger**publications

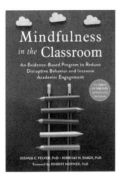

Did you know there are **free tools** you can download for this book?

Free tools are things like **worksheets, guided meditation exercises**, and **more** that will help you get the most out of your book.

You can download free tools for this book—whether you bought or borrowed it, in any format, from any source—from the New Harbinger website. All you need is a NewHarbinger.com account. Just use the URL provided in this book to view the free tools that are available for it. Then, click on the "download" button for the free tool you want, and follow the prompts that appear to log in to your NewHarbinger.com account and download the material.

You can also save the free tools for this book to your **Free Tools Library** so you can access them again anytime, just by logging in to your account! Just look for this button on the book's free tools page.

+ Save this to my free tools library

If you need help accessing or downloading free tools, visit **newharbinger.com/faq** or contact us at **customerservice@newharbinger.com**.